RELIGION AND REGIME

Religion and Regime

A Sociological Account of the Reformation

by
GUY E. SWANSON

Ann Arbor
THE UNIVERSITY OF MICHIGAN PRESS

To Mary Gray

Acknowledgment is made to the following for permission to quote copyrighted materials:

Ernest Benn Limited
> from Pieter Geyl, *The Netherlands in the Seventeenth Century*, PART ONE, 1609-1648 (revised ed., 1961)
> from Pieter Geyl, *The Revolt of the Netherlands* (2d ed., 1958)

Basil Blackwell, Publisher
> from Geoffrey Barraclough, *The Origins of Modern Germany*

Cambridge University Press
> from Wilhelm Oechsli, *History of Switzerland,* from Henri Pirenne's "The Low Countries" in *Cambridge Medieval History,* Vol. 8
> from T. F. Tout, "Germany and the Empire," and Stanley Leathes, "France," in *Cambridge Modern History,* Vol. 1

William Collins Sons & Company Limited
> from Alexis de Tocqueville, *The Old Regime and the French Revolution,* trans. by Stuart Gilbert

Doubleday & Company, Inc.
> from Alexis de Tocqueville, *The Old Regime and the French Revolution,* trans. by Stuart Gilbert. Copyright © 1955. Reprinted by permission of the publisher.

E. P. Dutton & Company Inc.
> from J. C. L. Sismondi, *History of the Italian Republics in the Middle Ages*

Harvard University Press
> from Eli F. Heckscher, *An Economic History of Sweden*

Rand McNally and Company
> from Vernon K. Dibble's "The Organization of Traditional Authority: English County Government, 1558-1640," in *Handbook of Organizations,* ed. by James G. March

Routledge & Kegan Paul Limited
> from J. C. L. Sismondi, *History of the Italian Republics in the Middle Ages*

D. Van Nostrand Company, Inc.
> from Nowell's *A History of Portugal,* copyright 1952

George Weidenfeld & Nicolson Limited
> from Ingvar Andresson, *A History of Sweden*

PREFACE

This is a study of the Reformation's beginnings: it is a test of an explanation for its appearance and for its measure of success. But that is not this book's main point. I want even more to explain a difference in experience having great consequence, a difference at issue in the Reformation: in some societies, Catholic nations being among them, people commonly feel they have direct, palpable contact with ultimate things, with spirits and with spiritual power. In other societies, including the predominantly Protestant states, most people feel in the presence of ultimate things yet separated from them. The problem of explaining this difference proves generally important for social science and not simply for studies of religion. It has special importance for sociology and, within it, for work in social psychology.

In studies of the intercourse between social organization and personality, two topics command greatest attention: first, among children or adults, the emergence of those social skills required of any person who communicates with others; second, the state of relations between men and the values ultimate in their societies. Between them, these topics embrace the most pervasive of social experiences.

The primary social skills include such generalized abilities as self-control, empathy, and the symbolization of experience. These skills are pervasive because they are employed whenever individuals participate in social interaction.[1] A society's ultimate values are pervasive because they define what is of ultimate concern, what goals should have precedence over all others. In most cases those goals are also defined as consummate: as capable of providing comprehensive direction and fulfillment to the careers of men and groups, as uniquely providing the most satisfying realization of all other objectives.[2]

In almost all times and places, including the societies of the modern West, a right relationship to spiritual beings and spiritual resources is presented as consummately valuable: as the only and sure means by which men and institutions are fulfilled; as the source, sustenance, and end of history. In our own tradition, communion with God or union with him is the end to be sought above all others.

Most studies of personality and ultimate values have suffered from an inability to specify what it is that such values represent. In an earlier book (titled *The Birth of the Gods*)[3] I sought to answer that question for theistic conceptions of the ultimately valuable. I offered empirical tests for the proposition that beliefs in gods or other spirits arise as symbols of men's experiences with the basic purposes and decision-making procedures of societies and of enduring and independent groups within societies. These basic procedures of societies and of other persisting groups were termed "constitutional arrangements" or "regimes." Differences in theology from one society to another were then explained by forecasting the kind of preexisting regime that would come to be symbolized by a particular and subsequent theological doctrine.[4]

In sum, men everywhere encounter ultimate values—the social formulae which state what should above all be sought, and they also encounter the things of ultimate concern to which the values refer—the objects, personalities, spirits, relationships, or whatever. We find that the things of ultimate concern are commonly spiritual powers or spiritual beings. There is evidence that belief in such powers and beings grows from experience with the constitutional arrangements, with the regimes, of societies and other groups.

Some spirits and spiritual resources, each possibly an object of ultimate concern, are believed actually incorporated in particular times, places, and things. Such objects are said to be "immanent." Other considerations equal, immanent objects are experienced as more immediately accessible, even as more palpable, than are things believed important for behavior and society yet always existing separated from time and place. Objects not immanent are impossible for individuals or groups fully to grasp or incorporate. They are more difficult to understand. The consequence is an anxiety in believers that must be overcome and the method for overcoming this must be institutionalized. It is this observation which brought me to a study of the immanence of objects of ultimate concern—to seek the conditions that determine whether such an object, in this case God, will itself be found present in the defining programs and purposes—in the "personalities"—of men and institutions or whether it will be considered as always influential over those programs and purposes yet separated from them.[5]

The Reformation of the sixteenth century provides one case in which the immanence of the ultimately valuable can be examined with relative ease. The great points then at issue concerned the extent to which God, the source of all value and himself consummately valuable, was immanent in his creation. The historical record of that period and of these controversies is ample, accessible, and reasonably objective. It allows one to judge which events preceded others. It provides a large number of cases for study. I used it to test an explanation for divergent experiences of God's immanence: for the experience formulated doctrinally in Catholicism that God's essence is embodied in the historically existing church and in the sacraments and for the contrasting experience formulated in the works of Luther and Calvin that God is omnipotent over his creation but that his personal essence is not to be found in any created thing.

I seek, however, an interpretation of immanence relevant not merely for societies and for deity but for groups of any sort and for the immanence of whatever objects they consider of ultimate concern. The general interpretation applied here to the Reformation will be successful if it applies to the "spirit," that is, to the things ultimately of concern in a corporation or a family, a political party, a voluntary association, or a community as it applies to the spirit of God.

My work on this topic was informed and corrected by many colleagues and was encouraged by institutions in which I worked. I began to develop the essential argument while a fellow of the Center for the Advanced Study of the Behavioral Sciences at Stanford, California. No member of the Center's fellowship can be grateful enough for the work of Ralph Tyler and Preston Cutler who there have brought to life the community among scholars of which every scholar dreams. I should not have dared to begin a study of immanence and the Reformation but for the support, and the help with bibliography, that I received from other fellows of the Center: Crane Brinton, Brainerd Currie, Louis Gottschalk, David Landes, Clarence Morris, Philip Rieff, and Fritz Stern. Later, I received funds to hire two readers who cross-checked the historical accounts I was developing and who sought further information to fill gaps in the record. These funds came from the Center for Research on Social Organization, Department of Sociology, The University of Michigan.

A first report of my findings was read by colleagues at Michigan, Harvard, and Berkeley. Their comments produced great improvements in the clarity of my ideas and the accuracy of my facts. I am indebted for this help to James Luther Adams, John Lofland, David McClelland, Neil Smelser, Sylvia Thrupp, and Harrison White.

I cannot say that any of these friends and colleagues fully agrees with what I now have to say, and I am certain that some of them have serious reservations about it. Without suggestions owing to their skills and consciences, there would be even greater room for reservations.

Everything I write benefits from my wife's critical pencil and her gentle, persistent skepticism. For this book I also drew on her specialized understanding of church history. But I dedicate it to her not for her colleagueship, but for the joy she brings to my life and to our children.

CONTENTS

[I]

Immanence and the Reformation Controversies

THIS IS A STUDY of a singular historical event for the sake of what may be learned from it about a common but puzzling experience. The event is the Protestant Reformation. The experience is that of the manner in which God—or other things people find of ultimate importance—are believed to be present in the world of men, nature, and society. In some societies people discover that what they believe of highest value is itself incorporated, is immanent, in persons, organizations, or various objects in the natural world. In other societies people never or rarely have any such encounter with what they value most. The division of Christianity in the sixteenth century concerned this difference in experience: all Christians held the presence of God to be their ultimate concern. Catholic doctrines declared that, as Christ, God's own spiritual essence was always present in bread and wine consecrated in the Mass and always embodied in the organization and acts of the visible church existent in time. Reformation Protestants denied those doctrines and any other which suggested that God's essential qualities were even partially embodied in "created things."

Most peoples, at most times in history, have considered spiritual resources or spiritual beings the most important of their concerns. If these supernatural resources and these spirits are immanent in the natural world, they are correspondingly more accessible to men and women: more palpable, more real. If they are immanent, it is easier to know when one is relating to them and how satisfactory that relationship is.

All, or nearly all, of magical practice seems to rest on a belief in the immanence of spiritual powers. Most religions, whether of ancient or of recent origin and whether primitive or comparatively modern, give to belief in spiritual immanence a central and honored place. Even many of the wholly secular philosophies important in modern societies contain some form of immanental doctrine.

Among the major religions, Protestantism is unusual in declaring that God, the source of all that is valuable and himself of all things the consummately valuable, is not immanent. He actively participates in the universe he created and controls it but is in no way incorporated in it. In the development of Western civilization and, through it, in the modernization of most human societies, the Protestant disbelief in God's immanence represents a new perspective from which interpretations in philosophy, science, and all other areas of culture have had to be rethought. It was from the consequences of that disbelief, more fundamental and distinctive even than Protestantism's ethics or activism, that the German historian-sociologist Max Weber constructed his now classic interpretation of the culture distinctive of the modern West.[1]

Weber himself did little to explain the rise or spread of Protestantism. Rather he described the movement and looked for its consequences. My purpose in this book is to offer an explanation for the Reformation and to examine the consistency between that account and the historical record. More generally, my purpose is to offer an explanation for the acceptance or rejection of belief in the immanence of whatever men consider of ultimate value and to provide one test of that explanation.

In this chapter, I first illustrate the idea of immanence as it appears in the magic and religion of primitives and in some major religions other than Christianity. In the course of these illustrations I define immanence. I then review the role of immanence in the Reformation controversies. Succeeding chapters contain my explanation for the Reformers' denial of God's immanence. They also present evidence necessary to judge in what respects that explanation is correct and whether it may account for the role of immanence in other religions and philosophies.

The Meaning of Immanence

In many primitive societies there is a practice that anthropologists call exuvial magic.[2] As the word "exuvial" suggests, this magic uses as ingredients natural products cast off by an animal, such products as the old skin shed by a snake. These products are exuviae. Into the sorcerer's bag go clippings of human hair, pairings from fingernails, bits of scab and skin, drops of excrement, any scrap or secretion from human bodies. From these ingredients the sorcerer makes his magic: magic with which he destroys men, changes their behavior, gains their powers, and restores their health. Cowards become brave when they drink the potion he brews from a hero's spittle. Patients smeared with the excrement of healthy men will regain their vigor. The sorcerer boils an infant's umbilical cord and the child dies, its abdomen seared by cramping pain. Or so the sorcerer and his neighbors believe.

They also believe that natural products of other animals can be put to similar use. A draught of lion's blood will serve to make the timid aggressive or give courage to a coward. In all cases, exuvial practice rests on two premises: the powers of one living creature can be appropriated by another and those powers are somehow embodied or contained in the creature's juices and tissues.

A man's powers, or an animal's, are not outward activities. Courage or health are foundations for behavior but not behavior itself. The powers should be thought of as capacities and abilities, as attitudes and motivations, as skills, knowledge, and wisdom, as interests, intentions, and commitments. They significantly determine what a man or animal does but are not the doing of it.

These several powers are not disconnected from one another but are organized attributes of a living creature. More exactly, they are attributes of what, if speaking of people, we usually call "personality"—the organization of an individual's powers to behave. In the languages of magic and of many religions this organization is conceived to be immortal and its immortality is stressed by calling it "spirit" or "soul" rather than personality. In these same languages the notion of spirit is often extended to include not only the immortal human personality but also the inner forces that underlie the action of all animals, plants, and inanimate objects. Through magical procedure or religious rite the powers of one creature's spirit become immanent within the spirit of another.

The notion of immanence resembles certain other ideas but is importantly different from them. Thus immanence refers to a real transfer of spiritual substances—of the powers of a spirit—and not merely to the influencing of one spirit by another. The lion's blood contains as substances the lion's powers of courage or ferocity and these are added to, or perhaps come to supplant, powers already part of the spirit of anyone who drinks the blood. We can imagine, by contrast, the existence of influence between spirits without the presence of immanence: for example, one spirit teaching courage to another or being of assistance by smoothing another's path.

Nor should immanence be confused with intimacy. Imagine, for example, that, upon drinking the lion's blood, the lion's spirit, or some attributes of that spirit, enter a man's body. Imagine further that there is no merger of properties between the spirits of man and lion, the two souls retaining their original integrity and proceeding to interact. Perhaps the lion's spirit alerts the man's to the presence of game or trains it in skills of slipping silently through dense underbrush. This relation between spirits is characterized by influence and intimacy. Immanence also involves both of those characteristics, but the form of their presence, if immanent, is that of the incorporation by a recipient spirit of powers formerly part of another.

A further difference between immanence and other forms of influence is this: immanence is never the production of a mere copy or duplicate of some attribute. If a lion's spirit trains a man's soul in stealth, the man's new ability in hunting is not the lion's, however much it resembles that of the lion. Were the lion's stealth immanent in the hunter's spirit,

it would be the lion's attribute as such—that is the lion's
very own skill in slipping up on prey—that now was an
ability of the man, becoming manifest in his behavior when
hunting.

Are a spirit's powers diminished when they become immanent in another soul? On that question there is no uniformity of belief. Some peoples believe that witches can
steal all of a child's spirit and enslave it simply by performing rites on the afterbirth. A contrary belief is that a man's
powers are fully and equally present in every cell and
secretion of his body. Those powers are in no way lessened
when he loses hair or sweat, scabs or urine, but they do become available to the sorcerer who collects these exuviae.

To this point we have talked of powers and of immanence.
We have found that powers are not behavior but are a
foundation for behavior; that they are the characteristics
of a spiritual personality. We have found that immanence
represents an intimate influencing of one spirit by another,
the influence occurring through the actual transfer of a
power from one spirit to another. The transferred attribute
merges with those already present in the spirit receiving it.
This transfer may or may not diminish the powers of the
donor spirit.

But we also found that magical practices employing
exuviae are just one instance in which something is believed to contain its spirit in the very elements of its natural
structure and exuvial practices afford just one example of a
belief in immanence. Not only a man's exuviae, but his
heart, blood, scalp, or any part of his body may contain his
powers. Not only the capacities for movement and change
to be found in men and animals, but also those perceived
in plants and in things not alive may be judged the attributes of an indwelling spirit and considered transferrable
to other spirits. Even powers of supernatural spirits, of the
gods themselves, are often believed capable of being immanent in the spirits of persons or places or groups or
trees or of any created thing. Perhaps the most extreme
form of this belief is a universal pantheism: the doctrine
that there is no distinction between the life of the infinite

godhead and the history of the universe itself: all things being but aspects or activities of the one god, their distinctive attributes or powers only special purposes of his, their careers determined by their service to his immutable nature. Such a pantheism dominated the thought of elites in India, China, and Japan from ancient times and continued to do so well into the nineteenth century. But almost all the major religions contain important doctrines of immanence; indeed, they provide too many examples. A few must suffice:

The theologies of early Judaism and of Islam placed a lesser emphasis on immanental ideas than did most of the other great religions. These theologies picture God as sometimes immanent and also portray the immanence of the spirits of men.

Current scholarship suggests that the two stones carried in the Ark of Moses' time, and eventually housed with the Ark in the Temple at Jerusalem, were believed to contain, and not merely to symbolize, the presence and person of Yahweh. When the Ark was carried into battle before the Hebrews' army, God himself led his people. God's will was discerned through many ritual procedures, among them the casting of lots, the consultation of oracles, and the act of divination. Such procedures rest on the assumption that a divine attribute, God's will, is linked in its substance to spiritual attributes of created things. By examining or manipulating those things, the divine attribute is revealed or evoked. (Although the Hebrews came gradually to reject and abhor such practices, they did not doubt their efficacy.) They also believed that ritual purity was a prerequisite to effective prayer and sacrifice and that a violation of the food taboos or lack of circumcision put a man outside the realm of divine concourse. God would not enter a defiled sanctuary nor be at one with impure men. The sins of the people could, by ritual means, be removed from them and placed upon a scapegoat. In driving the goat from their midst they drove out their sins. The blessing which God gave to heads of families and to other leaders of the people was not simply his goodwill but divine power to rule, decide, and overcome.

Islam is the community of Allah. The army and treasury are its major organs and Allah has laid down detailed principles for their operation. Mohammed considered himself a bearer of divine power and did not object when the people fought for possession of his spittle, hair, and bath water. The essence of Allah, or a part of it, is also in the Islamic community. Therefore the united community never errs, its preferred customs and laws not simply conforming to Allah's will but actually embodying it. Similarly, direct descendents of the Prophet embody his essence, including the divine force he received from Allah and which directed his conduct. As in Judaism there are practices formally ritualistic in character: prayer, alms, fasting, participation in holy wars, observance of food taboos, and, for the wealthy, the required pilgrimage to Mecca. The prayers, for example, are rituals rather than communion with God. To be effective they must be offered facing the holy city. The believer must first have cleansed his hands and marked off the place he will kneel. The prayers must be uttered exactly as written in the sacred text.

When Greece and Rome were at the height of their military power, their religions pictured the gods as investing the world with their presence and essence. For example, the gods of Greece had their home on Mount Olympus. There were sacred groves where they could be encountered. They spoke through oracles. The natural elements bespoke the indwelling nature of the deities who produced and controlled them. The gods fought beside the people and sometimes against them. Divine essence lodged in a stone or charm could be carried wherever one went. The divine will was in part housed and manifest in nature and one could discern it by examining nature: the entrails of fowl, the shape of clouds, the fall of dice, the birthmarks on a child. The gods could give powers to individuals: courage, skill in war, seamanship, wisdom, fertility, musical talents. The gods of Rome were like those of Greece in all these respects.

For anyone interested in understanding the meaning and origin of immanence, its very ubiquity is a problem. One can hope to find the sources only of those things that display some variation. Unless in some societies the doctrine of immanence applies to different things than it does in others, or unless this kind of belief is explicitly rejected in some societies, there is no effective method for judging what conditions might produce it. These facts lead us to consider afresh the origins and meaning of the Protestant Reformation because, alone among the world's major religious traditions, Protestantism—most dramatically Calvinist Protestantism—rejects all beliefs in immanence and particularly the Catholic belief in God's immanence in the visible church, the sacraments, and the soul transformed by sacramental grace. As Max Weber wrote of Calvinism:[3]

> . . . This, the complete elimination of salvation through the Church and the sacraments . . . was what formed the absolutely decisive difference from Catholicism.
>
> That great historic process in the development of religions, the elimination of magic from the world which had begun with the old Hebrew prophets and, in conjunction with Hellenistic scientific thought, had repudiated all magical means to salvation as superstition and sin, came here to its logical conclusion. . . .

Immanence as an Issue in the Reformation

The Protestantism of Luther and Calvin shared with Catholicism the general Christian view that God actively governed the world and that he was all powerful, all knowing, and everywhere present. Although rejecting Catholic doctrines of immanence, the Reformers declared that men can experience the consequences of God's presence, can come to know something of his character, can learn what he requires of them, and can interact with him. Neither Catholic or Protestant doctrine remained fixed.[4] In reviewing such parts of each as are relevant, I shall have in mind Catholicism as defined by the Council of Trent (1545-63) and the Protestantisms which, alone in this period, became the new official religions of some states, that is Lutheranism, Anglicanism, Calvinism, and Zwinglianism. The theologies of Calvin and Zwingli are identical in all relevant essentials and will be treated as one. For reasons to be given later,

Anglicanism will be treated as similar to Lutheranism in its views of immanence. It seems correct to treat Calvinism (and Zwinglianism) as least committed to a doctrine of immanence, Catholicism as most committed, and Lutheranism (hence Anglicanism as well) as an intermediate case.

The most relevant doctrines concern the nature of the Church and of the sacraments. Something must be said about the character of the Scripture in order to understand conceptions of the sacraments. Ideas about the church and the sacraments make sense only in the context of beliefs about law, sin, and the gospel and about will and reason.

1. Law, Sin, and Gospel:

Catholicism and Protestantism share the basic Christian outlook on history: at the time of man's creation, God established a Law governing human conduct. Because he violated that Law, man was cast out of Eden. Man, being free in will but finite in capacity, and being concerned primarily with his personal needs, continues to offend God. God, good and loving, cannot escape his own nature. He wants fellowship with man and seeks his creature's good. Man, dependent and full of guilt at his own rejection of God's perfect love, seeks to overcome his selfishness and sin, to find a way within his capacities to become reconciled with God. That effort is beyond man's ability. But God, incarnate as the Christ, provides for man's salvation. He offers a means by which man can be justified, that is, can become worthy of salvation. He also offers a means by which justified men can become sanctified, that is, can be purified from sin and its effects.

2. Will and Reason:

The Roman Catholic Fathers at Trent reaffirmed traditional doctrine: at its ground or depth, man's soul shares in the divine changelessness and is still. God is not immanent there, but the soul's fundamental qualities are compatible with God's character. The extent to which habits and acts acceptable to God develop from this ground depends on the way in which a man relates to his environment.

The soul's essence is more of a capacity than an ability. As a capacity, it is not justified or unjustified, but is neutral. (The souls of those who die before the "age of reason" are, correspondingly, consigned to Limbo, a vague, bland realm between Heaven and Hell.)

By contrast, Luther and Calvin found the soul ceaselessly alive and active and behind its activity the indivisible I, full of desire to assert a tough and narrow self-interest.[5] They declared that man is not an eternal spirit imprisoned in a material body nor an animal evolving toward pure spirituality. He is, instead, a unitary being affecting all of his natural life by his spirithood and all his spirithood by his natural life; sinning not because of his dual status but because of his proud unwillingness to accept it. There is no unspoiled divine nucleus at the deep center of man's individuality; no saving bridgehead to the Infinite.

3. The Church and the Sacraments:

a. Catholic Doctrine: "The Church," in Cardinal Bellarmine's well-known definition, "is a body of men united together by profession of the same Christian faith, and participation in the same sacraments under the governance of lawful pastors, more especially the Roman Pontiff, the sole Vicar of Christ on earth."[6] Christ is continuously incarnated in the Church, that is, in the organization of laity and clergy, which he established and which is his mystical body. Christ governs and teaches in and through the Church. Through it he administers the sacraments. The Church, being Christ's mystical body, cannot be less than infallible as a teacher, the sole true administrator of the sacraments, the only governor of man's relations with God. (At least since 1870 orthodox doctrine has specified that "Christ and His Vicar constitute one only Head" of the Church with comprehensive jurisdiction over its parts.)[7] The Church must, in this view, be visible so man can find it. Its vital force or soul, however, is the invisible Holy Spirit.

It is in the Church as a corporate body, not in its functionaries as men, that there reside Christ's presence, power, and activity. The cleric as a person is not especially fitted to act as an agent of the divine. He has such powers only in his position as a genuinely ordained priest, that is as a part of Christ's mystical body. As a consequence, the priest's ability to enact Christ's will is not invalidated by his own sin or by intellectual or physical incompetence or even by apostasy. If he has "at least the intention of doing what the Church does," and if the Church recognizes him at the same time as a legitimate priest, his sacerdotal actions are valid.

The Scripture is God's Word which, together with unwritten traditions, is the source of all saving truth and moral discipline. The Church is the only proper and infallible teacher of the meaning of Scripture and tradition. Tradition includes extra-Scriptural statements on faith and morals contained in the writings of the Fathers, the decrees of Councils, and official pronouncements of the Papal See. Since these decrees and pronouncements still come forth, one should think of tradition as including the current exercise of reason as inspired by the Holy Spirit. Tradition is not a proclamation of new doctrines but the discovery of doctrine implicit in truths which Christ proclaimed.

God's grace is of two kinds according to the purpose it accomplishes: actual grace and habitual or sanctifying grace. The first phase of justification is the bestowal by God of actual grace, a supernatural gift by which rational creatures are enabled to perform salutary acts. It renders man "capable of performing supernatural acts, so that he may attain justification." If a man so endowed chooses good rather than evil, he prepares himself for the reception of sanctifying grace: "A habit, a more or less enduring state, which renders man pleasing to God."[8] Reception of this sanctifying grace ordinarily requires one's participation in the sacraments. The sacraments convey or increase it and provide a recovery of justification if that is lost through mortal sin. Only the sacraments are a means of sanctifying grace. The Word is not. The sacraments contain the grace which they signify, conferring it in virtue of the ritual act performed and independently of the merits and disposition of the recipient, unless he is living in mortal sin. Moreover, they contain grace in a substantial form, that is in the form having the properties of a substance which can be assimilated by human spirits. Eternal life is gained only as man goes on in the power of sanctifying grace to perform meritorious works.

At no point in Catholic doctrine is an immanental belief more dramatically evident than in the tenet concerning Christ's presence in the Eucharistic bread and wine. This tenet states that Christ, as a person, is fully present in the elements of communion although existing fully and simultaneously at other points in and outside time and space.

A spirit is transcendent to the extent that it is capable of such full and simultaneous existence at more than one point in or outside time and space.[9] All Christians would agree that Christ, capable of existing at all such points, is completely transcendent. Catholics differ from Protestants in believing that, as in the Eucharist, he sometimes is present immanently. With respect to the Eucharist this means that Christ himself is believed present in the elements —his essence or some aspect of it is there and not just his influence or some one of his actions. Christ's essence replaces those of the elements themselves although their outward appearance persists. When the bread and wine are ingested, Christ's essence (in a sense not clearly specified) merges with (or places a mark upon, or shapes) the communicant's soul. The doctrine means, insofar as human analogues can portray the ineffable, that the bread and wine contain Christ's actual personality or character—his distinctive and living purposes, knowledge, commitments, standards, motives, judgment, and worth—and do not contain simply resultants of the exercise of that personality.

In sum, Catholic doctrines declare that God's character and purposing are themselves present, immanent, in creation. Specifically, they are present in the ground of the human soul shaped by habitual grace, in the visible Church, and in the sacraments. Because habitual grace is dispensed by the Church through its acts in the sacraments, the doctrine of the visible Church as Christ incarnate is the pivotal issue.

The Catholic position is unambiguous: When acting in its sacerdotal capacity, the visible Church is Christ incarnate, not as before in flesh but now in the purposes and organization of the Holy See. He sacrifices himself in the Mass; his is the judgment given from the lips of the priest in the confessional or from the Holy Father when indulgences are granted or anathemas pronounced; his is the authority and act that joins men and women in marriage, that accepts infants in baptism, that consigns the dead to God's care and intercedes for them in Purgatory; he is the infallible teacher of faith and morals whose doctrine Popes articulate.

b. Lutheran Doctrine: The Church is the congregation of those "whom Christ has rescued from the power and tyranny of Satan, sin, and eternal death and over whose hearts he has established his rule."[10] Membership is possible only by the Holy Spirit's call through the external means of grace: that is through hearing the Word rightly preached and receiving the sacraments.

The true Church is invisible, comprising all believers of all times. The true Church, but not the historically empirical Church, is infallible.

All believers are equally priests. All have the right to call and ordain ministers. The function of the ministry is to preach the Gospel and administer the sacraments. God ordains this public ministry of properly called men.[11]

Christ's Word in the Scriptures is the only religious authority, the only source and norm of truth. Wherever this Word is preached, it becomes the power of God, an active and creative Word, and it engenders the faith which accepts the Bible as Christ's inerrant and final Word. This belief does not depend on rational arguments but is a divinely wrought faith. The Gospel conveys to us Christ and the totality of his gifts as a present possession. The Gospel is not only the promise of God's forgiveness, but in reality the absolution itself. It actually creates faith. The Holy Spirit works "saving faith" solely through the Gospel. The Holy Spirit is always in the Word, therefore the Gospel is always divinely efficacious. All "enthusiasm" is condemned which teaches that the Holy Spirit operates outside the objective Word. But the Word is efficacious only if heard in faith. It requires and engenders faith.[12]

The sacraments are means of grace no more and no less than the spoken or written Word. Grace itself is a relation of God to man, not a substance or actual gift.[13] "Grace," said Melancthon, "is not medicine but good will."[14] Christ whole and entire, body and spirit, is present in the sacraments, but he is not infused into the recipient, entering rather into a relation of forgiveness and strengthening. Faith is unconditionally necessary for the salutary use of the Lord's Supper.[15]

Lutheranism breaks with transubstantiation—the Catholic doctrine that Christ's essence replaces that of the bread and wine leaving only their appearance. It declares instead for consubstantiation—the co-existence of Christ's eternal body and spirit "in, with, and under" the essence and appearance of the bread and wine.

To summarize, Lutheranism pictures God in Christ as actively governing his creation. He is present at all historical times and places yet separated from them. He is present as Savior in the visible Church, the Word, and the sacraments but in no sense "fused with" or "merged into" or "one with" the historically empirical agencies that participate in his work. Indeed, despite his presence, the visible Church may fail to represent him, the clergy may not obey his inspiration, and the laity may lack the faith requisite for an efficacious exposure to the Word and the sacraments.

c. *Calvinist Doctrine:* The true Church is the invisible body of the Elect whom God from eternity has chosen for everlasting life. But God has established a visible Church as the means through which he speaks to the world. The true visible Church has principally to interpret the Bible and to compel all men to live according to its precepts. Membership in the visible Church is an indispensable cause of salvation and even the nonelect must belong because membership is a tribute to God's glory.[16]

God's Word is normally heard through the word of a preacher of the Gospel, called and appointed by God to this task. The Word preached by man can become God speaking. Preaching should be undertaken and heard in the expectation that Christ will come and give his presence where the Gospel is preached and will cause men to hear his voice through the voice of the minister.[17]

The Word and sacraments are to men of all later times what Christ and his word and works were to men during his incarnation. They are his flesh—his lowly, humble form. They are the form in which Christ appears before men, but only those who see them with the eyes of faith discern their true nature.[18]

What God offers in words, he fulfills in deeds. When he speaks through the preacher offering forgiveness, those who hear the Word in faith are at once really absolved from their sins. This efficacy of the Word occurs only through a sovereign and free act of the Holy Spirit. Preaching may, thus, fail to be the Word of God.

The Bible is the only reliable source of God's Word. He will never speak again by other means. To men he commits instruction only. The Holy Spirit authenticates the Scriptures by giving inward testimony to the believer that they are the Word of God.

The ordinary member of the Church does not have the power to understand Scripture rightly. God has appointed an ecclesiastical government to teach and has given the Church the gift of interpretation. Men whom God calls to the ministry will have from him gifts sufficient for their task, but they must examine the objective Word and all of it, and must consider what the teachers formerly in the Church have said.

God speaks through words and through concrete signs. The sacraments are such signs. Revelation never takes place without a Word; there never is a genuine sign without a voice coming from God. Without the doctrine there is no sacrament. The signs draw attention to the Word that is spoken. The sign is to overcome the dullness of men's minds, preparing the way for doctrine.

Sacraments are appendages to the Gospel. They are like seals on a public document which are to no purpose if the paper is blank. There is no infusion of substance from Christ in Word or sacrament to the believer. Grace is not a substance, but the personal presence of Christ offering men a personal relationship with himself. In the sense of this relation, Christ is received by faith. Unbelievers cannot receive Christ.

Participation in the sacraments is not essential to salvation or to communion with Christ. The Word gives all that the sacraments contain. Nevertheless the sacraments should be employed because they are signs of God's grace.

We find that Calvinism thus joins in the Lutheran view that God is present but not immanent in the world. Like Luther, Calvin judged it unthinkable that God's power and character, infinite in goodness, complexity, and extent, could be encapsulated in any historical entity. Like Luther, he believed that men, whether as individuals or collectivities, differ from God not simply in finitude but in goodness as well. Men are inherently selfish. They actively oppose God's will. Therefore it is unthinkable that their character and actions should be identified as fundamentally congenial to God's, let alone as being instances of his own nature.

But the two Reformers also differed from each other. Luther's doctrine presents God as present in a more dependable and palpable form than does Calvin's. For Luther, the Word when preached is always God's power and is always consequential whether to condemn sin, to engender faith, or to absolve. For Calvin, the consequentiality of the spoken Word depends on the faith of those who hear it and on whether the Holy Spirit has directed the preacher.

The two Reformers disagreed on the importance of both baptism and communion. As we have found, Luther thought them equal to the Word as means of grace, Calvin judged them of no significance apart from the Word and the Word as giving all that the sacraments contain. In addition, although Luther had rejected transubstantiation, his doctrine of consubstantiation brought recipients of communion into contact with Christ's eternal body and not just his spirit. Calvin taught that Christ was present with communicants in spirit only, his eternal body being in Heaven.

d. Anglican Doctrine: I proposed earlier to treat Anglicanism as closer to Luther's ideas than to Calvin's. This proposal can now be justified. My rationale applies specifically to the Anglican position on matters related to immanence and given definitive formulation in the Thirty-nine Articles of 1563. (The Articles as a whole presented a theology blending ingredients from Lutheranism and Calvinism and offered doctrines of church government differing from both. My concern is with the theology.)

Like the Calvinists, Anglican authorities concurred at most points with the Lutheran Augsburg Confession. They went further than Calvin, however, in accepting Luther's view that the sacraments are not only badges and tokens of Christian profession, their observance ordained by God, but are, rather, "sure witnesses and effectual signs of grace . . . by which He doth work invisible in us and doth not only quicken but also strengthen and confirm our faith in him."[19] The Articles were Calvinist in their outspoken declaration of predestination and its meaning. They were purposefully made vague as between the Lutheran and Calvinist positions in describing the nature of Christ's presence in the Eucharistic bread and wine.

The Place of Immanence Among the Reformation Controversies

An account of the Reformation even in purely doctrinal terms will reveal the central position of disputes concerning immanence. But these disputes do not exhaust the Reformation's controversies. This fact is important for the chapters that follow because I plan to use a country's retention of Catholicism or its adoption of Protestantism as indicative of beliefs concerning immanence. Were immanence only a small or rather special aspect of Reformation doctrine, I might successfully predict the adoption of Protestantism because, unwittingly, I had found a way to forecast the spread of conceptions only slightly related to immanence.

There never is any final, decisive procedure for settling questions of this sort. If, however, we look at the several issues dividing Protestants from Catholics we find that the considerable majority flow directly from a view of immanence. Perhaps the doctrines most important in this connection concern the sources of truth.

In Catholic doctrine there are two sources of truth: the Scriptures and tradition. Tradition represents the accumulated wisdom drawn from the experience of Christians in the world and certified as truth by the Church, that is by Christ incarnate. Tradition consists also in periodic statements of truth newly revealed to the Church itself. It is evident that the authority of tradition rests ultimately on the belief that the visible Church is indeed Christ's mystical body. Once that immanental belief is challenged, all doctrines dependent upon it lose their foundation and the Scriptures remain as the sole source of truth. The doctrines which fall away when God's immanence is thus in dispute include the following: the clergy and only they are priests; there is a Purgatory; prayers and Masses initiated by the living may assist the dead in their progress through Purgatory; each Mass consists of a fresh sacrifice of Christ for the salvation of mankind; saints are those occasional men who have advanced so far in spiritual growth that they achieve a life without sin and no longer deserve the punishments merited for sins committed before they achieved sanctification; prayers to the saints or the Virgin are efficacious for man's spiritual welfare; the visible Church can remove by the issuance of indulgences or by other means some of the punishments merited for sin; a life of spiritual contemplation is superior to any other.

The two remaining Protestant doctrines seem not dependent upon immanence: the doctrines of salvation by faith alone and of predestination. I discuss them in the last chapter of this book and there indicate that they may be only different products of the same conditions that destroyed immanental beliefs. For the moment, it is important to recognize that the Reformers' rejection of Catholic immanentalism was not merely one feature of their position but central to it and, as indicated in the paragraph above, the source of most of their specific criticisms of Catholic tenet and practice. As a consequence we can be more confident that success in predicting whether a country accepted the Reformation or rejected it is appropriately an indicator of its stand on the belief that God is immanent in history.

[II]

The Roots of Immanence

A SATISFACTORY ACCOUNT of the Reformation would explain why the Reformers confronted a world without an immanent god; why they searched the Scriptures to learn the actual manner of God's presence. No such explanation exists. The causes of the Reformation as given in reliable histories are individually inadequate. More than this, no satisfactory combination of these causes has been effected.[1] It is useful, however, to review the standard lists of causes. A review justifies renewed search for an explanation and calls attention to proposals that may, at least in their present form, be safely left out of any account.

Many of the conditions most commonly given as sources of Protestantism prove equally prevalent in countries that remained Catholic. These conditions include: the decline of feudalism and of medieval kingdoms; the rise of some form of nationalism; the terror and the loss of population resulting from the Black Death; the start or conclusion of great wars; the replacing of cavalry with infantry as the foundation of military operations; the growth of a money economy; resistance by secular governments to ecclesiastical control; control by secular governments of ecclesiastical appointments, revenues, programs, and proclamations; the codification of laws; the bureaucratization of government; the settling of waste lands; the reception of the Roman law; a decline of disciplined performance of duty by clergy and laity; the struggle between conciliarists and papists for control of the church;[2] the practice of large-scale agriculture and the organization of the countryside into latifundia.

Certain purported explanations have the additional defect of picturing either Catholic orthodoxy or the Reform as but variations of earlier ideas that were, in fact, alien to both. One thinks, for example, of proposals that put forward the more extreme forms of humanism, skepticism, and individualism associated with Renaissance thought.

One cause that is frequently invoked, the growth of the middle classes, not only fails to distinguish Protestant from Catholic lands but constitutes a political and ideological development that had its great importance much later in European history. In most of Europe in the fifteenth and sixteenth centuries, kings, princes, and nobles were the politically significant elites whereas merchants and urban artisans were only a minute proportion of the population and were of comparatively little economic importance.

Much is sometimes made of the difference in Europe between cultures grown on the light soils of the Mediterranean as contrasted with those originating on the heavy and heavily forested earth of the north, the former being associated by one argument or another with Catholicism and the latter with Protestantism. Allusions may be made to the association between this difference in the character of the soil and the distribution of Germanic as contrasted with "Romance" language and culture. These points are interesting but probably of no importance for an understanding of the Reformation. They would not, for example, explain the strength of Catholicism in northern and Germanic Austria, Bavaria, or Inner Switzerland or in the northern but Celtic populations of Ireland and the Scottish Highlands. They are not consistent with the swift rise and, at one point, the predominance, of Huguenot Calvinism among the nobility in the south of France. Nor are they consistent with the rapid if temporary spread of Calvinism among the nobles of Poland or of Lutheranism in the Austrian nobility. What does seem true is that the religious persuasion which took root among the politically important elites of a country's richest urban and agricultural districts became the official doctrine for the country as a whole. Thus Anglicanism took hold on the rich "champion" lands of central England whereas, in France, Catholicism had its strongest bastions on lands of the same character.[3] Elites in these territories had the power to impose on dissenting countrymen the doctrine they preferred.

Although none of these several explanations is sufficient, some of them remind us of the decline throughout Europe of certain older institutional systems. It may be that the very pervasiveness of this decline was important. Perhaps, for example, the general loss of vigor and discipline in the Catholic Church facilitated a far-reaching reassessment of doctrine and practice impossible had only one or two countries been affected.

Another Interpretation

To find a new explanation for the Reformation, I begin with facts peculiar to it: with God and his immanence. Some findings from my own earlier studies of primitive and ancient religions provide a framework.[4]

In considering the Reformation we deal not with immanence in the abstract but with the immanence of a particular spirit and that spirit is a monotheism's great deity —what anthropologists call a "high god"—actively ruling the world he created. I began my earlier comparative studies with the notion that any conception of a spirit symbolizes experiences that men have with the purposes and activities of independent, organized groups and I then showed that the presence or absence of belief in a particular kind of spirit is associated with the presence or absence in a society of groups having properties attributed to that spirit. The evidence for these conclusions came from a sample of fifty primitive and ancient societies.

I showed, for example, that high gods appear in those societies in which a superordinate organization, that is, a society's central government, provides political coordination for the activities of at least two other types of organization, the latter being arranged hierarchically and each having some sphere of autonomy in making decisions. Thus a council of elders from several villages may coordinate decisions affecting all of those villages, and, in every village, a local council may develop policies affecting several organized clans of which each village is composed. Under these conditions, one over-arching source of decision and purpose provides unity among groups diverse in purpose. That, I suggested, is close to a description of what a high god does. All the societies of early modern Europe display belief in a high god and all have the form of political organization just described.

I also found that some high gods are believed indifferent to the world they created or are powerless to govern it. Others are believed creation's active governors. High gods prove to be active in societies that have specific groups which implement the purposes and programs of a central government. Cadres of military leaders or of agricultural advisors are examples of groups effecting the implementations I have in mind. All societies of sixteenth-century Europe contained such groups and, in each society, God was believed in active control of all creation.

These findings are important here because they suggest where one should look in explaining a high god's characteristics: one should look at some properties of central government. If the Reformers rejected the idea that God was immanent in creation, this should mean that the central governments of European societies had once been experienced as immanent in history and that, in some of those societies, this was no longer so.

My earlier work also contains information about immanence itself.[5] I found that an individual's soul is more likely to be thought immanent in his body, inherent in its fluids and tissues, if his intentions and abilities can be considered peculiarly his. Immanence of soul is most likely to appear, I discovered, if a man's personality cannot be readily construed as acquired through his importation of the purposes, traditions, and attitudes of groups to which he belongs. I was able to locate patterns of social relations associated with such immanence or with its absence.

These observations on immanence are important for our problem because they suggest, by extension, that a high god's essence or personality can be immanent in other things only if actions of a society's central government do *not* incorporate purposes that spring from other and independent sources. It is upon these ideas that I want to build an explanation for the rise of Protestantism.

In the remainder of this chapter I elaborate these ideas and describe which purposes of a central government are its own and which are not. I suggest that the Reformation arose in Europe in consequence of the growing penetration of central governments in some countries by purposes other than those of the governments themselves. On that assumption, I proceed in the chapters that follow to test two hypotheses:

1. There was a positive association in early modern Europe between (a) the extent to which external interests penetrated a central government's pursuit of concerns specific to it and (b) the replacement of Catholicism by Protestantism.

2. The greater such penetration, the more likely it was that Calvinism rather than Lutheranism (or Anglicanism) would be adopted.

(Fortunately it is not necessary for our purpose to explain why, in Catholic Europe, God was believed immanent in the church but not in secular governments. The causes of the separation in the West between religious and political institutions are imperfectly understood. Such a separation is not usual in this period in other parts of the world.[6] But here we need reason only as follows: if belief in a high god's immanence depends upon certain features of a central government, we can predict the presence or absence of that belief without considering what conditions determine those things in which the god, if immanent, will dwell.)

Embodiments of a Spirit
or of Relations Among Spirits

All Christians believe that God actively rules his creation. Catholics believe he sometimes exercises his powers in immanental form. Protestants do not. From earlier studies of primitive men we can say that a man's soul is believed immanent in his body if it appears that the powers behind his actions are peculiarly his. Are these several facts related? I propose that they are.

Immanence always refers to the manner in which a spirit dwells within something else, whether that something be another spirit, a person, a group, a mountain, or whatever. It dwells there immanently if the activities of its host are embodiments of the spirit's own powers. A spirit may be present in a host and may influence its host without being immanent. Exactly that situation exists when the host's activities are the overt expression of inner powers not directly those of the indwelling spirit.

Consider an example. Suppose a spirit named Poseidon is immanent in all water. If he is, then the running of tides, the texture of fluids in sea and stream, the fall of dew or rain, and every other characteristic and change of water will be externalizations of Poseidon's personal attributes, of his powers. Given these beliefs it makes sense for men to feel that, in possessing water or in drinking it, they control or ingest something that is given its distinctive properties by the continuous presence and activity in it of Poseidon's powers. If something is water it contains those powers. Remove those powers and all water would vanish.

Suppose, however, the properties and activities of water have a different origin. Suppose Poseidon is only one of several spirits each of whom has all water as its host. Suppose the characteristics of water come from the influence of all these spirits. By what process might that occur?

The process must be such that the influences of these spirits are stable and coordinated. Otherwise we could not by this reasoning explain why water tends always to be where, when, and as it is. In short, because water and its occurrence display regularities, we must assume that relations among the spirits which produce it are neither capricious nor inchoate. There seem only two means by which such order might occur among spirits.

A first possibility is that one of the spirits, say it is Poseidon, obtains all relevant powers from the others and exercises them together with powers originally his own. Poseidon's personality then includes and coordinates these several powers and, through his immanence in it, water gains its properties and regularities. Thus we again have immanence, only this time the powers concerned have their origin in several spirits rather than in the one through whom they were made immanent in water.

It might be wondered why each of several spirits could not immanently contribute its own power, the combination of all their contributions forming water. The chief reason for thinking this implausible rests admittedly on conjecture, not observation. If I am right in thinking that the powers of a spirit are attributes of an immortal personality, then the coordination of those powers, as powers, can occur only insofar as they are attributes of some one personality. As shown in the preceding example, that coordination requires that attributes of several spirits must become immanent in some one spirit.

There is, however, a second plausible way to explain how several spirits might jointly form water. Suppose the spirits work out a relationship among themselves such that each retains his distinctive powers but each continuously so relates to the others that water is created. Its creation may be either the purpose of the relationship or an unintended by-product. The lawfulness of water's properties would be explained as rooted in the stability of the relations among the spirits.

By this second explanation, water is a product, not of the spirits directly but of a relation they have with each other. An analogous relation among people may clarify what is involved.

Suppose three men are constantly in association and engage among themselves in buying and selling. Each man wants certain things and, to obtain them, must give something acceptable to another who can supply what he wants. Personal attributes of each man—each man's desires, for example—are embodied in his acts. In this sense, those attributes are immanent in behavior. There is, however, a complication. As the men buy and sell, one man may be found to have more power in exchange than the others and a second man to have more than the third. This ranking may become a fact with which all must cope. It may become a source among them of differential prestige. It may provide a basis for the future phasing of their bargains such that the most potent individual always states his terms first and then the second man, leaving the third no choice but to comply. The third man is then not only the least powerful but is in a minority. He is unable, that is, significantly to influence certain standards by which he must live.

The ranking just described is no personal attribute of any man involved. It is a relation among them. It may not be desired by any one of them. It may not even be recognized by the participants, yet it exists and has consequences as illustrated above. Its independence from the three participants' personal traits can be illustrated as follows: the same ranking might appear in another group of three, each man having a personality quite different from any of those in the first group. The ranking reflects their positions relative to the needs and abilities of other participants and not the specific contents of their personal traits. A second illustration of the independence between the ranking and personal attributes is provided by breaking up the original group of three and involving each man with two new participants. It is quite possible that, in his new group, the man formerly most powerful would now be in a minority position; that the man once least influential would now be dominant. One can likewise show that the level of prices which will emerge in exchange is also a characteristic of an interrelationship among participants and not directly of the traits of the persons involved.

Now what I have proposed is that, among spirits, water might, like a system of ranking or a level of prices, be a relation among the spirits rather than itself an act of one or all. Alternatively, water might be like prestige or a minority position, that is it might be a secondary consequence of a relation among spirits. In neither case would the spirits' powers be immanent in the water. Water would, rather, be an interrelationship among their acts. A man who drank water produced by this process would ingest a relationship among spirits but not the powers or personalities of those spirits: he would drink a pattern among, or a product of, acts which flowed from the spirits' several personalities but not the acts or personal traits themselves.

Fanciful though all this may seem, it is at least consistent with the evidence from primitive societies concerning belief or disbelief in exuvial magic and related practices. The evidence is that if conditions exist which make for doubt that a man's behavior embodies purposes and powers distinctively his, then primitives do not believe his spirit is immanent in his organism and acts. Rather his acts are conceived as produced by interrelations between his spirit and others, all perhaps residing within his body, but none immanent in his bodily tissues or in his behavior. If, however, conditions that raise such doubts are absent, the belief is general that each man's soul is immanent in his own body and behavior.

Building upon earlier studies I extend this reasoning to high gods. If such gods represent experiences with the unifying activities that central governments exercise over groups subordinate to them, then whether an actively governing high god will be judged immanent should depend on whether the actions of such a central government are believed to embody only that government's purposes and other attributes or to represent a compromise between the government's attributes and the programs and character of other and independent agencies. Such a compromise would be a relation between government and these agencies.

Consider a pair of illustrations that catch this difference in political structure: in the first, a government's acts are considered to implement its own purposes. In the second, programs of government are believed to reflect a relation between its purposes and those of other agencies. In both, the common good or common interests of a society's people will be taken to constitute distinctive purposes of a central government. Later I will be more specific about a government's purposes, but this will do for the present.

It is clear that we often wonder which, if any, aspects of governmental action represent the legitimate common good, which actions embody both common and special interests, and which promote special interests only. Under some circumstances the suspicion may arise that the machinery of the state has been prostituted to promote only the latter. Now to the first illustration.

In a classic absolute monarchy, the legitimate central government is solely in the hands of the king and his agents. Apologists commonly legitimize such a regime by saying that the vitality of the society itself, of the whole, is of more importance to all concerned than the achievement by groups within the society of objectives peculiar to them. The crown is above such special interests—above partisan politics. It represents the society's general and enduring interests and purposes in the sense of being responsive to, and responsible for, the whole round of a society's life and for the indefinite course of its future existence. The crown is not the agent of just some of the society's people or activities. Ideally, the judgments, policies, and activities of the crown are unswayed by special interests (indeed are irrelevant for and disinterested in them) except as those interests are important to the vitality and maintenance of the whole society. If this is true, then, in principle, the crown's purposes —the central government's—are immanent in its institutional structure and are manifest in the exercise of its powers.

For a contrast we may consider a representative, federal regime like the government of the United States.[7] Such a regime no doubt originates and persists for the pursuit of interests common to its constituent states, but the states themselves are organized bodies having particular concerns. Their representatives in Washington are expected to pursue those concerns as well as the nation's common good, indeed they are to define the common good as in part the good of each of the several states taken separately. Because unanimous agreement is rarely possible, the decisions and acts of this regime represent compromises rather than consensus. As a result, those decisions and acts bear only an uncertain relation to the society's common purposes. In a compromise no one view of those purposes is actually realized in the collective decision. Conceptions of the common good, each held by its advocates to be true and desirable, are approximated in varying degree but are not fully expressed in the actions of government. Policies are adopted by means of coalitions which shift and change considerably from one issue to another. These several political conditions have certain consequences: participants are justified in seeing present policy as possibly temporary. They are, thus, encouraged to hold their particularistic views in the hope that those views will be adopted later as central policy. Participants must work together but need not agree, their independent powers enabling them to perpetuate the representation of their special interests and to avoid their seeking a principled resolution of differences that would transcend particularisms by identifying the common good.

Merely because a regime institutionalizes the promotion of special interests through the apparatus of the state it does not follow that there is absent a vital society, its people bound together by strong and supple ties. As American history testifies, a stable and powerful society may be of this order. There is, then, no doubting the existence of American society itself, and, hence, of common purposes and the common good, nor is there any mistaking the strong influence of these on daily operations of our central government. Nor is there doubt that the primary reason for establishing that government was to promote common interests, those interests being that government's distinctive purposes. On the other hand, in a regime in which the exercise of government is not, in principle, separated from the influence of special interests, the common purpose, that is, the regime's own distinctive purpose, is difficult to separate from the special. Compromise decisions are not statements of shining and absolute Truth, but only current operating procedures representing perhaps momentary distributions of power. Rule by majorities obviously leaves the minorities' "truth" out of account. The true standard, the common purpose, remains hidden yet potent.

The Purposes of a Central Government

If successful, these illustrations of political arrangements suggest what is meant by saying that the institutional structure and acts of some governments seem to embody purposes distinctive to those governments and also suggest, by contrast, what is meant by saying that the structure and acts of other governments seem to reflect relations between the character distinctive to those governments and the character of other groups. To obtain a standard that will enable us to assess in these terms the acts of governments that existed in a period far removed from our own we must pass from illustration to some general rules. Our next step, then, is to determine in a general way which attributes of a central government can be considered its own and which cannot.

Governments are organizations. It seems simplest to get at the issue of their attributes, of their powers, by employing certain notions that apply to all social organizations: the notion of an organization as an association and the notion of an organization as a social system. All organizations are both associations and social systems.

The root idea of an association is this: people form organizations, join them, and remain in them in part for what they individually get from them. If the organization no longer profits them, they will abandon it if they can. Other things being equal, an organization's strength and stability depend on its importance as a source of things people want. An association is a relationship among its participants, each being tied to the others because dependent upon them for the satisfaction of his own needs.

It happens, however, that to get what they want from an association, its members must also make an effort to maintain it. They must consider the special problems of keeping it in operation and must devote time, effort, and other resources to that end. They must be willing to undertake assignments in its service. In large organizations some people come quickly to have special responsibility for the tasks of maintaining the organization. They speak in the interest of those tasks and not simply in their own personal interest. They submit to the demands and constraints required of those who serve as agents of the organization and they seize upon opportunities to serve it more effectively. They can act effectively on the organization's behalf only by acting under the discipline of their organization's needs.

But in any organization all participants must on occasion do likewise. In the degree an organization and its needs are thus identified and served, in the degree, that is, to which people act as agents of the organization itself, the organization becomes a social system. As a social system, it does not cease being an association as well.

In any organization, whether it be a society or a community or a family or whatever, there will be some procedures for making decisions which define and promote the interests of its several members and of their organization as such; which advance the interests of its members as partners in an association and as participants in, and as the agents of, a social system. Those procedures are the organization's political system or polity. I shall follow Easton[8] in distinguishing between the polity of an organization as an association and its polity as a social system, referring to the first as a political community or body politic and to the second as a regime. Rightful power exercised in the conduct of a political community is what, in medieval times, was called "jurisdictio" whereas rightful power exercised in the conduct of a regime is what medieval thinkers called "gubernaculum."[9] This distinction between jurisdictio and gubernaculum helps us understand what is meant by speaking of a central government's own purposes and of its incorporation of purposes that spring from other and independent sources.

When Bracton wrote (circa 1250-56) of the king's role in gubernaculum and of his role in jurisdictio he offered ideas common in Europe during the preceding century and for three or four hundred years to come. Reading him today we may appropriately substitute for "crown," "king," and "royal" the prerogatives of any regime in its definition and pursuit of the interests of a society's social system. Gubernaculum, Bracton declared, stands for "Those things which belong to jurisdiction and the peace, and those which are incidental to justice or the peace," and these[10]

> pertain to no one except to the crown alone and to the royal dignity; nor can they be separated from the crown, since they constitute the crown itself. For the *esse* of the crown is

to exercise justice and judgment and to maintain the peace; and without these the crown could neither subsist or endure. Moreover the rights of this kind, or jurisdictions, cannot be transferred to persons or to fiefs; they cannot be in the possession of a private person, neither the enjoyment nor the exercise of the right, except where this has been granted to him from above as a delegated jurisdiction, and it cannot be delegated in such a way as to prevent the ordinary jurisdiction's remaining in the king himself. . . .

Gubernaculum, then, pertains to the rightful, the legitimate, powers of a regime and a regime is the political machinery by which decisions are made to advance the interests of a social system, decisions, that is, which will sustain the interests peculiar to an organization as such rather than those peculiar to its constituent members. Because the members need to maintain the organization in order to fulfill their personal desires, and because they are committed to that end lest the organization fail, the interests of the organization are also interests of its members.

Bracton and other writers tell us that the powers of a society's central regime always include judicial procedures for settling disputes among its members, methods for maintaining internal order, and devices for protecting the society against external enemies. In medieval and early modern Europe a central regime's exercise of gubernaculum commonly included its right, on its own authority to make war or conclude a peace, to create supreme magistrates, to establish a system of judicial appeals, to pardon adjudged offenders, to coin money, to have allegiance or fealty or homage, to grant patents including those of monopoly, and to convoke and control the militia of the state. One simple method for distinguishing the strong regimes of this period from the weak is to count the number of such powers held and observe the effectiveness with which those powers were exercised.

What of jurisdictio: the rights in government of a society's association, of its political community? These are especially the power to define the spheres in which the regime may legitimately govern and the manner in which it may legitimately exercise its powers. Jurisdictio also includes the power to define some spheres of action as reserved to particular members of the political community. Although written constitutions were rare in the fifteenth and sixteenth centuries, those which were later adopted by various Western states usually drew these distinctions between the powers of a regime and those of its underlying political community.

I have stressed that in a society, as in any organization, both an association and a social system are in some degree present and indispensable. Likewise, the rightful decisions made by a society's government will consist of actions both of the society's political community and of its regime. Except perhaps in revolutionary situations, these two sources of authority will be articulated with each other.

There seem only two viable arrangements for effecting such an articulation. In one, the regime comes in practice to exercise all powers of gubernaculum and jurisdictio. In the other, the regime has primary control in gubernaculum, the political community has primary control in jurisdictio, and one or both have some share in the implementation of the other's powers. Bracton describes the second type of articulation. Jurisdictio, he says, is a function shared by a regime with others. It concerns the exercise of, or changes in, the prescribed rights of particular tenants or subjects. (Men of a later age added to his list the prescribed rights of citizens.) To be legitimate, definitions of such rights must be approved by the consent of those to whom they are given and must be confirmed by the regime itself. Changes in such rights again require the consent of those affected and confirmation by the regime. In gubernaculum, said Bracton, the regime's discretionary power is legitimate, complete, and shared with no one but God. In the exercise of jurisdictio there are positive and coercive bounds to its discretion. The regime appoints the judges, but they are bound by oath to determine the rights of subjects according to the law and not the regime's will. The regime must govern with the advice of vassals, citizens, kinsmen, and the like in matters respecting their lands, persons, chattels, and tenurial rights.

Law, as known in medieval times, often consisted of contracts between the king or another officer of the regime and
one or more subjects. To make such law legitimately, the
regime had to proceed by means of consultation and agreement with those of its people who had rights that would
be affected, that is in concord with relevant persons or
groups in their status as members of the political community. The principal objective of the English barons in
forcing King John to sign *Magna Carta* was to end the
king's usurpation of jurisdictio and confine him to the exercise of gubernaculum.[11] The law, whether enacted or grown
imperceptibly from popular traditions, was interpreted in
the West as the rightful will of the political community.

There is a rough correspondence between gubernaculum
and what today are considered powers conventional to the
executive branch of a government and to the higher judiciary. Similarly, the powers now thought peculiarly those
of a legislature or of constituent citizens are somewhat like
the rights earlier enumerated under jurisdictio. But the correspondence is rough at best. The separation of executive,
judicial, and legislative powers was rare in medieval or
early modern times. In those periods, laws were often considered to have been "discovered" or "recognized" rather
than enacted; parliaments and related bodies frequently
served more as a monarch's personal council or as high
courts rather than as law-making assemblies; kings were
often supreme judges and, within such constraints of
jurisdictio as they encountered, supreme law-makers as well.
Kings frequently had, in principle, supreme powers of
policy formulation and execution as well as of routine
administration, there being, for example, no effective requirement that they consult their vassals before making war
or concluding peace or before establishing a police or a
system of courts. On the other hand, the sphere of action
of many central regimes was far more restricted than that
over which modern governments make decisions.

Given these complications it seems better to list those
specific actions generally believed in the fifteenth and sixteenth centuries to constitute either an exercise of guber-

naculum or of jurisdictio and to note separately the various agencies which exercised those powers. Wherever the rights of the political community, that is jurisdictio, were exercised, they included all or most of the following: approval of the making or changing of laws; consent to codifications of law; exercise of the very highest judicial functions (for example, the making of decisions in cases of treason, rebellion, or lese-majesty); approval of declarations of war or of treaties of peace; approval of proposals to levy or renew taxes or to make or obtain loans.

For reasons to be given in the next chapter, it is not possible to list all rights thought proper to a regime. It happens, however, that one can enumerate those rights in gubernaculum which came in some societies to be exercised not only by a regime but also by members of the political community. Those rights are of special interest for our purpose. I can offer a fairly comprehensive list only in the next chapter and after introducing certain new ideas. At this point I can say that the more important rights in gubernaculum sometimes shared by both a society's regime and its political community included the following: the right of selecting or removing principal officers of the regime and of holding them responsible for their actions; the right to determine what administrative or judicial agencies a regime might establish and to supervise the operation of such agencies.

This discussion of association and social system, political community and regime, jurisdictio and gubernaculum can now be made to serve our need for a definition of powers specific to a central government and of powers embodied in its acts but originating outside it. We are looking for the characteristics of a central government that may be associated with belief in the immanence of God.

I have argued that immanence refers to the presence of one actor's powers, of attributes of his personality, in the personality of another. I propose that the presence of a social system's powers in its regime is what we seek. I conclude that the regime's rightful powers, gubernaculum, are those it has as the political agent of the social system and that the social system will be considered immanent in its regime when the regime alone exercises gubernaculum.

Consider the reasoning behind these conclusions:

1. A high god symbolizes the control and coordination in a society of two or more types of subordinate organization by a central government.

2. A central government, hence a high god, will be considered immanent to the extent its structure and acts embody only its own distinctive orientations and purposes.

3. The orientations and purposes involved in a government are those connected with each of its two aspects: a political community and a regime.

4. The orientations and purposes in a political community are those of its several constituent members.

5. The orientations and purposes in a regime are those of the society as a social system which, apart from the requirements of its participants, has special requirements for its operation, maintenance, and enhancement.

6. Therefore the orientations and purposes in government as a political community are not distinctive whereas those in government as a regime are distinctively its own.

7. The orientations and purposes in government as a political community are exhibited in the exercise of jurisdictio; those in government as a regime are embodied in the structure and acts through which gubernaculum is exercised.

8. Therefore a central government, hence a high god, will be considered immanent to the extent the structure and acts through which it exercises gubernaculum embody only its orientations and purposes as a regime.

9. Conversely, a central government, hence a high god, will be considered present and active, but not immanent, to the extent the structure and acts through which it exercises gubernaculum embody the orientations and purposes of particular members of the political community in addition to those distinctive of its regime.

There is another line of reasoning that leads one to decide that the distinctive orientations and purposes of a
government will be found in its regime rather than in its
political community. Regimes may appropriately be conceived to have personal attributes, whereas, apart from their
individual members, political communities may not.

The participants in a political community are tied to one
another individually and are dependent upon the persistence of the whole web of their mutual bonds. They are
affected by new opportunities, demands, and allegiances
developed by their fellows. They are not, however, as an
association, capable of formulating choices or developing
joint programs of action. Only as they become a social system does their relationship have the qualities of a collective personality, a collective actor, rather than merely the
attributes of a web of participants. A regime is the "head,"
the directing decision-making apparatus, of a social system.
Its function is to formulate and implement the interests of
the system. Through its regime a social system can function
as a corporate personality. Through it the system speaks
and acts. Through it the system makes choices; amasses
resources and expends them.

The importance of these new distinctions for questions
concerning the immanence of a high god is this: if a high
god symbolizes the purposes and actions of a central government in unifying relations among groups subordinate
to it, then that god will be experienced as immanent if the
programs and actions implemented by the central government are seen as peculiarly those of the government itself.
We have just seen that, as a political community, a government is not appropriately conceived as having programs or
purposes, that is as making choices or pursuing objectives
or utilizing knowledge. By contrast, to the degree a government is a regime such conceptions become appropriate
because the polity now has a collective character or personality. These observations provide an additional reason
for thinking that the distinctive purposes implemented by a
government are those which it has as a regime.

I concluded earlier that, if a government implements

purposes other than its own, this occurs as its regime is employed to serve private and special interests. In some governments, persons or groups participate in the regime not as its members or agents but as members of the society's political community and, when they do, the acts of the regime represent not an embodiment of the common interest but of relations between the regime and the several special interests now involved in its affairs. In such acts there cannot be said to be immanence because the structure and acts of government embody not the personal traits of a single collective actor but the interrelations among several actors. This last conclusion needs further development.

The inner life of every polity is something of a shoving match, its participants trying to use the powers and machinery of government to advance personal ends. Were the presence of these internal struggles taken as evidence of a regime's permeation by external interests, it would be difficult to distinguish one regime from another. Regimes do differ, however, in the extent to which members of the polity find it possible to relate effectively to the regime only in their capacity as that regime's members, subjects, and agents. In some political systems, men and groups come legitimately to serve as executives and agents of their regime because of their special positions in the political community. Before explaining further and more generally what I have in mind, I will give two illustrations.

In the sixteenth century, Venice was an independent city-state and the supreme authority in Venice was its Great Council. This council had to approve all important policies of government. It served as the highest legislature and highest court. It also served as the highest executive, selecting all important officers of the state, requiring that they be responsible to it, defining, on occasion, the policies which those officers might pursue, and allowing most of the important officials to hold office for very short and nonrenewable terms—terms of from two to twelve months. The significant point for us is that all males who were full citizens of Venice, that is who were full members of the city's political community, were members of the Great

Council. I think this point important because it indicates that participation in the operation of the Venetian regime was open to men in their capacity as members at large of the political system and not because of any traits thought peculiarly theirs as particular individuals in the political community or as representatives of particular groups in that community.

Consider, for contrast, another city-state of the same period, the Swiss canton of Zurich. In Zurich, the supreme authority was again a council, its powers closely resembling those of the Great Council in Venice. Its membership, however, consisted of representatives elected by the several mercantile and artisan guilds into which the whole population of male citizens was divided. Under this system, a role in the central operation of the social system, in its regime, was open to men only in their capacity as representatives of organized groups, those groups not being themselves agents or creations of the regime but, rather, existing independently. They thus were bodies in the political community.

In Venice, men participated in their regime only as members of the social system, only, that is, by virtue of what they had in common with all other members of the political community. And in Venice as everywhere else it was exactly those common interests that had given rise to the social system and to the regime that served as its political head. Moreover, in Venice, certain formal controls were applied to insure that persons in responsible positions in the regime would not use those positions for personal rather than common advantage. Among those controls were short, nonrenewable terms of office and the responsibility of the officials to the Council. It is perfectly true that in Venice as everywhere else, each member of the polity had some interests and purposes peculiarly his. In this sense there were special or selfish interests rather than common interests. But, in Venice, the institutional structure provided no legitimate place for the exercise of those special interests in determining who would man the regime or in what cause the regime would act. The Venetian regime was, in this sense, insulated from the effects of special interests: from the effects of interests held by its participants as members of the political community. Moreover, in their operation of the regime, participants were defined by this procedure as essentially sympathetic to it. They had much to learn about its needs. They would need to be trained and corrected. They must come to discriminate with increasing precision between the regime's requirements and their own. But, given their basic commitment to act as the regime's members and agents, their continued life within it and their service both to it and from it would produce steady improvement in these matters.

In Zurich, matters were different. Men participated in the regime to support the common undertakings on which all depended, but they participated only if they also served and supported special interests in the political community—the interests of the guilds—making certain that the regime served those special interests as well as the common interest. Let it be clear that important common enterprises were present in Zurich, else the state would not have survived. But men related legitimately to the regime in a manner which indicated that their special interests were not foregone in pursuing the common undertakings. Indeed, this structure recognized that those special interests were organized, perpetuated, and fueled by groups in the political community, groups having a considerable autonomy. Participants in operating the regime might, in its name, coerce and encourage and implore and seduce one another's support for it and, because the regime was important to all, they often were successful. On the other hand, they had always to reckon with the presence in their fellows of persistent, ineradicable special interests and with the likelihood that such interests would conflict with those of the common enterprise. The coherence between participants' purposes as members of the political community and as agents of the regime would never be complete. The most that could be achieved would be an ever-strengthened accommodation between the two concerns founded on an increase in participants' commitments to the importance for each of the common interest and on their determination and skill in helping to control such of their own special desires as conflicted with the common interest.

To summarize once more: I have suggested that societies, like all organizations, consist of two formations: an association and a social system and that there corresponds to each formation an organization through which decisions are made. These are, respectively, a political community or body politic and a regime. I have proposed that social systems as institutionalized in regimes have the properties necessary to a corporate actor—a collective personality— and that associations and political communities lack those properties. Therefore social systems and regimes, but not associations or political communities, can have the powers, the attributes, of an actor. The powers of a social system can possibly be immanent in its regime and in the acts of that regime, that is immanent in the regime's exercise of gubernaculum. That possibility, I proposed, is destroyed when men or groups participate legitimately in a regime not solely as its officers or agents but also in their status as members of the body politic—the political organization of the society's association—and hence as promoters of legitimate special interests that exist independently of the common interest, the latter being the special province of the regime itself. This reasoning leads me to define the penetration of a central government by autonomous powers as the formal sharing of a regime's exercise of its special and distinctive powers, of gubernaculum, by persons or groups in their status as members of the political community.

I can now recast the two hypotheses stated early in this chapter and tested in those that follow:

1. There was a positive association in early modern Europe between (a) the extent to which a regime's exercise of gubernaculum was controlled by a political community and (b) the replacement of Catholicism by Protestantism.

2. The greater such control, the more likely it was that Calvinism rather than Lutheranism (or Anglicanism) would be adopted.

In the next chapter, I sketch the varieties of regime found in Western Europe immediately before, during, and soon after the Reformation, specifying the principal patterns which did or did not involve participation by individuals or groups as members of a political community. It is fortunate for our ease of understanding that each of the societies we study can be characterized as having one of only five basic varieties of regime.

[III]

European Regimes in the Fifteenth Century and After

HAVE WE CORRECTLY DESCRIBED political developments in countries that later adopted Protestantism? Did countries with other types of political structure remain Catholic? An answer requires examination of the central governments of European states adhering to Roman Catholicism in the fifteenth century. We shall look at the form taken by those governments in at least three periods: first, in 1490, a point in time well before the Reformation began; second, at the time each country reached its final Reformation settlement; third, in 1780, a date sufficiently later than the Reformation to help us estimate the stability of relations between religious doctrine and government as established at the Reformation.

Societies and Central Governments

How many societies and central governments were there in Europe in 1490? In the sixteenth century? There is no way to tell. But the number was far greater than today. In early modern times, Europe was divided into independent and quasi-independent states of many kinds: kingdoms and republics, duchies, baronies, principalities, lands of tribes, lands of clans, city-states, rural cantons, free cities, bishoprics and archbishoprics, empires, provinces, and lands disputed over by any or several of these. My rule of thumb is to count as a society any population acknowledging a particular secular government as legitimate and as ultimately controlling in its affairs.[1] In practice I judge that such a government exists if it grew naturally from the population whose common affairs it conducts and if it conducts foreign and domestic affairs without the permission and supervision of another power. This means that I shall consider as societies not only well-defined states like England, France, or Portugal but also the unnumbered "clans" of Ireland and of the Scottish Highlands, the major German principalities, and the several Swiss cantons. Each was, for all practical purposes, an independent political entity.

The English government had no effective control over Ireland (except for a small area, the Pale, around Dublin) until well after the Reformation became established in Europe. The Scottish government at Edinburgh had only loose and sporadic power in the Highlands. In most of Ireland and in the Highlands, the ultimate powers of government rested in each of the numerous, localized groups now popularly known as clans. Similarly the German territories were under several independent governments, not one: the Holy Roman Emperor having given up his control over the internal affairs of the major German principalities by 1356 and having lost control over their conduct of foreign affairs by 1520.[2] In Switzerland, each canton was a sovereign state, allied with the others for the common defense but having exclusive control over its internal affairs and often undertaking an independent foreign policy.

If one thinks of central governments as I suggest, he will not count as separate the governments of those countries generally under the effective control of other powers. Thus Belgium should not be counted because Austria and, later, Spain controlled its territory. I do not count Norway which lay under Danish sovereignty; Finland governed by Sweden; Wales held by England; the principalities of German Austria or the territories of western Hungary controlled by the Hapsburg emperors. I also do not count separately the many cities or kingdoms of Italy ruled from Paris, Madrid, Rome, or Vienna; Lithuania under the Polish kings; Esthonia and Latvia variously controlled by Poland or by German nobles. Some countries must be counted independent in one period and not another. These include: Bohemia, an independent and Protestant kingdom subsequently conquered by Austria; Prussia, Mark, and Cleves, all of which fell under the sway of Brandenburg during the period of the Reformation; the duchies of Jülich and Berg which came under Bavarian and Hapsburg domination in the seventeenth century.

Special problems arise from the fact that some lands were organic states, others were dynastic unions—that is a collection of territories united only by their having the same overlord, and still others were only cartographic labels under which existed a variety of independent governments. There is also the difficulty that the central governments of the multitudinous, smaller societies have never been tabulated, let alone individually described. These would, as previously mentioned, include the clans in Ireland and Scotland and the many states on German territory. The following are decisions I made about questionable cases:

Austria:

In the period of interest here, Austria was in the process of changing from a dynastic union to a unified state. My picture of its central government refers to the relations between the Hapsburgs' imperial administration and the several quasi-independent Austrian states whose joint enterprises that administration controlled. These states each had a powerful diet which shared jurisdictio in its territories with the imperial government. At one period these provincial diets also participated in the emperors' central exercise of gubernaculum over the whole of Hapsburg Austria. It was Ferdinand II's achievement in 1620 to establish the imperial sovereignty over the interrelations among these states, definitively institutionalizing that sovereignty and excluding the local diets from a share in the imperial exercise of gubernaculum whether at central or local levels.

Denmark:

My descriptions refer to the government of Denmark itself. The Oldenburg dynasty also ruled in Norway and in Schleswig-Holstein, but under rather different terms in each.

France:

The data I shall cite refer to the government operating over the great bulk of the country. In the period of interest, most of France was directly under the crown. Certain territories, the *pays d'état,* although under the crown, were administered in some important local matters with participation in jurisdictio by their own diets.

Ireland:

The indigenous government of Ireland consisted of groups of kinsmen and their dependents; each group organized as a sept and administered by a chief. The so-called "kingdoms" native to Ireland consisted of very loose and shifting alliances among septs and unions of septs. The "kings" were more largely ceremonial symbols than secular rulers. I have taken the septs as the units of government to describe, but count them together as only one case.

Germany:

In early modern times, Germany was divided into many states. I shall examine only the ten that were the largest, wealthiest, and politically the most important.

Brandenburg-Prussia: These two lands under Hohenzollern rule had separate but essentially similar governments until after the Thirty Years' War when they were united in one administration. The evidence I review for 1490 and for the period of the Reformation is intended to refer to each land separately. The evidence for 1780 refers to the unified state.

Poland:

I shall refer to the administration of the more traditionally Polish lands themselves. The integration of Lithuania into these lands varies considerably from one time to another and is not taken into account.

Scotland (Highlands):

The native regime in this territory is quite similar to that in Ireland. Here too the septs are the units described and they are counted as only one case.

Spain:

My descriptions of government refer to the central Spanish administration based on Castile. This administration, which gradually extended over all of the Spanish lands, became, under Ferdinand and Isabella, the clearly dominant partner in a dynastic union. The rulers gained sole control over gubernaculum in Castile early in our period. In their other territories (Aragon, for example) their regime was at first monarchic but not absolutist. By 1780 their rule was absolute even in these lands.

Switzerland:

For reasons already given, I count separately each of the thirteen original Swiss cantons. To these I add the Canton of Geneva, the long-time ally of the thirteen. On the other hand, I do not describe the several quasi-states (the Grisons, for example) then developing on what later became Swiss territory.

Canton of Appenzell: Following the development of a political stalemate between Protestants and Catholics, this Swiss canton divided in two for certain purposes of internal administration. I shall not distinguish between the two, however, because the canton retained a single central government and because the two sub-cantons appear to have had similar political structures.

Canton of Unterwalden: From a time before our story begins, this Swiss canton had been divided into two half-cantons, Obwalden and Nidwalden. Each had almost complete autonomy. Their governments appear similar in form and I shall count them as only one case, not two.

United Provinces:

My information refers to the internal administration of the counties of Holland and Zeeland (as well as to that of most other members of the Dutch confederation). These two counties were the overwhelmingly dominant members of the confederation. During much of the period of interest here, the union of confederates had itself only feeble powers and no continuing organs of government.

By applying these standards, one obtains a list of forty-one "societies." (Swiss cantons are indicated by an asterisk (*), Germans states by a cross-hatch (#)):

*Appenzell	#Mark
Austria	Poland
*Basel	Portugal
#Bavaria	#Prussia
#Berg	#Saxony
*Bern	*Schaffhausen
Bohemia	*Schwyz
#Brandenburg	Scotland (Highlands)
#Cleves	Scotland (Lowlands)
Denmark	*Solothurn
England	Spain
Florence	Sweden
France	Transylvania
*Fribourg	United Provinces
*Geneva	*Unterwalden
*Glarus	*Uri
#Hesse	Venice
Hungary	#Württemberg
Ireland	*Zug
#Jülich	*Zurich
*Lucerne	

Central Governments at the Reformation

My immediate objective is to examine the central governments of these forty-one societies *at the time of their final Reformation settlement,* and later to see what those governments were like in 1490 and in 1780. I am evaluating an explanation for Protestantism which predicts a relation between the nature of a society's central government and its citizens' experience of God's immanence.

I count a society as Protestant or Catholic when either was its official doctrine. If a country lacked such a doctrine, I classify it according to the apparent preference of its citizens. If sixty percent or more of its citizens had a particular preference, I take that preference to be the country's. (We almost never have reliable evidence concerning the religious preference of the mass of common people. Sometimes the preferences of special or elite groups can be documented. It is my impression that the vast majority of people in most societies adopted the official doctrine, whatever their earlier preferences may have been. There also is scattered evidence that such doctrines, whatever the reluctance displayed at their initial adoption, came in a relatively short time to be the focus of strong popular commitment. In any case, the explanation for the Reformation that is being examined here makes official doctrine especially important because, being official, that doctrine is a direct empirical link between religious persuasion and the fundamentals of political structure.)

What shall be considered the date at which a country arrived at its final position on the Reformation controversies? A case can be made that certain European states, the Netherlands for example, have yet to do so. Luther made public his quarrel with Rome in 1517, but the great European wars of religion continued to 1648. Protestantism, having for a time enjoyed official toleration in France, was newly proscribed in 1685. That date is a significant marker. After 1685 no officially Protestant society became Catholic, no Catholic society became Protestant, and none of the forty-one societies proscribed a faith to which it had afforded toleration. Therefore, in these societies the most violent conflicts over Protestantism were concluded by the end of the seventeenth century. For that reason, I take as the date of a country's Reformation settlement the year prior to 1700 at which it achieved the official religious policy still in force in 1700. The earliest date of settlement is 1524 when Appenzell accepted Zwingli's reformed doctrines and the latest, as stated above, is 1685 when the French government revoked the Edict of Nantes. The regimes of those Catholic societies scarcely touched by the Reformation must also be described. I describe them for the period 1500-1550.

Components of a Central Government

We know at this point that a society's central government has two major components—a political community or body politic and a regime, and we have identified the rightful powers of a body politic as jurisdictio and those of a regime as gubernaculum. Hypotheses have been stated that Protestantism appeared in societies in which some citizens had earlier acquired a formal role in the regime's exercise of gubernaculum as members of the body politic and not merely as "at-large" members of the society or as agents of the regime. Now each government must be classified in a fashion which reveals such participation or its absence.

To develop this classification, it is necessary to decide exactly which parties are members of a body politic. All of a society's members never qualify, children and many others usually being excluded. It is also necessary to judge whether a regime is headed by a governor, that is by a king, prince, executive council, or some other central agency having a considerable independence of action. This judgment is important because the presence and powers of a governor importantly limit the possible ways in which members of the body politic can formally participate in a regime.

A society's political community or body politic consists of all parties recognized in it as its members *and* as free. The body politic does not include parties who are members of a society but unfree or free inhabitants who are not members. Among the forty-one European societies are some in which many inhabitants have only limited freedom but nonetheless are defined as members of the society. They are liable, for example, for taxes and for military service. This was the position of landless peasants in Denmark, Prussia, and Hungary. There are also societies, typically the smaller ones, having more free permanent inhabitants than members. This situation arose in several of the Swiss cantons and, in each, the distinction between the rights of mere inhabitants and those of citizens was sharpened in favor of the latter.

Parties who legally were both members of a society and free tended to have certain civil and political rights: the right to own land and/or business enterprises; the right of access to the central government's courts for the adjudication of civil, political, or criminal actions brought under laws administered at least in part by the central government; the right to protection by the central government against foreign powers; the right of participation, as legally possible, in whatever procedures existed for exercising jurisdictio. (In some countries there were no routine procedures by which members of the body politic could exercise jurisdictio. In others, those rights were very limited or ineffective. In only some countries was there a parliament or a council or an assembly of all citizens, this body exercising the rights of the political community.)

I shall regard the aggregate of all parties having all of these civil and political rights as constituting a society's body politic. Any one of those parties is a constituent body in the body politic. (I refer to parties and constituent bodies rather than to persons because, in some governments, groups as well as individuals were full participants in the body politic.)

A society's regime consists of all parties rightfully exercising powers of gubernaculum, that is, powers of a central government other than powers constituting jurisdictio. (Powers in jurisdictio were enumerated in the preceding chapter.) As we discovered in Bracton's sketch, powers in gubernaculum correspond roughly to the executive and the higher judicial functions of a government. Later in this chapter I list specific powers in gubernaculum important for a test of our hypotheses.

Some regimes are headed by a governor. An example would be the English regime under its king. Other regimes, like those in Venice or Zurich, lacked a governor. A governor may be an individual or a group. In either case, a governor is organizationally separated from the body politic and from agencies through which the body politic may exercise jurisdictio, for example, from legislatures. A governor has independent rights in the exercise of gubernaculum.

To be organizationally separate from the body politic and from a legislature, an agency must have six characteristics:

1. *Term of office:* A governor may come to office by one of many routes. He may come by inheritance or by the choice of his predecessor. He may be chosen by a legislature. He may be selected by the entire body politic. Whatever the route by which a governor comes to his post, he must obtain the right to a term in office exceeding two years. The point of this minimal requirement is to insure that the governor not be too immediately dependent on the wishes of some constituency.

2. *Tenure in office:* A governor must have the security in office provided by a stated term and by the rule that he can be removed from office, if at all, only if he violates such conditions of office as are established when he accepts it and if that violation is determined by due process, that is by some judicial procedure which protects the governor's stated prerogatives as well as prerogatives of persons who challenge his continued right to office.

3. *Confidentiality of procedures:* The incumbent must not be legally obliged to provide any other person or any official body with such information as it may desire concerning the procedures by which he and his subordinates exercise his rights, nor may he legally be called upon to do so upon the completion of his term of office.

4. *Guaranteed support:* There must be some guarantee prior to his taking office that resources needed for the discharge of his responsibilities will be supplied him. These may take any appropriate form: income from a crown's hereditary lands, feudal dues or services, or taxes and aids.

5. *Separation from the body politic:* If the governor is a group it must not consist of more than ten percent of the members of the body politic.

6. *Separation from agencies specifically those of the body politic:* The governor must not be an agency through which the body politic exercises jurisdictio.

The Great Councils of Venice or Zurich were not governors nor were officials empowered by them. Both councils were agencies through which the body politic exercised jurisdictio. The Venetian Council contained not ten percent of the body politic but all of it. Most officers chosen by these two councils had terms in office of one year or less. In Venice, administrative officers typically lacked the right of confidentiality of administrative procedures and could be removed by the Council at its pleasure.

By contrast, the kings in England or the Small Council in the Canton of Lucerne had all the powers of a governor. The terms of both were for life. In neither case was there the legal possibility of removing an incumbent by judicial action. Neither was formally obligated to reveal the procedure by which policies in gubernaculum were formulated. Both had guaranteed sources of support and both were separated from the body politic and from agencies through which the body politic participated in jurisdictio.

But a governor is not merely independent in organization from other agencies. It also has independent rights in the exercise of gubernaculum. These include:

1. *Scope of initiative:* A governor has all aspects of gubernaculum within his purview and may take the first steps toward action with respect to any or all of them.

2. *Administrative independence:* A governor has sole authority to administer at least some of the significant policies that guide the exercise of gubernaculum. He may, for example, have the decisive word in determining how a system of provincial courts shall be organized or how policies regarding foreign trade shall be implemented or how a newly created army shall be trained.

3. *Executive authority:* No one has the right to disobey a governor's decisions except by authority of established judicial procedures which protect the governor's rights as well as those of complainants.

By these three criteria, every head of government is not a governor. The dukes (doges) of Venice, like the kings in modern England, reigned but did not rule. All effective powers in Venice were reserved to the Great Council and to agents empowered by it. Similarly, in some periods of Polish history, the kings lost effective legal powers over gubernaculum: the nobles deprived them of any clear rights in administration and reserved to themselves the right at their individual discretion to ignore the monarch's administrative orders and to rebel against him.

By these same criteria, a governor need not have exclusive competence over gubernaculum. A king or self-perpetuating oligarchy may, for example, be forced to exercise gubernaculum in some matters with the consent of a council, that council consisting of representatives of a legislature and responsible to it. This came to be the position of kings in Hungary. But the existence of this council need not infringe on the organizational separation of the governor's other powers from the legislature's or on the independence of his rights in gubernaculum.

Gubernaculum

Having in hand the concepts of a constituent body and of a governor, we can itemize actions commonly considered an exercise of gubernaculum in the fifteenth and sixteenth centuries. As indicated in Chapter II, it is impossible to construct a complete list of such actions. That list would have to include any steps that might be taken by a government on behalf of a social system. It is possible, however, to do what is needed for our work: to list powers in gubernaculum that were often exercised by participants in the body politic, that is by constituent bodies. Some of these powers affected the staffing and operation of the government's central executive and judicial agencies. Other powers shaped the policies for staffing and organizing the agencies that applied the central government's policies to special groups in the society: for example, agencies that applied those policies to guilds or to localities. Among agents who applied central policies to special groups we commonly find local judges, militia, police, and tax collectors.

In Europe at the Reformation we can observe here and there constituent bodies exercising over central operations of government such powers as the following:

1. Maintain the regime
   a. Elect governor
   b. Share in exercise of regencies
   c. Possess the right, as an assemblage of constituent bodies, to rebel against a governor who breaches their privileges
   d. Possess the right, as individual constituent bodies, to rebel against a governor who breaches their privileges

2. Control over administrative staffing
   a. Name some or all major officials, these then being responsible in some measure to the constituent bodies
   b. Remove major officials who breach the law
   c. Name some or all major officials
   d. Nominate a slate of candidates for some or all major official posts, the governor then making his appointments from this slate
   e. Consent to the accession to office of major officials named by the governor

3. Supervision of administrative operations
   a. Supervise the collection and/or the expenditure of taxes and aids
   b. Supervise trade and commerce
   c. Establish and/or support the maintenance of armies, militia, or fortifications
   d. Determine the uses made of armies or militia
   e. Consent to the establishment or revocation of alliances

4. Comprehensive powers: Constituent bodies select or comprise authorities having independent and original jurisdiction in regime.

Some of these powers are more important than others. Control over administrative staffing provides a continuing influence over the operations of the regime. So does the lodgment in the body politic of comprehensive powers in gubernaculum. In both cases, these powers enable constituent bodies significantly to influence the regime's policies and not merely the administration of those policies. Similarly a right of rebellion constitutes a more continuously important power than does the right to elect a governor or to share in regencies. In sum, the more important of these powers in gubernaculum are 1 c and d; 2 a, b, c, and d; and 4.

Just as we can find governments in which constituent bodies participate in the central operation of the state, including rights in gubernaculum, so we can find governments in which constituent bodies share, with a governor, control over the application, to subdivisions of the population, of policies developed by the central regime. The following are the more common forms of such control:

1. Control over staffing of local units of a national administrative structure
   a. Name some or all major local officials, these then being responsible in some measure to the constituent bodies
   b. Name some or all major local officials
   c. Consent to major local officials named by the governor
   d. Nominate a slate of candidates for major local official posts, the governor making his appointments from this slate
   e. Governor must choose major local officials from among that locality's inhabitants

2. Control over the operation of local units of the national administrative structure
   a. Control all or a large share of the local administra-

tion of the national system of justice and general
administration

b. Possess the right to subject the local administration
by national officials to judicial review

Five Types of Regime

One finds that each European society had at the time of its
final Reformation settlement one of five types of regime:
commensal, heterarchic, centralist, limited centralist, or
balanced. The first two lack a governor. In commensal
regimes, Venice being an example, participants in the body
politic participate in the regime only as that regime's members and agents. In heterarchic regimes, Zurich being an
example, constituent bodies participate in the regime as
representatives of their own or others' special interests.

The three remaining types of regime have governors. They
differ from one another according to the governor's powers
in gubernaculum. In centralist regimes he alone exercises
those powers. He may, however, share jurisdictio with
constituent bodies. In limited centralist regimes, the governor
shares with representatives of constituent bodies the application of his policies to those bodies. In balanced regimes,
the governor shares with constituent bodies the central
formulation and administration of policies in gubernaculum;
specifically the governor shares with constituent bodies those
central powers in gubernaculum itemized above as the most
important.

Each type of regime is described more fully in the chapters
that follow. Those chapters also contain brief accounts
of the political and religious developments in each of the
forty-one societies selected for study.

In interpreting so fluid a period of political history as that
from the fifteenth through the eighteenth century, there are
special problems in deciding just what kind of regime a
society had. I rely whenever possible on accounts of the
structure of power and the practices of government actually
in operation at the time and on descriptions of traditions,
laws, or constitutions generally accepted in a society. When

these two kinds of evidence are in agreement there is no problem. When they give discrepant pictures, one must make a choice. I employ certain rules to guide that choice: first, I try to avoid making any decision on the basis of knowledge about the fate of a government after the period in which a society's Reformation settlement occurred. I use, instead, only information from that period and from earlier years. Second, I pay little or no attention to the effectiveness of government, relying instead on accounts of the political structure employed for making decisions whatever the success or failure it encountered. Third, I give more weight to actual practices of government if it is evident that written legal prescriptions for government or fondly cited traditions have been dead letters for some time or if there recently occurred a struggle in which supporters of some prescriptions or traditions were decisively beaten or relegated to minority status.[3]

At least for my purpose and for this period of history, these three rules work quite well. There probably is a special reason why they do: by choosing to examine the regime in power at a society's final Reformation settlement, to 1700, I pick a regime which weathered a great social upheaval and was associated with a balance of social forces capable of achieving some measure of religious stability, in most cases for a century or more. As we have seen, no society that adopted Protestantism before 1700 later adopted Catholicism, nor did any Catholic societies later adopt Protestantism.[4]

It is my thesis that commensal and centralist regimes provide no legitimate role in gubernaculum for special interests, that is for constituent bodies, as such. I assume, therefore, that these regimes will be associated with the persistence of Catholicism. I propose that, by contrast, heterarchic, limited centralist, and balanced regimes each provide such a place for constituent bodies and that they will therefore be associated with the adoption of Protestantism. Finally, I propose that the role of constituent bodies in gubernaculum is greatest in heterarchic and balanced regimes because they there join in the formulation of central policies by which the state is guided and administered. By contrast, in limited centralist regimes constituent bodies participate only in the application of such policies to subdivisions of the body politic. Because Calvinism is an even more drastic denial of immanental doctrines than is Lutheranism (or Anglicanism), I conclude that Calvinism will appear with disproportionate frequency in countries that adopted heterarchic and balanced regimes; that Lutheranism will appear more often than Calvinism under limited centralist regimes.

As I evaluate the evidence, 21 of the 41 societies under study had commensal or centralist regimes. All but two of these societies remained Catholic. Of the 20 societies I judge to have had heterarchic, limited centralist, or balanced regimes, all adopted Protestantism. All societies with limited centralist regimes adopted the Anglican or Lutheran reforms. All societies with balanced or heterarchic regimes adopted Calvin's doctrines. The evidence for these conclusions is given in the next five chapters.

[IV]

Centralist Regimes

THE GREATER STATES of Europe and some lesser states had regimes headed by a governor. Because the greater states so largely determine the history of all other societies, I begin by describing their regimes and something of their political histories. It is convenient to describe centralist regimes first, then limited centralist regimes, and, finally, balanced regimes.

Regimes Having Governors

Feudal lordships and feudal, medieval, and absolute kingdoms were the most common varieties of centralist state in the fifteenth and sixteenth centuries. On occasion one finds instead rule by tyrants or by small self-perpetuating groups. All these systems of central government are similar to one another in that, in each, there is a governor and the governor alone, or through agents responsible to him, exercises the central regime's powers in gubernaculum. Constituent bodies do not share the exercise of those powers at either the central or the local level. At the time of their final Reformation settlement, eleven of our forty-one societies had centralist regimes. All of these societies remained Catholic.

Feudalism was a method of government which arose to perform essential political functions in a period of great disorder occasioned by the breakup from within of the Carolingian Empire and by incursions of Northmen and of Asiatic tribes into France, Italy, and Germany.[1] In those chaotic times, public authority came to be treated as a private possession, and public duties were performed as a result of private contracts. As a return for the protection and order a man could provide on lands under his control, or in compensation for rights to work the land and to gain a share in its produce, other people attached themselves to the owner. They pledged to support him by rendering him obedience, military service, the payment of fees, the granting of economic aids in times of emergency, and the provision of assistance with the local conduct of the lord's government. "Vassal homage was a genuine contract and a bilateral one. If the lord failed to fulfill his engagements he lost his rights."[2]

Whether greatly elaborated as a feudal kingship or confined to local relations among nobles and vassals, the feudal order gave gubernaculum to the lord, and did so by contractual definition. However, it reserved certain rights to the lord's subjects and, in matters connected with those rights, in jurisdictio, lord and vassals had in principle to reach a joint agreement.

In a *feudal* kingdom, the monarch exercised gubernaculum equally over many vassals, by virtue of having *with each a special* contractual arrangement terminable by reason of the parties' failure to fulfill their respective obligations or by either party's extinction. The lord's contractual arrangements often differed considerably from one vassal to another.

Most kingdoms were not purely feudal. In what may be called *medieval* kingdoms, there existed in addition to feudal ties an awareness among vassals of problems and interests they had in common even though these vassals did not jointly comprise a unified state. They looked to their common lord to develop and implement policies appropriate to serve their joint interests as well as their separate, individual needs. Gubernaculum over both was in his hands and in those of officials chosen by him.

In feudal and medieval kingdoms (or in duchies or other lordships of considerable magnitude), the lord received homage from the great men of the land. Subordinates of those men owed allegiance, however, to their immediate superior and not to their superior's lord. This meant, in principle, that the overlord's exercise of gubernaculum did not extend to his vassals' subordinates and, in practice, that struggles often ensued between overlords and their immediate vassals for control over the mass of the population. Technically, however, only the lord's own vassals constituted the body politic of his regime.

Absolutism is one type of centralism. The most common variety of absolutism in early modern times was that of a monarchy in which the king had exclusive rights over jurisdictio as well as gubernaculum. On occasion, however, a tyrant or a self-perpetuating oligarchy occupied that position. It is true that even strong and effective autocrats were unlikely to make laws diametrically opposed by their more powerful subordinates and that weak or indolent rulers might use little of the power legitimately theirs, leaving its exercise to others able to grasp it. Nonetheless, the principle of absolutism is that of the formal supremacy of a governor over both gubernaculum and jurisdictio.

Centralist regimes may be contrasted with limited centralist and balanced regimes. At the time of their final Reformation settlements to 1700, eight of our forty-one societies had limited centralist regimes. These were Brandenburg-Prussia, Denmark, England, Hesse, Saxony, Sweden, and Württemberg. In each regime, the governor was a king or nobleman. All but England adopted Luther's Protestantism, the English developing a faith, Anglicanism, that we have found to have doctrines of immanence resembling those of Luther.

Limited centralist regimes are identical with centralist regimes in all respects but one: constituent bodies have a guaranteed, formal role in the application to particular subdivisions of the body politic (guilds or localities, for example) of policies and orders in gubernaculum originated by the governor. This criterion requires that the governor be able on his own authority to originate such policies and orders and that the subdivisions of the body politic be at once required to implement them and empowered to act as the governor's agents supervising that implementation.

We shall find that some regimes, those to be termed "balanced," do not permit a governor this right to originate policies solely on his own authority. Centralist regimes, by definition, provide the governor such a right. In some centralist regimes the governor's policies are applied to subdivisions of the body politic through agents appointed by him and responsible only to him. We shall find that this was the situation in Bavaria and in Portugal. But in other centralist states, France, Spain, and most notably, Austria, at least some subdivisions of the body politic were largely and independently responsible for the application to their members of policies devised by the governor. How do these three countries differ from limited centralist states?

In all three of these countries, but not in states I term limited centralist, there persisted some remains of feudal arrangements: specifically, in each country, the monarch had to negotiate separately with local governments in each of several territories, this on the grounds that his rights of government over each had been acquired by a special arrangement and those rights differed somewhat from one territory to another. Thus, although the French kings had by the fifteenth century attained an absolutist rule over most of the country, there were still a few important French territories, the *pays d'états*, having a different relation to the crown. Among these territories were Brittany and Languedoc. The kings could, solely on their own authority, administer, legislate, and tax in other areas of France. In the *pays d'états*, however, they had to negotiate special arrangements with local legislative bodies, arrangements concerning the tax each territory would accept as its rightful share of the national total and concerning the procedures to be employed in administering policies related to taxation and other matters. As a rule, once the administrative procedures were agreed upon, agents acceptable to the local legislatures and partially responsible to them then implemented the new policies. The Spanish kings had an absolutist base in Castile, but had more traditionally feudal relations with such of their territories as Aragon and Catalonia. The Hapsburg rulers of Austria were forced to engage in such special, contractually obligatory negotiations in each of their several Austrian lands.

In limited centralist states there is no need for such separate negotiations with particular formal subdivisions of the body politic. Instead, each relates to the governor under the same terms as the others and a policy which he establishes for all is equally binding upon each. The subdivisions have come to be defined as administrative units of the central state and hence as its creatures rather than, as in the case of vassals or of vassal states, each having a special contractual agreement with its overlord. The local authority exercised by these subdivisions is authority as the overlord's agents.

Nonetheless, the subdivisions in a limited centralist state do serve as the governor's agents in applying his policies to their local affairs. This is not a trivial power. The governor has, in principle, either to appoint as his agents residents of the localities which those agents are to administer or to utilize nominees of already existing and otherwise autonomous local bodies for that purpose. These agents and bodies are required, for their part, to implement the governor's orders: for example to allocate and collect taxes levied, to appropriate or expend funds for public works constructed in the locality, to create and instruct and maintain police and militia, to hold courts of law and execute their decisions, to organize works of public charity, to support and supervise the extra-sacerdotal aspects of the local churches, to report to the governor and advise him, and to supervise trade and other economic activities. And all these functions are in principle performed at the governor's command and under his supervision.

The regimes I have called limited centralist provide some formal guarantee that these local agents have significant autonomy in implementing the governor's programs. In our period, such guarantees usually took one or both of two forms: (a) the composition by local representatives of a strong national diet with which the governor was forced to share his role in legislation or (b) the governor's empowering of local bodies to form the agencies and select the persons who would administer central policies on the local level. Under these conditions, representatives of subdivisions of the body politic, that is of special interests, have an important share in the central government's exercise of gubernaculum, but they must encounter, take account of, and compromise with the central regime, a power which, in principle, represents the common interest—which is designated normatively as above the differences among these subdivisions. Conversely, that power must temper its directives to make it likely that subdivisions will enforce them.

Balanced regimes, like centralist and limited centralist regimes, have a governor. They differ in that constituent bodies—subdivisions of the body politic—have a formal role in shaping the governor's central administration and not merely in the local application of that administration's policies. All the societies in our sample having a balanced regime adopted Calvinist doctrines.

The crucial feature of a balanced regime is that the governor shares his general and central exercise of gubernaculum with persons chosen by some constituent body or bodies, those persons then reporting to such bodies as well as to the governor, or receiving their advice as well as his, or being removable by them. Thus the kings of Hungary had for a time to employ as their administrators in each Hungarian county local notables responsible to local groups, and had also to share their administration of the central executive and judicial organs of the state with men elected by the Hungarian parliament and responsible to it. The parliament, in turn, consisted of representatives elected by the landowners of each Hungarian county. In our period, the governments of six other societies appear to have had balanced regimes: those in Bohemia, Geneva, the Scottish Lowlands, Transylvania, Cleves, and Mark.

It was not uncommon in the fifteenth and sixteenth centuries for a parliament or diet to elect a nation's king and to require that he submit for its approval the persons he desired as principal officers. However, once the monarch and his lieutenants came to office, their exercise of gubernaculum might thereafter, and by right, be in their hands alone. According to the criteria set for a balanced regime, constituent bodies in such governments have a role not simply in installing the governor and his principal agents but also in continuously sharing with them the central formulation and administration of policies requiring the exercise of gubernaculum.

But these generalized descriptions of regimes come to life only when one examines the histories of particular societies. In the remainder of this chapter are short sketches of essential political and religious events in each society that was centralist at the time of its final Reformation settlement to 1700. These sketches begin with the period 1490 or earlier and extend at least to 1780. In some cases there was a change in type of regime from one period to another and in other cases there was not. The significance of those changes for our explanation of the Reformation are discussed in Chapter IX. In this chapter and in Chapters V through VIII, I group countries according to whatever form of regime was in power at the time of their final Reformation settlement. The next chapter, Chapter V, presents histories of countries having limited centralist regimes. Histories of countries with balanced regimes are given in Chapter VI.

Centralist Regimes

The centralist societies vary in the date at which each by indigenous processes attained a resolution of the Reformation issues. In five societies there was never, to 1700, a significant Protestant movement: Ireland, Lucerne, Portugal, the Scottish Highlands, and Spain. Their regimes are here described as centralist at least in the period 1500 to 1550. Protestantism made important inroads in the bodies politic of the remaining societies. Their regimes are here described as centralist at least at the time the Reformation struggles were concluded in each. The respective dates are: Austria —1620, Bavaria—1564, Berg-Jülich—1614, France—1685, and Solothurn—1533. I interpret in Chapter IX the conspicuous oscillations in religion and regime that occurred in several states. One of those states, Austria, is described in this chapter.

Of the eleven centralist regimes in our sample, six were

absolutist or nearly so, the governor having over most of the body politic exclusive control over jurisdictio as well as over gubernaculum. These were the regimes in France, Ireland, Portugal, the Scottish Highlands, Solothurn, and Spain. Seven of the eleven governors were individuals: kings, emperors, or noblemen. This kind of governor was found in Austria, Bavaria, the Rhenish territories of Berg and Jülich, France, Portugal and Spain. Two governors were groups of kinsmen: those in Ireland and the Scottish Highlands. Two were self-perpetuating councils: the governors of the Swiss cantons of Lucerne and Solothurn.

We have already seen that three centralist states, France, Austria, and Spain retained important features of feudal kingdoms, the monarch in each having to negotiate and renegotiate separate adminstrative arrangements with at least some important provinces in his realm. Several centralist governments would also at times involve the body politic or some of its members in exercising jurisdictio. In two cases, the Austrian duchies and the canton of Lucerne, this involvement of the body politic on certain issues was constitutionally mandatory.

I shall describe the essential political structure of each centralist regime, beginning with Austria. In describing the centralist German states—Bavaria, Jülich, and Berg—I first sketch something of the general political situation in all of Germany, this being a necessary context for understanding events in her several constituent societies. Similarly, when describing Lucerne and Solothurn in this chapter, I begin with some necessary observations about the political situation in all of Switzerland. In a later chapter I give a comparable overview of politics in the whole of Italy before turning to individual Italian states.

Austria

In early modern times and well through the eighteenth century, the unified state we know as Austria did not exist. Instead there were a series of duchies and other small territories, each owing allegiance to a member of the House of Hapsburg as its hereditary overlord. Sometimes all the territories were under the same overlord and sometimes they were divided among different members of the House. The exact arrangement depended on the wish and will of the previous rulers, on their success in rearing children to maturity, and on the vicissitudes of death, longevity, and madness in the ruling house.

The archduchy of Austria itself was called Lower Austria and was divided for purposes of administration into Austria above the River Enns and Austria below the Enns. Each section had its own officials and a diet of its own Estates. (The archduchy of Austria and the duchy of Styria were the nucleus of Hapsburg power in Germany.)

There were, in addition, the Tyrol and Vorarlberg, known jointly as Upper Austria, the three duchies of Styria, Carinthia, and Carniola called "Inner Austria," and the Hapsburg lands in southwestern Germany termed "Further Austria." The Hapsburgs had governed most of these lands since the fourteenth century.

By the late 1400's, and despite a variety of local differences in government, all the Austrian territories had developed similar patterns of internal administration and a similar relation to their rulers. In each there were active and powerful diets of Estates from which, with the exception of the Tyrol, all elements but the nobility had been stripped of effective power. The Hapsburg overlords, perpetually short of funds as a result of their own impecuniousness and of wars against European powers and against Turkish invaders, were forced to come to these diets for support and had to grant concessions in return.

The diets were further strengthened by quarrels and divisions within the ruling house in the period from 1379 to 1526, a period in which the Estates frequently played the role of mediator and arbitrator. The diets had to be consulted before taxes were levied or renewed. In many cases their assent had to be obtained before the lord declared war or concluded a peace. Most diets had created standing committees to manage local finances when the full diet was not in session and to represent local interests to the overlord and supervise the local preservation of public order.

Indeed, in the sixteenth century, the Hapsburgs usually depended on the diets and the diets' agents for all local administration.[3] The ruling house did appoint a governor for each territory and provided each governor with an advisory commission, but in most cases the diets gained the right to approve or disapprove the appointees and it was the Estates and their agents who governed effectively in local matters.[4] They established police, passed measures to promote public health, appointed printers, master builders, house painters, teachers, and even cooks. They created militia and raised the funds for their support.[5] They allocated, collected, and, in part, administered taxes to which they consented.

With the exception of certain major crimes, such as treason, or of legal cases in which the prince himself or his major vassals were the parties, the administration of justice outside the cities was primarily in the hands of the Estates.[6] The officers of the courts were local lords exercising a hereditary jurisdiction or were agents of the diets, applying customary law or statutes enacted by the diets themselves.

To this point we have found that Estates in the Austrian lands exercised rights of jurisdictio in dealing with their lord and far-reaching rights of gubernaculum in internal affairs. Despite their best efforts, they were unable to go further. The several territories were unable to develop and implement a foreign policy other than that of their Hapsburg overlord. They gained neither the right nor the power to employ militia outside their own boundaries except with his consent and under his general supervision. They were not represented in a diet of all the Estates of the Hapsburg realms, a diet capable of exercising jurisdictio in matters of common interest to all the Austrian lands. They were unable to participate by right in the establishment, staffing, or operation of the lord's central administrative councils, although subject to decisions and actions of those councils.

They never gained the right to insist upon redress of their grievances before affording the lord the subsidies he demanded. The time finally arrived when their lord had at his disposal military forces independent of theirs and far more powerful.

From 1437 to 1742 and from 1745 to 1806, a Hapsburg ruling in Austria also occupied the throne of the Holy Roman Empire. Incredible as it seems by modern expectations, it was not until the reign of Maximilian I (1486-1519) that a serious effort was made to establish some central institutions capable of administering either Austria or the Empire.[7] Maximilian concentrated on the organization of his Austrian lands. In 1490, and with the permission of the several diets, he substituted a council of government nominated by himself for one elected by the Estates and he entrusted general matters of finance to a commission of four members. This new system met growing resistance from the Estates of Lower and Inner Austria. Resentment increased when he created in 1498 two agencies for the whole Empire including his Austrian lands: a treasury and a supreme council, the latter also acting as a court of last appeal. Unable to pursue the reorganization of the Empire in the face of chaotic conditions that spread in Germany between 1499 and 1502, he turned to matters in Lower Austria, establishing a central court and a treasury.[8] He chose as judges, not local nobles but trained jurists.

The Austrian Estates fought each of these changes and, to gain their aid in financing a war with Venice, Maximilian was forced to restore their traditional provincial courts under local control and to assent to the codification of local customary law. He did manage to retain the central treasury and the council to supervise government in all his Austrian provinces. These bodies included representatives chosen by the Estates.[9]

In his last year of life, his financial resources were again exhausted and Maximilian was forced to convoke an assembly representing all his Austrian Estates. He asked them for money and he proposed the creation of a permanent council to help in the government of Austria and of the Empire. The

Estates at first demurred, trying to limit his powers and to dominate the new organs of government should they come into being. Maximilian was at length given the money he sought but he granted nothing to the Estates.

Charles V, Maximilian's successor as Holy Roman Emperor, became increasingly preoccupied with his inheritance of the Burgundian lands and of Spain, and he divided the Imperial responsibilities. In 1521-22, he gave his brother Ferdinand (Ferdinand I: 1521-64) title to rule in Germany, in Austria, and in the Hapsburg lands in eastern Europe. Ferdinand continued Maximilian's council and treasury for Lower Austria, developing them as permanent commissions having collegial responsibility for their internal operations.

At Ferdinand's death, the Austrian territories were divided among his three sons, each of whom maintained an independent government within his domains. Each did, however, establish organs of administration which, ready to hand, were available to be fitted into a larger whole when the Austrian lands were once again under a single ruler able to control his patrimony.

Such a ruler was long in coming. The Emperor Maximilian II (1564-76) may himself have been Protestant in outlook. In any event he was not anxious to curb the several Austrian Estates, themselves now largely Protestant, upon whose support he relied in his competition with Charles V's son Philip II for control over the Empire. The Emperor Rudolph II (1576-1612) was weak, vacillating, often immobilized, and finally mad, his government exercised by a regent. It was only with the accession of Ferdinand II (1619-37) that the Austrian lands were again united under a single lord who also was capable of governing and of extending a pattern of central institutions that might outlast his own reign.

Ferdinand I had removed the representatives of the Estates from the central council and court for Austria. Ferdinand II reinvigorated both bodies and linked them to administrative offices in each of the several territories, each under a governor fully empowered to represent the Emperor.[10]

By gradual stages the organs of central direction were extended, the monarch's privy council being the chief instrument in this work. The administration of the most important political and judicial affairs of the various provinces of the monarchy was withdrawn from the influence of the Estates. Although the Estates still maintained their rights in principle, after the middle of the sixteenth century their real influence in all but economic affairs was gone.[11] Even in that department their power was not great, for while they accompanied their grants of money with complaints and petitions, it was by no means determined that grants were dependent on redress of grievances. In actual practice the Estates did not refuse the demands of the crown in matters touching on the general government of the Austrian lands.

But if the effectiveness of the central authorities in exercising gubernaculum was extended in matters of general policy for all the Austrian territories, the diets of local nobility long continued to be influential in purely internal matters. Even when, under Maria Theresa (1740-80) and Joseph II (1780-90), the Austrian rulers turned definitively from their prerogatives in the Empire to organize their Austrian possessions, the Estates retained a great and independent force. Maria Theresa made only a beginning at requiring that sentences of manorial courts be confirmed by a representative of the Imperial government.[12] She was forced to recognize the right of the diets to levy and collect taxes and she agreed to publish no decree concerning taxation without the consent of the Estates.[13] Joseph II emancipated the peasants and greatly extended central control over the provincial courts and administration, yet had to face the fact that his monarchy depended on the cooperation, or at least the acquiescence, of the organized Estates. At his death, many of his reforms were overridden as the provincial diets and the principal ministers of the central government regained the initiative from the crown.

Despite the great size and complexity of the lands involved, the form of government prevailing in Austria during most of the period from 1450 to 1790 was that of a

feudal state gradually becoming a unified centralist kingdom as centralization changed the component lands from
mutually independent realms to provinces of a single
monarchy. The indications of the growth of this regime
are as follows: government over relations between the emperor's vassals and between them and the emperor was in
the latter's hands and, with the short-lived exception of
Maximilian's council for Austria, was the emperor's alone.
Ruler and Estates exercised jurisdictio jointly at all periods.
Until the reign of Ferdinand II, and especially before that
of Joseph II, the Estates had the larger part of the government of their own dependents in their own hands. The
segregation of the emperor's rule from that of his vassals is
seen with special clarity in relation to the vassals' dependents. The Imperial courts did not adjudicate matters
concerning those dependents nor could such dependents
appeal to these courts. The emperor could not tax such
dependents directly, having to work through the often
unwilling local diets. He could enact statutes binding in
local affairs only with the consent of those diets. The diets
and their officers, not the emperor, had the right to regulate
the enlistment and quartering of troops and to organize a
local police, regulate trade, and develop programs for the
public welfare.[14]

The Estates fought every effort to centralize the Imperial
government or make it effective, and, when that government
was extended despite their protests, they sought representation in the emperor's exercise of gubernaculum. In that
they finally failed. During these struggles, the greater part
of the nobility seems to have embraced Protestantism.[15]

The Great Synod of Salzburg in 1549 indicated that
Styria, Carinthia, and Carniola were completely infiltrated
by Protestantism. The diets of all these provinces asked
their ruler, Charles II, to establish the Reformation. Urban,
Bishop of Gurk, wrote in 1572 to Albrecht of Bavaria saying
that one Austrian city after another was embracing the new
doctrines, official action having been taken at Graz,
Marburg, Loeben, Judenburg, Radkersburg, Fürstenfeld,
Rottenmann, Noitsberg, Aussee, Neumarkt, Eisenerz, Weis-

senkirchen, Feldbach, Oberseiring, and Obdach. Klangen-
furth, capital of Carinthia, had hardly one Catholic within
its borders. All public offices were in Protestant hands.

In that same year, while admitting Jesuits to Graz,
Charles of Styria had to promise not to eject the Lutheran
preachers. He renewed his concessions to Protestantism in
1578. In 1581 the Town Council of Graz imposed a fine upon
those who attended a Catholic sermon. Charles began to
regain control for Catholicism in 1582, imprisoning the
mayor and decreeing that attendance at Catholic services was
obligatory for all. In 1587 he vetoed the erection of new
Protestant churches and insisted that all judges must be
Catholics. However, after his death in 1590, the Reformation went forward with new vigor. Attending Mass at Graz
on Easter Sunday in 1595 after his accession in Styria, Duke
Ferdinand found that he and his entourage were the only
communicants.

It is estimated that by 1567 only five noble families in
Styria were Catholic, four in Carinthia and three in Carniola
and that the ten cities and eight markets of these territories
were thoroughly Protestant. In Upper Austria only one
Catholic family remained among the older nobility and the
delegates to the diet from the seven newer cities were all
Protestants. The Styrian diet in 1580-81 consisted of forty to
fifty Protestants and of five or six Catholics. All twenty
Styrian towns and markets were represented by Protestants.
In 1609 the diet of the Archduchy of Austria consisted of
three hundred Protestants and eighty Catholics.

Ferdinand of Styria, later to be the Emperor Ferdinand
II, led the movement against Reformed doctrine. Acceding to rule over Inner Austria in 1595 he set about a
systematic campaign for Catholic revival. In this he had
military aid from Bavaria. In 1598 he ordered the departure
of Protestant preachers from all towns in his domains and,
having succeeded in this, declared that all townsmen must
return to Catholicism or must sell their goods, hand over a
tenth part of their property's value, and emigrate. When
the Estates protested he declared he was free to act as he
pleased in his own lands. Protestant books were burned,

teachers expelled, and a public oath in support of Roman doctrine exacted of all. The Estates renewed their protests. Ferdinand refused to receive their deputation. Within a decade all public display of Protestant worship had been suppressed.

Meanwhile, in Vienna and Lower Austria, the Archduke Ernest took similar measures. His effort to root out the Protestants among the formerly Catholic clergy proved slow work, having to await the training by Jesuits and other Catholic Orders of a sufficient number of worthy candidates for the priesthood.

When Ferdinand became Emperor in 1619, the Protestant majority of the Estates of the Archduchy of Austria refused him homage. They retired to Horn and there prepared a defense against their prince, concluding an alliance with the Bohemian Estates (likewise Protestant) and with their coreligionists who formed a majority in the diet of Austria above the Enns. They required that the entire administration of the archduchy be carried on with their advice, claimed freedom from taxation, the right to meet at will, the authority to administer the archduchy when the throne was vacant, and the prerogative of making alliances.

Ferdinand, heir to Bohemia as well as to Austria, collected a great army consisting of Austrians loyal to his cause and contingents sent to his aid by the Spanish branch of the Hapsburg family, a branch not suffering in its dominions from difficulties with Protestantism. Aided also by Polish troops, Ferdinand crushed the Protestant Estates of Bohemia in 1620, imposing a strong centralist regime. With that victory, rebellions against him in Austria collapsed and Protestantism was forcibly extirpated. Its adherents were required to become Catholics or to leave the country.

Pending the detailed historical studies that have yet to be made, we may note that the rise of Protestantism in Austria coincided with a struggle between the Hapsburgs and their Estates for control over government in the several Austrian territories, that the Estates sought either some large share in the new central organs exercising gubernaculum or an even greater exercise of gubernaculum in their own affairs

—even to the extent of gaining control over their own foreign policies. It is true that Imperial control was often feeble as the emperors sought to fight in the great wars that exploded in Europe and to defend their eastern frontiers against the Turks. But Imperial weakness seems not to have been the critical and governing condition that accounts for Protestantism's rise. The Imperial power had been dangerously weak at other times in the past. What seems distinctive at this time was, rather, the novel effort of the Hapsburgs to create central institutions, an effort which seriously threatened the feudal privileges and rule of the Estates and which raised for them the whole problem of their relations to the dynasty.

In any event, the triumph of Ferdinand in 1620 was simultaneously a triumph for a centralized regime and Catholicism. That double triumph was never upset whatever the vicissitudes of Austrian history during the next century and beyond.

France

The long and troubled development of French government from the first feeble Capetian kings to the Battle of Agincourt (1415) is in part a story of struggles among the nobility, towns, and crown. Two features of that struggle are of considerable importance for us. The first is the persistence of sectionalism and separatism: a large part of the French nobility sought for themselves a local hegemony rather than control over the national government. The second feature, related to the first, is the establishment of feudalism in France to a degree perhaps unequalled anywhere else in Europe. The gradual development of powerful centralized political institutions in France occurred only through the defeat of separatism and feudal anarchy, whereas, in countries like England, the machinery of the state grew with the collaboration of nobles and townsmen.

The English invasion of France in 1415 did much to strengthen French national feeling, this sentiment spreading through all classes and regions.[16] By 1453 the English were expelled from all of France but Calais. The Hundred

Years' War was over. There emerged a new political situation.

> Communal, feudal, representative institutions have proved too weak to withstand the stress of foreign and civil war. The monarchy and the monarchical system alone retain their vitality unimpaired, and seem to acquire new vigour from misfortune. Under Charles VII the new *regime* was begun; under Louis XI and his daughter the ground was ruthlessly cleared of all that could impede regal action at home, while the wars of Charles VII and Louis XII, purposeless and exhausting as they were, without seriously diminishing domestic prosperity, satisfactorily tested the strength and solidity of the new structure.
> . . . The sacrifice of individual and local liberty is hardly felt. In the splendour and power of the monarchy the nation sees its aspirations realised. Nobility, clergy, commons, abandon their old ideals, and are content that their will should be expressed, their being absorbed, their energy manifested in the will and being and operations of the King.
> Institutions of independent origin give up their strength to feed his power, and exist if at all only by his sufferance. Time had been when clergy, nobility, even towns, had been powers in the State with which the King needed to reckon, not as a sovereign, hardly as a superior. Before the Reformation two of these powers had been yoked in complete submission, and the third was far on the way to final subjugation.[17]

Despite his vacillation in war, Charles VII (1429-61) proved effective in regaining control of France after the English were dispelled and in repairing the worst ravages of the Hundred Years' War. During that war, control by the central government had nearly disappeared over large areas of the country. Powerful nobles and municipal and regional corporations had assumed almost regalian rights over local affairs. Events were to prove, however, that the crown had several important and decisive sources of strength. The local forces opposed to it were numerous but disorganized. They had no program for the nation, desiring primarily to retain their local prerogatives. There were no established national institutions capable of challenging the monarch's authority. The bulk of the population gave the crown at least passive support as the single agency capable of quickly restoring order after a century of disruption. By inheritance, treaty, right of conquest, and dynastic marriage, the ruler had come to control vast patronage and wealth. Most of the land itself had become his personal possession, lordships being let by the crown and escheating to it on the extinction of the noble vassals.[18] The highest offices of the church as well as of the state were in the king's gift. If his finances were in ruins, his opponents' were equally deficient and of far smaller value.

In this situation, Charles VII was able to rule with the aid of bourgeois advisers, to suppress efforts by disaffected nobles to gain control of the government, to control the bands of unpaid soldiers and robbers roaming the countryside, to repair roads and harbors, and to revive the economy. The Estates General gave up their control of the purse, voting that the basic land tax, the *taille*, could be levied in perpetuity.[19] Charles' policies were continued and the authority of the central government extended under his successors, Louis XI (1461-83) and Charles VIII (1483-89). The essentials of the polity which was then developed persisted despite internal and external challenge until the end of the monarchy in 1789.

For all practical purposes the central government was in the crown's hands. It was not always strong government, but what national government existed was the king's. The nobles were made a part of his principal councils only at his instance, not by any hereditary right, a development made easier by the extinction, in the reign of Louis XI, of most of the great feudal houses.[20] In their place grew up a cadre of professional, middle-class advisers, creatures of the king.[21] The royal council was the supreme court of appeal, being able to set aside the judgments of all ordinary courts. It was the highest administrative authority. Subject to the king's approval and delegation, it had the power of legislation.

Besides the monarchy there were, at the center of the state, the Parlement of Paris and the Estates General. By the sixteenth century, neither retained significant authority independent of the king's.

The Parlement was a court for administering the highest justice throughout the realm. It could evaluate royal edicts and ordinances and it supervised economic policies and municipal administrations. It judged cases among subjects and between the king and his subjects. By tradition, the Parlement claimed the right to correct errors in the king's applications of principles of law and equity, and to enregister, as having the force of law, only those royal edicts and ordinances consonant with law, with established usage, and with principles of right and natural law. It also sent remonstrances to the king concerning his exceeding his prerogatives. On the other hand the court declared in (1580) that unregistered royal enactments, although expiring at his death, were binding on the king's subjects as his express commands. The king had, in principle, the right to appear in the court in the ceremony of *lit de justice* and there to order the enregistration of his edicts. In his presence, all powers reverted to him, the Parlement's authority being held from him and not an independent force in the constitution of the realm.[22] Faced with a recalcitrant Parlement, some rulers (for example, Henry III [1574-89]) employed the *lits* with great frequency.

The Estates General first met in 1302. Unlike the English Parliament it never developed the right to assent before an order had the full force of law, and in the sixteenth century legal writers of almost all persuasions were emphatic in denying the Estates any authority in framing ordinances independent of the king's will. The Estates' *cahiers* constituted advice and petitions, but were in no way binding on the monarch.[23] Charles VII convened several large representative assemblies of his Estates and apparently had some thought of establishing a regime patterned on the English, but he concluded that the Estates were incapable of effective collaboration with the monarch. He thereupon undertook a system of personal rule.[24] Louis XI convened the Estates General in 1468 to ask its advice on settling the armed rebellion of his brother Charles. Around 1483 he asked persons who might normally have been called to a meeting of the Estates to meet in their several towns and bailiwicks and approve the treaty which ended the struggle for the Burgundian succession. Charles VIII met with his Estates in 1484 to give them an opportunity to meet their new sovereign and pledge their loyalty to him. There were no further meetings of the Estates until 1560 when the Wars of Religion stimulated the holding of sessions aimed at developing consensus around a religious settlement. To that end meetings were held in 1561, 1576, 1588, and 1593. The Estates met in 1614 for the last time before the French Revolution.

These several meetings in the fifteenth and sixteenth centuries had one major purpose in common. In each case the king sought to associate the Estates with some great new national policy affecting the internal integration of the state or its relations with major foreign powers. In matters of foreign relations it was sometimes a foreign government which pressed for such an association, hoping thereby to insure the stability of settlements it made with the French crown.[25]

Government of the provinces and of smaller administrative units was shared in varying measure by local authorities and by crown officials. Strong enough to keep local interests from having any systematic control over the central government, the crown found itself unable to ignore the many traditional rights and powers that had grown up concerning local control of local affairs. Thus under Charles VII regional royal parlements were created at Toulouse, Bordeaux, Grenoble, Dijon, Aix, and Rouen.[26] From the fifteenth century to 1789 Estates met in several of the provinces and in some smaller administrative districts. Their powers varied widely, but in territories like Brittany and Languedoc the provincial Estates debated all matters of local importance. With the king's approval, they planned, carried out, and financed public works, they levied royal taxes in a manner chosen by themselves, and they established public credit.[27]

Inhabitants of lands that had become a part of the royal domain continued to elect local officials who apportioned the royal direct taxes and who, in time, served as judicial officers in cases arising from the collection of those taxes. By the seventeenth century, however, the elective character of the office was eliminated and the offices were filled by purchase from the crown.

In the fifteenth century, the kings divided the royal domain into sections and appointed provincial governors. The whole country was divided into twelve jurisdictions, each ruled by a prince or magnate who exercised or sought to exercise every nonjudicial prerogative of the crown. In 1499 these officers had to be denied such regalian powers as pardon, ennoblement, and legitimization.[28]

The towns resisted royal control with fair success until the reign of Henry IV (1589-1610). Villages gained freedom from their seigneurs and felt the crown's authority only with respect to taxes.[29]

Deprived of any formal rights to participate in the central government, the nobility was, nonetheless, the chief source of the manpower appointed to high office: to the military and judicial post of royal bailiff in the domain lands; to an increasing number of municipal offices; to posts in the standing army.[30] In the sixteenth century, seigneurs exercised rights of the lower jurisdiction and of police in their domains. These powers were used with the king's consent and under the close supervision of royal officers. Sentences could be appealed to a royal judge.[31] Even and up to the years immediately before the Revolution, nobles imposed the corvée on their personal lands, levied dues on fairs and markets, enjoyed exclusive rights of hunting, forced farmers to bring their wheat to the lord's mill and their grapes to his wine press, levied an impost on transfers of land within their domains.[32]

The crown established its own officers in titular control of every major division of local government, a process which was accelerated during the Wars of Religion. This control was at first often titular only, but the system steadily improved at the expense of traditional local authorities until, under Louis XIV (1643-1715), the country's provinces were each governed in minute detail by a powerful royal intendant.

Did the nobility's privileges mean that the local lord ruled his peasants? Tocqueville provides a classic summary in speaking of the smallest administrative units, the parishes:[33]

> In the eighteenth century all that touched the parish, the rural equivalent of the township, was under the control of a board of officials who were no longer agents of the seigneur or chosen by him. Some were nominated by the Intendant of the province, others elected by the local peasantry. . . . as for the lord, he rarely figured as the King's representative in the parish or as an intermediary between him and its inhabitants. He was no longer expected to see to the maintenance of law and order, to call out the militia, to levy taxes, to publish royal edicts, or to distribute the King's bounty in times of shortage. All these rights and duties had passed into the hands of others and the lord was in reality merely one of the inhabitants of the parish. . . . his social rank was higher, but he had no more power than they. . . .
>
> When we turn from the parish to the larger territorial unit, the canton, we find the same arrangement; the nobles play no part, collectively or individually, in the administration of public affairs. This was peculiar to France. . . .
>
> England was administered as well as governed by the great landed proprietors. . . .
>
> . . . .
>
> True, in the eighteenth century we still find great lords bearing the title of Governors of Provinces. . . . But though they still were treated with deference, they had ceased to have any power now that all real authority was vested in the Intendants.
>
> The Intendant was a young man of humble extraction, who had still his way to make and was never a native of the province to which he was posted. He did not obtain his office by purchase, by right of birth, or by election, but was chosen by the government from amongst the junior members of the Council and he was always liable to dismissal. . . .

At the Reformation the crown had succeeded in securing a monopoly on legitimate initiative at the center of the state. It had well begun the extension of control over local affairs but still shared that control with a great congeries of authorities, individual and collective, bound to it by feudal obligations or by inheritance or by traditional alliance or by delegation or by tenancy. The reigning monarch, Francis I (1515-47), went from one military and diplomatic success to another, constantly strengthening his house. But France was far from being a unitary polity. For example, it was only in 1539 that French was legalized as the official usage of the realm, thus sanctioning the decline of literary Provençal.[34] Local legal customs were published in 1550, and in 1582 the process of rationalizing and systematizing these into something like a nationwide code was under way. Yet even their publication was a hindrance to such systematization, tending rather to crystallize the many local differences.[35] Not even by the time of its extinction had the French monarchy issued a complete code of its edicts and ordinances.[36] Not until Napoleon's regime was the distinction abolished between a northern region of common law and the predominance of Roman law in the south.[37]

The king, the royal council, or even the Estates General might set military quotas or levels of revenue to be obtained from provinces, but where local assemblies and officials functioned, the central government had to negotiate separately with each concerning the men or money it would endeavor to raise and the manner in which these targets were to be achieved.

Francis I began his reign by signing a Concordat (1516) with the Vatican which ended the conciliar flavor of the French Church and its relative independence from Rome. The same agreement legitimated many long-standing royal practices, giving the crown almost full control over the Church's officials and wealth. The king obtained the right to name all archbishops, bishops, and abbots in his realm. Almost all benefices among the lower clergy were part of the patrimony of local notables. The king had the right to tax the Church and did so without mercy in order to avoid the bankruptcy of his government. Thus the Church became one of the monarchy's great resources and proposals to reform the Church took on the aspect of rebellion.[38]

Although seeking to minimize disorder and bloodshed, the central government moved persistently to suppress first Lutheranism and, after the publication in French in 1541 of the *Institutes of the Christian Religion*, Calvinism as well.

Protestantism was always a minority movement in France,

but the minority became powerful enough to force the government to grant it liberty of conscience and worship in 1589 and to uphold its full civil rights. (These guarantees were revoked in 1685 at the instance of Louis XIV.) Although there is no adequate study of the spread of Protestantism in France, certain judgments seem well supported. The peasantry was scarcely touched, but those peasants who were converted remained among the movement's most faithful adherents. The more prominent adherents seemed to include disproportionate numbers of doctors, lawyers, notaries, merchants, the lower clergy (especially the friars), and the lesser nobility. The movement also seemed strongest in the long arc of territory extending along the Atlantic Coast and swinging east through the southern provinces. It may be important that these were precisely those sections of the country with the largest number of jurisdictions still enjoying a considerable autonomy in their local affairs and providing the major recruiting grounds for noble resistance to the centralization of the state.[39] However, Protestantism made no significant inroads in the north and east of France, where lay the most ancient and centralized lands of the royal domain, the greater part of the population, and the richest agricultural territories—in this period the greatest sources of wealth.[40]

Germany

In our period, only three of the ten major German states were centralist. Before reviewing political and religious developments in these three states, I shall describe the context of German politics in which all ten states developed.

The constitutional history of Germany up to 1500 is one of unification followed by progressive fragmentation and climaxed by an effort at reunification. Much of the German land was once a part of Charlemagne's empire, the provinces of eastern Franconia, Saxony, Thuringia, Swabia, Bavaria, and Carinthia passing under the rule of his grandson Louis the German in 843. Otto the Great (936-73) and his successors expanded the size of the domain and retained royal authority over it despite persistent efforts by certain of the nobility to unseat them. The lot of the German kings was not easy, what with strong and restive nobles at home and with enemies perched along their borders. None of these rulers succeeded in gaining firm control over his territories or in so institutionalizing the choice and rights of his successor that the transfer of central authority in the kingdom went unchallenged. To complicate his situation, the German king was nominal ruler of the Holy Roman Empire and had to spend time and some resources in efforts to govern Italy. Some emperors were fortunate enough and strong enough to provide considerable domestic stability in Germany. Many were not. The progressive decline of the monarchy's control over the nobility became increasingly apparent after the reign of Frederick Barbarossa (1152-89). When Charles IV proclaimed the Golden Bull in 1346 he sought to gain stability and unity in German politics by explicitly recognizing the powers of the major nobles. From that time until the Empire was dissolved in 1806, a small body of the greater nobles became the legal Electors of the Emperor and were able, constitutionally, to set limits on the authority of the candidate they selected.

In this situation, the post of emperor became most onerous, having limited and uncertain powers and entailing considerable expense to its occupant. Only rulers of the larger principalities found it possible to assume the imperial title, and these came to regard the role as a means for furthering the dynastic ambitions of their own principalities and houses rather than an opportunity for benefiting all German territories.

What kept the Empire together?

> . . . There was a monarchy whose great history was still remembered even in the days of its impotence and ruin. There was a real sense of national life, a consciousness so strong that it could bend even the selfish instincts of feudal nobles into cherishing an ambition wider and more patriotic than that of making themselves little kings over their own patrimony. The strongest of the German feudal houses was less well organized on a separatist basis than the duchy of Brittany or the duchy of Burgundy. And few indeed of them could base their power on any keenly felt local or national

tradition, or upon anything more solid than the habit of respect for an ancient house. Moreover, the ecclesiastical States might have been, and both the small nobility and the wealthy numerous and active free towns actually were, permanent counterpoises to the absolute supremacy of the greater feudatories in a way to which French history supplies no parallel. . . .

Even in its worst decay the German kingship still counted for something. "The King of the Romans," as the German King was styled . . . , was still the first of earthly potentates in dignity and rank. And feudalism was still sufficiently alive in Germany to make the traditional feudal sources of income a real if insufficient substitute for grants and taxes of the more modern type. The imperial Chancery issued no writ or charter without exacting heavy fees. No family compact between members of a reigning house, no agreement of eventual succession between neighbouring princes, was regarded as legitimate without such dearly purchased royal sanction. Even where the Emperor's direct power was slight his influence was very considerable. He no longer controlled ecclesiastical elections with a high hand; but there were few bishoprics or abbeys in which he had not as good a chance of directing the course of events as the strongest of the local lords, and his influence was spread over all Germany, while the prince was powerless outside his own neighbourhood. All over Germany numerous knights, nobles, ecclesiastics, and lawyers looked forward to the Emperor's service as a career, and hope of future imperial favour often induced them to do their best to further the imperial policy. If indirect pressure of this sort did not prevail, the Roman Court more often than not lent its powerful aid towards enforcing imperial wishes. There was no great danger that the feeble monarchs of this period would excite general opposition by flagrant attacks on the traditional authority of their vassals; and in smaller matters it was more to the interest even of the greater princes to keep on good terms with Caesar, than to provoke his hostility by wanton and arbitrary opposition to his wishes.

Another weighty advantage accrued to the German monarch from the circumstance that his chief rivals were every whit as badly off in dealing with their vassals as he was with his. The well-ordered territorial sovereignties of a later generation had not yet come into existence. The strongest of the imperial vassals were still feudal lords and not sovereign princes. The resources at their disposal were those of a great feudal proprietor rather than those of an independent ruler. Outside their own domains they had few means of exercising any real power.

Their vassals were as hard to keep in hand as they were themselves impatient of control by their sovereign.[41]

The dying Albert of Brandenburg declared in 1486:

> All projects and all warlike preparations . . . were of no effect
> so long as Germany as a whole had no sound peace, no good
> law or law-courts, and no general currency.[42]

The rudiments of such reforms had been laid before the
Imperial Diet in 1485 by Berthold, Count of Henneberg and
Elector of Mainz. He proposed a single national system of
currency, a universal *Landfriede*, and a Supreme Court of
Justice charged with carrying out the Public Peace. Later,
the reformers agreed to the levy of a general tax throughout
the Empire. Their proposals amounted to:

> a scheme for the constitution of a federal state, in which the
> administration was to be taken out of the hands of the mon-
> archy and placed in those of an imperial council of seventeen
> members, of which the president alone would be the emperor's
> nominee.[43]

The project of reform "won the support of practically every
prince and estate" in the Diet of 1495.[44]

Three forces have been proposed to explain this effort to
revive the Empire. Tout suggests that its leading pro-
ponents, such as Berthold himself, were of the second rank
of the nobility.[45] They could not hope for absolute domination of their own lands, yet were strong enough to aim at
successful common action. Further,

> Berthold and his associates were in the same position as the
> English baronial leaders [of the thirteenth and fourteenth cen-
> turies who accepted the centralized institutions of the monarchy
> as ultimate facts, and aspired only to keep the centralized
> power under their own control]. As Archbishop of Mainz
> Berthold might either be a petty prince holding sway over
> scattered regions . . . or a great political ecclesiastic. . . . The
> wider career appealed alike to his patriotism, his interests, and
> his ambition. As feudal sovereigns the Rhenish Electors stood
> but in the second rank of German rulers. As prelates, as coun-
> cillors of their peers, as directors of the Diets, and as effective
> and not merely nominal Chancellors of their suzerain's domains,
> they might well emulate the exploits of a Hanno or a Ranald
> of Dassel. . . .[46]

In addition to the personal aspirations of the second rank of the nobility, it has been suggested that internal disorders and, during the first half of the fifteenth century, losses of German lands by reason of foreign invasions and separatism had stirred popular German nationalism to a degree unknown since 1338.

It was now that the saga of the emperor Frederick Barbarossa, slumbering on the Kyffhauser waiting to restore the empire to its old glory, took hold over popular imagination . . .

and

a number of pseudo-Fredericks appeared and secured a following.[47]

All of these tendencies were reinforced by the desires of the House of Hapsburg. Acceding to the post of Holy Roman Emperor, the Austrian dynasty had managed to retain and expand its ancestral holdings including, in 1477, far-flung possessions stretching from the lower Rhine and the Scheldt to the Upper Rhine, to the eastern Alps, and along the Danube. It had to retain the Imperial title if only to rule in these scattered lands and to prevent a challenge to its rule by some other dynasty which might ally itself with France. Under the Emperors Maximilian (1493-1519) and Charles V (1520-58), this Hapsburg policy was in the hands of strong and able rulers.

Any proposal to strengthen the central institutions of the Empire while reserving control over their functioning to a council responsive to the nobility foundered on many difficulties, but none was greater than the determination of the Hapsburg emperors to become absolute rulers of their own domains and to shape Imperial policy to their own desires. Emperors and reformers wanted peace and union for the empire, but their terms were radically different.

. . . The creation, in 1500 and 1512, of ten provincial districts . . . comprising each a number of separate principalities, was, despite its limited objects, a step towards greater territorial cohesion, just as the proposal at the [diet] of 1522-23 to raise a general imperial customs duty . . . implied recognition of the empire as a single economic unit. All this went beyond the immediate dynastic interests of the princes, as fundamentally did the plans for the reconstruction of imperial taxation. . . . the very fact that they were willing to put imperial finances on a stable foundation showed that the princes still accepted, and were prepared to make tangible concessions on behalf of, a form of federal state which transcended the boundaries and immediate interests of their principalities. . . . the attempt at reform was serious; . . . the responsibility for the failure to give it a trial rests with Maximilian and his successor, Charles V. . . . When Charles V, opening his first diet at Worms in January 1521, stated that "the empire from of old has had not many masters, but one, and it is our intention to be that one," and when he added that he was not to be treated as of less account than his predecessors, but of more, seeing that he was more powerful than they had been, he was accusing himself of crass historical romanticism or outlining a policy of compulsion or both. In either case, he was . . . announcing a trial of strength with the princes. . . .[48]

The vicissitudes of these efforts toward national unity occurred when Germany:

was in a state of political crisis, which was fanned by the work of propagandists and satirists who, in widely read verse, attacked Rome and the great prelates, the higher social classes and the corruption of the bourgeoisie by money. . . . Ulrich von Hutten, whose *Epistolae obscurorum vivorum* published in 1514, raised hostility to Rome to a new peak of violence, also bitterly reproached all classes within Germany with betrayal of their country for their own selfish interests. . . . But, after the disappointments on the political plane, the frustrated hopes of constitutional reform, it was in the religious reformation that the new spirit of German nationalism found expression.

[Luther's] challenge to Rome appealed to the national consciousness. . . . His belief that the essence of religion lay in an inner experience was in the German tradition. . . . His appeal was to the "German nation," to the "Christian nobility of the German nation." He planned, of course, to reform the universal Church; but the resistance of Rome threw him back increasingly on German support and gave his propaganda a peculiarly German flavour. "It is for you Germans," he wrote in 1531, "that I seek salvation and sanctity."

. . . .

. . . The conflict of German and Hapsburg interests was the stumbling-block. Charles V, the King of Spain, whose real power derived from his non-German lands, could not afford to compromise his position outside Germany by placing himself at the head of a German movement directed against Rome. . . .[49]

When the great religious struggles ended in 1648 with the Peace of Westphalia, the Protestant princes and cities on the one hand and the Hapsburg emperors on the other had fought to a stalemate. The next one hundred and fifty years saw the territorial princes as sovereign in their respective territories. The spirit of German nationalism lay quiescent. That it was not dead is apparent in such movements as the continuous development by German scholars of the theory of "the nation as a federation" and in the spontaneous and popular revival of nationalism which occurred under the stimulus of French conquest and exploitation after 1806.[50] None of the German states

had succeeded in taking over, even within the limits of its own territorial boundaries, the loyalties which had formerly animated the Reich; they had existed, most of them, as independent political units since 1648, but none had established that identity of government and people, of state and folk, which gives endurance and stability to political society. They were still, at the end as at the beginning, the arbitrary product of accidental contingencies, superimposed on the population regardless of race, geography or history; they were able to interfere with the economic and social life of the people . . . but they were unable to gather the life of the people around them, to make themselves the centres of popular life and activity, expressing the common interests of their inhabitants. They had, for more than a century after 1648, undermined the sense of common German nationality which had been vigorous as late as the sixteenth century, but they had failed to set anything else in its place. And even that piece of destruction, which for long seemed permanent, proved transitory. . . .[51]

In 1500 there were many autonomous or semi-autonomous territories in Germany. I deal with the ten principalities which then and later were the most populous and, politically and economically, the most important: Bavaria, Saxony, Württemberg, Brandenburg, Prussia, Hesse, Cleves, Mark, Jülich, and Berg. All were governed as lay principalities. All but Bavaria, Jülich, and Berg adopted the Protestant reforms. Of the Protestant lands, all at first became Lutheran except Cleves and Mark which opted for Calvinism. It happens that only the three Catholic states also had centralist regimes. They therefore are of concern in this chapter.

Bavaria:[52]

The Bavarian lands were ruled by members of the Wittelsbach dynasty from 1180 to 1918. The many partitions of Bavaria in the fourteenth and fifteenth centuries caused endless conflicts among members of that dynasty and facilitated the rise of the Estates in various Wittelsbach territories. In 1505 the Estates of these several lands declared themselves one body and the Duke, Albert IV, who had reunited the country in the Landshut Succession War, granted them important privileges: succession to the throne would follow primogeniture; the Estates would meet as one corporate body; conflicts over succession within the ruling dynasty would be settled by the Estates; on his accession a new duke was to confirm the liberties and customs of the duchy as, simultaneously, the Estates rendered the oath of allegiance to him.

Albert died in 1508 leaving a minor son to succeed him. During this minority the Estates reached their greatest power, six of their representatives exercising the regency with the young duke's uncle. In 1511 the regency ended and William IV assumed the government of his realm. Thereupon followed a struggle for supremacy in which the Estates steadily lost such powers as they had had. Those rights had included that of administering taxes on central and local levels. By 1545 the ducal government had gained clear control. It levied and renewed taxes without consulting the Estates and appointed councilors without abiding by the demand that a majority be natives. Agitation grew for the introduction of Lutheranism with at least a strong minority among the nobles and burghers favoring it. However, after many Lutheran nobles were arrested and convicted in 1564 for a plot against the state, religious agitation ended. There was no meeting of the diet from 1612 to 1669—a time when its counterparts in other German principalities were still gaining strength. During the 1580's the Estates had lost control of the financial administration. The Privy Council and War Council likewise were created without reference to the diet and leading officials were often foreigners. The duke legislated on his own authority. Nobles exercised the lower jurisdiction on their own estates, but had no other judicial or administrative authority, all such matters being controlled by ducal officials.

In the days of its power, the diet had established a Small Committee to administer its affairs and to treat with the Duke when the parent body itself was not in session. At the diet's last meeting the Estates accepted the Duke's order that this committee determine with him what taxes and other financial arrangements should be enacted and that members then on the committee be allowed to fill any vacancies that might occur in their organization (with the restriction that appointees be from the same Estates and districts of the country as the previous holders). This Small Committee retained some powers to the end of the eighteenth century. It met once or twice a year to supervise the financial administration of the Estates and the work of their officials and was by no means entirely pliant when the government demanded new monies. Its members continued to petition for a diet to be summoned. They rejected an effort to include ducal commissioners among their number. The dukes continued to be dependent on their collaboration and consent in matters of taxation. The Small Committee passed on the drafts of new legal codes in the 1750's. However, its greatest special powers were the appointment of its own officials and tax collectors. In each local district several members of the Estates appointed by the Committee were responsible for the levying of taxes granted. In the capital, four members received the money and checked accounts. Although the Committee gained no new powers and often seemed automatically to approve what a duke proposed, it was not formally abolished.

Neither the towns nor the nobles, and certainly not the peasants, had developed any great strength in Bavaria. The towns did not become free Imperial cities nor were the nobles free Imperial knights. Apart from Munich, which in 1500 had a population of twelve thousand, the thirty-

four towns were small. The duke always retained the higher
jurisdiction except in a few leading towns. His lands were
so extensive that about half of the duchy's peasants were
under his immediate control. The nobility were very numerous and most of their estates were both small and
scattered. In the fifteenth and sixteenth centuries they were
increasingly impoverished. Their peasants, personally free,
were under the lower jurisdiction which nobles exercised
on their own manorial lands, but, in practice and in law, the
obligations of peasants to noble landlords were modest and
did not increase. In short, there were in Bavaria no great
centers of power and no communal institutions which might
have provided an effective counterpoise to the ducal administration.

Jülich and Berg:[53]

These two Rhenish duchies were united by dynastic inheritance in 1423. From 1510 to 1609 they were part of a
dynastic union with the neighboring territories of Cleves
and Mark. The latter territories had been united since 1368.
Even when all four were united, however, they retained
their separate governments and institutions. The diets of
Cleves and Mark usually met in common as did those of
Jülich and Berg. In the sixteenth century a common diet of
the four principalities was held frequently. Although only
Jülich and Berg are of interest in this chapter on centralist
regimes, their history is so interwoven with that of Cleves
and Mark that all must be treated together. Cleves and
Mark developed balanced regimes. I begin with them.

Cleves and Mark, two duchies near the Netherlands'
frontier, became a property of the Hohenzollerns in 1666.
By that time, however, they had gained a character which
even the centralizing dynasty in Berlin could not extirpate.

Unlike the predominant Junkers of Brandenburg with
their subservient burghers and servile peasants, the nobility
of Cleves and Mark did not dominate the diet or possess
private jurisdictions. The nobles were not exempt from all
taxes and customs duties. Demesne farming was unimpor-
tant. Nobles received dues rather than labor services from the

peasants who leased their land. The towns were important and prosperous, producing cloth, linen, and leather, and during the fifteenth century they participated in the growing wealth of the Netherlands. Most peasants were tenants holding leases which, in practice, were hereditary. There was rural self-government in which peasants participated side by side with resident noblemen and local officials. The main business of such government concerned the local requirements: roads, bridges, salaries, jails, and the relief of the poor. Accounts from the preceding year were audited and approved.

In both duchies commoners were able to purchase noble estates. The dukes of Cleves had created a modern bureaucracy and eliminated the remnants of feudal ties.

During the 1400's the diets of Cleves and Mark gained great powers. In the latter part of that century they forced their rulers to reorganize the administration of finances. In 1486 and 1489 the duke promised to rule "according to the decisions of his four principal councillors." Against ducal opposition the Estates succeeded in extending their influence into the field of administration: twelve of their members were to be appointed as ducal councilors and as cosigners to all important actions. They were to nominate a treasurer who was to receive all revenues and be responsible to the prince and his councilors. In 1505 a committee of the Estates was entrusted with putting the ducal finances in order and with the levying of taxes. In 1517 the diet came to be composed of representatives from the thirteen principal towns and of all members of the nobility who met certain qualifications of ancestry and property.

As in Cleves and Mark, Estates appeared in Jülich and Berg during the second half of the fourteenth century. The duke became increasingly dependent on the Estates for financial support and the diet met regularly at its own initiative. In 1478 the Estates were granted a passive right of resistance against unjustified tax demands and began to exercise influence over foreign policy. In 1511 the ruling duke promised not to start a war or feud without asking their advice. He was able, however, to prevent the diet's exercising control over the financial administration. Members of the nobility took part in the levying of taxes by ducal officials but did so as appointees of the ducal government and not as members of the Estates. The nobility in these two territories was more numerous than was that of Cleves and Mark and much more important politically than were the towns. The nobles were also exempt from taxation.

The Reformation gained a firm foothold in the towns of Cleves and Mark but the tiny duchies were a battleground for the major powers and, against his will, Duke William (1539-92) was forced by the Holy Roman Emperor not to permit the introduction of Protestantism.

In 1569 Wesel, the leading town of Cleves, forsook Lutheranism and adopted Calvinism, an example quickly followed by other towns of the duchy. Refugees from the Netherlands poured over the border. In 1577 the diet demanded that the free exercise of the Augsburg Confession be allowed. This demand was repeated in 1580 and 1583. In Cleves and Mark, and to some extent in Berg, these were years in which the ducal government, although officially Catholic, allowed a de facto tolerance of Protestantism.

Finding Jülich and Berg more congenial to their rule, the dukes governing the four now united provinces set up their capital at Düsseldorf in Berg. Constant warfare, lack of funds, and the recurrent madness of heirs to the dynasty greatly weakened the ducal sway over Cleves and Mark, these two duchies developing quite independently of the central administration. (In both duchies, the towns were in practice small republics united for purposes of general government.) The diets of Cleves and Mark became responsible for measures of defense and taxation.

The ducal government headquartered in Berg retained generally effective control there and in Jülich. The nobles of Jülich remained predominantly Catholic. The nobles and towns of Berg included a substantial Lutheran population and some Calvinists. The Catholics in both lands demanded that services be held in German rather than Latin and that the laity be given the wine as well as the bread in communion. The religious situation in Jülich and Berg appeared fluid in the middle of the sixteenth century, the outcome uncertain. The fortunes of war and inheritance turned the outcome in favor of official Catholicism.

In 1614 John Sigismund of Brandenburg, a Calvinist, was accepted as ruler of Cleves and Mark; Wolfgang William of Neuberg, recently reconverted to Catholicism and allied to Bavaria and the emperor, received Jülich and Berg. Through the Thirty Years' War their nominal rulers usually had little control over the duchies, Dutch, French, and Imperial armies using these lands as staging areas. From this period religious developments in Cleves and Mark were determined by their gradual absorption into the growing system of the Prussian state; developments in Jülich and Berg by their dependence on policies originating in Bavaria and Vienna.

Ireland

From the ninth to the twelfth centuries, Ireland was organized as a pyramided series of groups founded on locality and kinship which formed five kingdoms, all acknowledging some vague primacy to the ruler of Meath as king of all the Irish people.[54] Norman invasions launched from England in 1166-72 broke only the superstructure of native Irish government—the provincial kingdoms and the sway of the High King at Meath. The Anglo-Norman rulers, settling in on their conquered lands, became assimilated to the Irish system rather than imposing their own feudal patterns on it and the understructure of the Irish polity continued to function undisturbed. Beginning in the late thirteenth century, mercenaries from the Hebrides were imported to serve the Irish chiefs and Anglo-Norman lords and there began that revival of Irish power against the English which, by the time of Henry VIII, limited English authority in Ireland to the Pale, a small area around Dublin. Early in the fourteenth century Norman nobles all over Ireland renounced their allegiance to England and adopted native Irish principles of succession to lordship and land.[55] By this means the lords became autonomous kings instead of feudal vassals.[56]

By 1530 Ireland outside the Pale consisted of ninety states of varying size and enjoying de facto sovereignty.[57] They were small lands, peopled by landed freeholders and ruled by hereditary families. Each state was united with others in varying measure and for varying purposes. Over them all appeared once again the remote, symbolic High King at Tara in Meath. As the sixteenth century progressed, increased elements of feudalism appeared. The chiefs became more autocratic. Lands once considered those of freemen were now alleged to belong to chiefs. The mercenaries were fighting wars in the chieftains' interests, not those of the people.[58]

It is the substructure of Irish politics which will concern us most because it is the resilient, continuing force which the Normans and later the Tudors found possible to suppress but not to kill, the organization which absorbed the Normans and which actually governed Irish lands until the early seventeenth century.[59]

Although often described as an organization of clans or tribes, ancient Ireland might better be described as a series of chieftainships, each headed by a dominant extended family and containing, together with relatives of that family, many dependents unrelated by kinship. Within a chieftaincy there was no belief that all members descended from a common ancestor. Land was owned privately by small family groups—extended households—rather than by individuals and was inheritable, grantable, and salable. The owning family, not merely an individual, had to consent to such changes in the status of its lands.[60]

Following Skene's analysis, it is convenient to begin with the Tuath, a unit intermediate between the High Kingship and the Finés or septs which were the smallest political units.[61] A Tuath contained several septs. It is estimated that the typical Tuath could muster seven hundred fighting men without special effort.[62] From an early period the Tuaths appear grouped into Mortuaths, unions of three to seven Tuaths over which a king presided. Unions of the Mortuaths constituted the five provincial kingdoms of Ireland all under the High King himself.

The septs are most readily understood through a description of their creation—a continuous process in Irish society. We begin with the observation that Tuaths had members of varying wealth and that the recapitulation of the formation of a sept requires our tracing the possible history of the son of a poor family. At 14 years of age the boy was freed from his parents' control. At age 20 he was given a separate residence and a share of the Tuath's land. If the family he founded retained possession of its land for three generations, it gained legal right to that property. If the family prospered it entered the ranks of boaires or cowlords. There were six grades of boaires, representing increasing amounts of property owned by the family. The highest class of boaires were termed the grad flaith. Such families possessed tenants to whom they gave their surplus cattle in return for rents, services, and homage. These tenants might themselves be free or in bond to the owning family, a relationship determined by the extent to which the flaith furnished the stock necessary for the tenant's support.

A Finé or sept consisted of a boaire together with his nearest agnates and his dependents. (Ireland's population of small, independent landholders was gradually extinguished as the septs spread. Free tenants also declined in number, generally preferring the greater security afforded in the status of a bondsman.) As the boaire's wealth increased, he settled followers from other septs upon his wastelands.

The sept was governed by its chief, his kin, and by a body of rules granting rights and duties to certain of his kinsmen. These kinsmen were an artificial group of seventeen persons which extended across five generations. These seventeen formed the sept in its narrowest sense.

The seventeen were divided into four groups termed respectively the Geilfine, Dierbhfine, Iarfine, and Indfine. The founder and his four youngest children comprised the Geilfine. As each new person was born into the Geilfine, whether as a child of the founder father or of his four youngest children, the oldest member remaining passed into the Deirbhfine until that group numbered four persons. As new members were born into the Deirbhfine older members passed into the Iarfine and so until the Indfine was formed. Finally, a man passed into the commonalty of the Finé leaving a residuum of seventeen persons behind him. These complex relationships depended thus on kinship with the chief of the Finé. The Geilfine were the youngest cadets of his line and the Indfine the oldest. As those longest separated from the chief and having had the most opportunity to develop their own resources, the Indfine were the most powerful branch of the family next to his own.

Each of the four groups had some special responsibilities for its members and each possessed mutual rights of a complex sort in the inheritance of land vacated by the extinction of the other groups. Further, when a sept's chief died, the members filled the office by electing one of the seventeen as his successor. It became customary simultaneously with a chief's election to name his successor. The latter, called the Tanist, was selected from the new chief's Indfine.

Succession to the title and lands of the several grades of Irish chieftaincy and kingship followed these same principles of artificial kinship and Tanistry.

The Tuaths, Mortuaths, and provincial kingdoms were tied together by gifts and subsidies and alliances for war and participation in the symbolism (originally pagan) of the High Kingship.

The English understood the integrative force of these many ties of kinship and alliance. When Strafford's armies finally smashed the Irish militia, the ties of kinship which bound septs and chiefs were declared to have no place in English law. Succession by means of Tanistry was voided.

There was no important spontaneous acceptance of Protestant doctrine in Ireland. Successive English governments sought to impose it on the Irish people, but, generally employing only indirect means toward this end, they failed. Thus the Irish were not required to become converts, but were required to support an Anglican establishment in Ireland with their tithes and with periodic attendance. Roman Catholics who practiced privately were not usually bothered by the authorities. (Freedom of Catholic worship was not restored officially until 1791.) Catholics were barred from the important professions and from participation in the new government.

Scotland: The Highlands

Scotland underwent conquest by English invaders in the thirteenth century. Following prolonged struggles with the English kings, Scottish forces led by Robert Bruce won independence in 1328. There were, however, two Scotlands: the Lowlands over which successive kings gained some respectable degree of control and the islands and especially the mountainous territories in the north and along the English border over which a continuous royal authority was exercised only from the seventeenth century and effective royal control established only in 1745.[63] At the Reformation, the Lowlands became Protestant while the rest of the country remained Catholic.

The essentials of the political and social system of the islands and Highlands have already been given, for these peoples closely resemble the Irish in organization by septs.[64] Both of these Celtic peoples had Tuaths, but the Scots were affected more strongly by feudalism than the Irish and among them the Tuaths disintegrated leaving their constituent septs as independent bodies. It is these which came to be called the Scottish clans. The chief, his kinsmen, and his dependents from other septs all bore the name of the chief's clan. A semi-Tanistry governed succession to chiefdoms. While in office, the chief exercised an arbitrary authority over his subordinates, determining the outcome of all disputes among them, levying taxes upon such extraordinary occasions as the marriage of a daughter or the building of a house. He could not, however, alienate the clan's lands and none but a clan member could succeed him in office.[65]

Portugal

Portuguese national history begins in the twelfth century when Afonso Henriques broke with Spain and assumed the title of King of Portugal. The country was defined and united in the course of wars against Saracens and Spaniards. What emerged was a kingdom modeled on traditional feudal lines, and characterized by the typical struggles of the Estates and the monarch. When, early in the fifteenth century, Portugal had repulsed yet another Spanish attempt at conquest, the crown found itself in a position to enlarge its powers over the rest of the country. A considerable part of the nobility had taken the side of Spain, and the king now ceased to employ nobles for his administrative work, appointing, in their place, lawyers from the middle class. New nobles were created who were loyal to the king.

> The coming of the House of Avis [1411] meant a definite swing toward royal absolutism. The cortes continued to be very important and was called many times in the reign of João I [1385-1433] and frequently by his successors. But it is possible to note a slight decline in its influence, setting in almost as soon as the new dynasty had firmly grasped the throne. It had met almost constantly in João's early years, but then the intervals between meetings began to lengthen, and once, from 1418 to 1427, Portugal went nine years with no cortes. Later kings . . . ordinarily assembled the cortes frequently near the beginning of their reigns and after that dispensed with it as much as possible. Shortly after the death of João I, the cortes lost an important fight when it demanded and failed to gain the right to be summoned every year. More than this, the kings gradually succeeded in having cortes business limited to an agenda prepared by themselves, and in this way eventually drew most of the august body's teeth. Although the time was still far distant, the Portuguese cortes was destined ultimately for the oblivion suffered by the states-general of France in the generations before the French revolution.[66]

By the early sixteenth century, the government was essentially that of an absolute monarchy.[67]

The powers of the Portuguese monarchy grew steadily in the fifteenth and sixteenth centuries. In the reign of Edward

I (1433-38) the kingdom's laws were revised and codified.[68] Of even greater importance was an action remaining in force to 1832: all grants of land by the crown were made inalienable and indivisible and were to revert to the crown in default of a legitimate male heir to the grantee.

John II (1481-95) allied himself with the towns and asserted the crown's authority over nobles grown strong by reason of a long royal extravagance. The nobles were deprived of the higher jurisdiction and feudal courts were subjected to royal tribunals with provision for the gradual extinction of the former.[69] Royal magistrates were established throughout the country and given the right to enter the lands of all crown tenants and to inspect the private administration of justice wherever it occurred When the nobles rebelled against these and other restrictions on their powers, they were crushed.

John's successor, Manuel I (1495-1521), brought about a reconciliation between crown and nobility without restoring the latter's powers.[70] He made his nobles part of a magnificent court society supported by the riches that came from the Portuguese outposts in Asia. A new revision and systematization of the general laws was begun in 1505 and completed in 1521. There was a separation of the public and royal operations of the magistracy and treasury. Royal justices were placed in the smallest communities. The towns, having gained many local rights during the reconquest from the Moors and the consolidation of the country in preceding centuries, now lost most of their independence. Manuel ordered a review and redrafting of municipal charters which reduced them to little more than royal codes of taxation.[71]

As in Spain, the voyages of exploration were almost exclusively ventures of the crown. It gained the wealth and prestige they brought. But, in Portugal, new wealth was soon followed by extreme poverty. The state alone could not supply trading vessels and protect its outposts. The population was too small for the military ventures required. By 1518 the flow of wealth from Africa was subsiding and in another twenty years the country's finances were in great disorder.

The Portuguese cortes had a long history but seems never to have gained any stable corporate character or privileges. The kings often called it into session as a consultative body. In minorities or during difficult periods of royal succession it provided members of the government of regency. During weak monarchies it declared itself to have such rights as that of approving taxation and being consulted in matters of war and peace but it had no clear powers. It apparently did not attain a definition of those individuals or groups having settled rights of participation in its work. Its composition was determined from one session to another by the king's will. Legislation could and did get enacted through the sovereign's direct and sole action.[72] The cortes had no continuing machinery to conduct its business when the entire body was not in session and the sovereign had no obligation to convene a cortes at specified intervals.

Portugal fell to Spanish conquest in 1580 and remained a subject state until 1640. The restoration of independence meant no growth in the regime's liberality and, from the accession of John V (1706-50), royal centralism prevailed, being supported by the gold of Brazil and lasting until the liberal movements of 1820.[73] Towns regained some rights over local affairs and the royal administrative courts and councils were staffed largely from the nobility. The cortes was, in principle, to approve any new taxes that might be levied and the king had to promise to respect natural law and the rules and customs of the country. However, in principle and in practice, there was no serious challenge in this period to royal centralization and initiative. After 1697 and until 1820 the cortes vanished altogether, not destroyed but stripped of all power and never convened.[74]

The Reformation made no serious inroads in Portugal. The crown and nobles were united in suppressing any symptoms of religious dissent.

Spain

The realm which Ferdinand and Isabella began to rule in 1479 and which they freed completely from Moorish occupation in 1492 was not a united country. Instead, it consisted of five territories, different in custom and government and united, not with each other, but with the dynasty. Of these, Castile was clearly dominant in territory, population, and wealth, a dominance increased when the resources of the Spanish territories in the New World became the private property of Castile.[75] As the Hohenzollerns first organized Brandenburg and Prussia and then extended more effective control over their other domains, so the Catholic Kings set about the subjugation of opposition to their rule in Castile and from this base their successors were able to control the whole peninsula.

The problem of retaining their newly won hegemony was complicated by constant threats of Turkish attack by land and sea and by the large minority of resident Moorish converts to Christianity who conformed only from necessity and were a potential fifth column.[76] It was to control these converts that the crown petitioned Rome in 1478 for the establishment of an Inquisition under royal control. These extraordinary courts were commissioned to override all local deterrents. They not only maintained the "purity" of faith but provided in common religious devotion a substitute for a sense of Spanish nationhood.[77]

Something of the problems and achievement of Ferdinand and Isabella can be seen in a resume of major steps taken by them between 1479 and the Queen's death in 1504.[78] The crown recovered royal estates seized by the nobles, annexed the grandmasterships and estates of three semi-autonomous military orders, demolished castles of rebellious nobles, and pursued a steady process of turning over important political offices to jurists of humble birth. In 1480, with concurrence from the cortes of Castile, the monarchs banned private wars, they revived and then, after its success, disbanded the Hermandad, an organization of cities for policing the countryside and controlling the nobility. They eliminated municipal autonomy in favor of royal control; appointed royal officials to municipal councils; appointed a corregidor to every council in Castile. The corregidors were omnicompetent servants of the crown—unconnected with the locality to which they were appointed—keeping close watch on finances, revenues, common lands, religion, gambling, taxation, and justice. The composition of the royal council was changed, again with consent from the Castilian cortes. The council's hereditary noble members were first deprived of their vote and later of their places. In their stead were appointed lawyers not of the nobility.

The cortes of Castile reached its greatest power in the fourteenth and fifteenth centuries.[79] By the middle of the fifteenth century the great nobles were the major power in the cortes and the state. At this time the Castilian monarchy was weakened by minorities and disputed successions and the towns were too weak to restrain the aristocracy. There were, however, some constitutional features which lent themselves to exploitation by the crown. The kings had no obligation to summon their cortes at regular intervals and no one had, in principle, a right to attend, the kings summoning whom they pleased.[80] Because the crown gradually found alternative means of obtaining subsidies, it could avoid convening the cortes. (Thus the chief tax, the alcabala [a levy on sales], became set at a fixed and perpetual sum in 1494. The crown had also the revenues from the customs, the subsidio [a tax on clerical income], and the cruzada [a tax on the sale of the indulgences which everyone was expected to buy at regular intervals].)[81] When in session, the cortes could only consent to the revocation of existing laws, the ruler having the right to proclaim new legislation at his own pleasure. The nobles and clergy gradually ceased to attend meetings of the cortes because it was summoned only to grant funds and they were exempt from taxation. Only the cities remained in attendance and they were dominated by the crown.

In 1496 a standing army was established and a twelfth of all men aged 20 through 40 years were made liable for service.

These several developments gave the monarchs exclusive control over the central government in Castile and, hence, over the only general government in Spain. They did not eliminate the existence of considerable local autonomy in their other provinces or curb, in Castile, the minor local powers in the hands of nobles.

Next to Castile, Ferdinand's Aragon was the most important Spanish state. Its internal organization perpetuated feudal practices.[82] The king was obliged to convene the Aragonese cortes at regular intervals. The towns had great power and were an effective counterweight to the nobility. On their own estates, the nobles exercised powerful seigneurial justice, having almost absolute power over their vassals and exercising the higher jurisdiction. A freeman arrested by royal order could put himself under the jurisdiction of the Aragonese kingdom's highest judge who was independent of royal control.

From the thirteenth century, the major economic activity in Castile was the production of wool from merino sheep, a pastoral system better suited than grain agriculture to the country's arid lands. The Castilian crown supported the pastoralists against all opposition, receiving a constant and assured revenue from taxes on sheep and on the sale of wool. On this economic base the aristocracy, including the gentry and a noble urban patriciate, and comprising in all perhaps two percent of the population, came to own 95 to 97 percent of the land. A small group of the nobility within this landed population obtained vast, even fabulous, prestige and wealth.[83] Beginning early in the sixteenth century, so much of Castile was given over to grazing that Spain began a long period of suffering from a serious shortage of grain.

In the late fifteenth century the crown was not able to make a direct assault on the private jurisdictions associated with the lands of great nobles.[84] Towns and villages under noble or ecclesiastical jurisdiction were nominally outside the system of royal justice and administration. The monarchs did insist, however, that the private jurisdictions maintain high standards of justice and were prepared to intervene when a miscarriage of justice was alleged. Over the years, this insistence by the crown on its own judicial primacy sapped the aristocracy's independent judicial power as did the greater competence of royal justice in many fields of litigation. By the end of the sixteenth century, the influence of the corregidor and royal justice extended to every corner of Castile. The process of compiling the royal ordinances was begun in 1480 and a codification of Castilian laws was finally achieved under Philip II in 1565.

During the interregnum from Isabella's death in 1504 to the accession of Charles I (1516-56), towns and nobles managed to subvert some of the monarchy's control. Charles' authority restored that control from 1521 and it was never seriously shaken again during the reigns of the Hapsburg kings (1516-1700).[85] (The Spanish states other than Castile came gradually under the central organization. Their lesser economic and political importance did not justify the monarchs in undertaking a head-on confrontation.) After 1538 the nobles were no longer called to the Castilian cortes and that body in effect abandoned its powers. The monarch established the exclusive right to make and promulgate laws. No cortes was called for all Spain until 1709.

The local judicial powers of the greater nobles waxed under feeble monarchs in the seventeenth century, but the aristocracy was not able to establish power at the center of government.[86] By 1787 the smaller towns were predominately seignorial and this situation continued well into the nineteenth century. It was not until 1911 that a series of laws began to whittle away at the nobles' private jurisdictions. However, the nobles exercised only the lower jurisdiction. Their real strength lay not in political or judicial power but in the sheer size of their estates. A third of the cultivatable land was in the hands of four great houses and the nobility found in their control of municipal councils opportunities for maximizing their advantages in marketing the products of their estates.

The crown had obtained in 1486 the right to name candidates for all vacant bishoprics in the newly reconquered lands in the Peninsula. In 1516 this privilege was extended to the whole of Spain.[87] The Catholic Kings also obtained a large degree of control over the wealth of the Church. From 1494 they received a third of all tithes paid in Castile. In the sixteenth century taxes on the Church provided a very important part of the crown's income.

The Reformation made few inroads in Spain and was persistently opposed by the regime. It was also opposed by the Spanish Church which had already undergone a considerable reform and revival.[88] The Spanish Dominicans had reformed themselves morally and intellectually before the end of the fifteenth century. The Thomist theories of natural law, strongly attacked in the universities of northern Europe during the fourteenth and fifteenth centuries, became the focus of a new intellectual flowering in Spain. Led by Cardinal Ximenez, Biblical studies of great penetration were flourishing before the Reformers began to claim the Bible as their own.[89] One needs only to recall the intellectual and devotional events of sixteenth-century Spain to recognize that this religious renaissance still continued then and was no mere conformity to a Counter-Reformation. This was the century of Saints Peter, Teresa, and John of the Cross. The Society of Jesus and the Dominicans revived theology. The Polyglot Bible, a scholarly edition prepared to give the most adequate text possible, was published in 1522. ". . . the Spanish reform was initiated under royal auspices and independently of Rome, whose own religious revival it anticipated by many years."[90]

Switzerland

In this chapter only Lucerne and Solothurn, the two centralist states among the thirteen Swiss cantons, are of immediate interest. Descriptions of their histories are introduced by a sketch of the larger context of Swiss politics.

At its inception in the Everlasting League of 1291 and during its many years of expansion, the central Swiss regime was a shifting confederation of towns and rural districts all forced into mutual alliances to defend their liberties. By 1513 the Confederation consisted of thirteen cantons, each with equal representation in a common diet. Each canton, alone or in combination with various of the others, controlled domain lands. All cantons were governed by some or all of their own inhabitants.

The Swiss had once retained a kind of moral tie to the Holy Roman Empire. This was broken late in the fifteenth century when their hereditary enemy, the House of Hapsburg, came into possession of the Imperial throne. In 1499 the Confederation became, de facto, an independent union. Its independence gained formal recognition at Westphalia in 1648.

The structure of the Confederation was little altered from 1513 until the French invasion in 1798. The national diet discussed matters the cantons found of common interest, making its decisions by majority vote. Each canton was completely self-governing within its own borders. The diet might properly be considered a congress of sovereign states discussing problems of mutual concern: defense, the administration of lands that had been either conquered or purchased by all acting together, diplomacy, the regulation of a coinage, and, on several occasions, the mediation of disputes among member states. Although usually acting in concert in foreign affairs, the cantons could, and sometimes did, have individual relations with other powers.

Certain small, neighboring states were quasi-members of the Confederation, being nearly always allied to the Swiss and usually sharing Swiss positions on foreign policy. Of these states, Geneva was the wealthiest and most populous.

Two facts about the Thirteen Confederates and Geneva determined many of the political developments I am about to describe: even by standards of that period, each canton was small and none was economically self-supporting. In the sixteenth and seventeenth centuries when cities like Amsterdam, Antwerp, and Vienna had populations in excess of fifty thousand and major German centers (including Cologne, Augsburg, Ulm, Brunswick, and Lübeck) or the Flemish city of Bruges had more than twenty-five thousand people, the largest Swiss communities never exceeded seventeen thousand. Here are some estimates in thousands:[91]

Basel: 1400's − 8 to 10
               1450 − 9

Bern: 1400's − 3 to 4
               1450 − 5 to 6
               1558 − 5
        late   1700's − 12

Chur: 1481 − 1.5
               1499 − 1.5
               1799 − 2.5

Fribourg: 1444 − 5.2
               (Growth then ceased until 1794)

Geneva: 1404 − 6.5
               1589 − 13
               1698 − 17
               1700's − 20 and more

Lucerne: 1352 − 3
               1798 − 4.3

Schaffhausen: 1392 − 3
               1521 − 2.5
               1798 − 5

Solothurn: 1481 − 2
               1798 − 3.4

Zurich: 1408 − 5 to 6
               1450 − 4
               1467 − 4.5 to 4.9
               1529 − 4.6 to 5.5
               1637 − 8.6
               1682 − 10.8 to 11.4
               1762 − 11.4

The growth of these towns was arrested in the fifteenth century when the ratio of the town dwellers to the farmers in their surrounding countrysides became exceedingly high. For example, this ratio was 1:2 in the canton of Fribourg and 1:3.5 in Bern and Zurich.[92] The Alpine cantons around

Lucerne had long suffered from their paucity of natural resources. Population pressures now forced them to export men into foreign military service along with their more traditional exports of dairy products and cattle.[93]

The period of the Thirty Years' War (1618-48) was a time of prosperity for most of neutral Switzerland. When the war ended and Swiss sales to combatants stopped, many cantons were thrown into a desperate economic situation. In town and rural cantons alike a movement grew to close the lists of full citizens in order to limit those who might claim a share of limited resources in trade, agriculture, and state service.[94]

At the Reformation certain cantons adopted Calvinism, others remained Catholic, and two, Appenzell and Glarus, split into a Calvinist and Catholic sector. The Protestant cantons were Basel, Bern, Geneva, Schaffhausen, and Zurich. The Catholic cantons were Fribourg, Lucerne, Schwyz, Solothurn, Unterwalden, Uri, and Zug.

Lucerne:[95]

Originally a dependency of its Benedictine convent, Lucerne became a fief of the Empire in 1277, and later, a tributary of the Hapsburgs. Together with the neighboring Forest Cantons, Lucerne gained de facto independence after the Swiss victory at Sempach in 1386.

In 1252 the town had a council of eighteen members and a burgomaster, these officials serving for terms of six months and exercising the higher and lower jurisdictions. By 1281 burghal statutes had come to have the force of law before Imperial courts. During most of the period of Austrian control, the duke named the burgomaster. The ducal bailiff had the right to veto actions of the town council. Retiring members of the council elected their successors. Records show that by 1334 the council had the right to assent to or decline the nomination of a burgomaster proposed by the duke. In this same period, former members of the council had the right to sit as members of councils elected after their retirement from office. In 1385 the town asserted the right to elect its burgomaster and to do so once every six months.

The stages by which the Great Council emerged are unclear. One can say that it appeared between 1336 and 1343 and apparently was intended as an intermediary between the old, now Small, council and the burghers. Its members were selected by the Small Council to consult with them on matters of community importance. The General Assembly of the burghers was forbidden to take actions or discuss problems except under the guidance and with the consent of the Councils.

The burghers of Lucerne apparently met in General Assembly to participate in jurisdictio, but their powers were considerably more circumscribed even at an early date than was the case in most Swiss communities. They had been prohibited in 1252 and again in 1343 from forming groups or alliances, for example, guilds, among themselves. The community of all burghers was declared the only politically legitimate corporation. Guilds were restricted to the conduct of trade and business and were never of great importance even in such matters. Moreover, both during and after Austrian rule, the Small Council alone had exclusive rights to exercise gubernaculum. It was successful in defending both this monopoly and its right to self-renewal despite serious challenges in 1396 and 1424. Its success in 1424 was complete.

This regime continued to develop its institutions. In 1431 the Great Council received the right to cast formal votes. By 1491 the Great and Small Councils acting together were electing the town's administrative, military, and judicial officers. Authorities disagree as to whether the Councils still had to get approval from the burghal Assembly to decide on matters of war and peace, alliances, taxation, or the acquisition of property. The bulk of the evidence suggests that the Assembly's consent was required in most of these matters—all relating to jurisdictio—through the eighteenth century.[96] In 1492 elite control even over the Great Council was increased, its membership being reduced from 100 to 64. At this time the Small Council had 36 members.

Thus we find that Lucerne had a centralist regime even before 1500, headed not by a noble lord but by a self-perpetuating Small Council, that body, together with its agents in the Great Council, exercising all rights of gubernaculum and many of jurisdictio. This pattern was only strengthened by developments in the sixteenth, seventeenth, and eighteenth centuries. By ordinances passed in 1569, 1576, and 1594 a narrow patriciate fastened itself on the city. The bailiwicks owned by the municipality were assigned to members of the Councils. Membership on the Councils came to be for life. The town's administrative officers came to be chosen by the Great Council which restricted its selections to members of the Small Council. In 1773 full burghal status was restricted to members of 29 families, new families to be added only upon the extinction of the old. The patricians of Lucerne took on the title and style of nobility in the mid-seventeenth century, calling themselves "junkers."

Solothurn:[97]

Certain data useful for our analysis cannot be obtained because a fire in the fifteenth century destroyed many of the city's historical records. Fortunately, most facts essential for our purpose are available.

Solothurn, ruled by feudal powers, gained a Council of twelve members around 1330 and, in 1347, the right to elect its burgomaster.[98] The composition and selection of the Council are unclear, but it appears that noble families controlled it. The town's guilds revolted in 1347, and, as a result, gained the right to nominate candidates from which the existing council would choose the members of a new council of twenty-two. The new councilors served concurrently with the members of the old council. Each of the town's eleven guilds was to be represented on this new combined or "Great" Council by two members. Thereafter the Great Council nominated candidates for the Small Council who then were elected by the citizens, one representative coming from each guild. The Small Council continued to elect the Great Council from the guilds' nominees.[99]

The guilds in Solothurn served as military rather than economic or political groupings. From 1500 burghers were not obliged to be members of one guild in particular but might choose freely from among them. In this period the guilds came to engage mostly in social and religious activities.

The burghers of Solothurn met in General Assembly to elect their burgomaster and discuss important affairs. When the Reformation began they gave it strong support, contingents from Solothurn aiding Zwingli in the First Kappel War. Immediately after the defeat of Zurich in the Second Kappel War and the resultant immobilization of the Swiss Protestant cantons, Catholics in Solothurn seized control of the city's government. Their regime was in power from 1533.

The new rulers added a third council, larger than its predecessors and elected by the Small Council. The new body superseded the burghal Assembly in almost all matters, the latter being reduced to confirming communal officers (burgomaster, banneret, and others) chosen by the councils. The new Grand Council was allowed to consider only those matters sent it by the Small and Great Councils, but its participation was required in deciding on war and peace, in making treaties, in concluding alliances, in granting civil status to new residents, and in creating constitutional institutions.

Under this new regime the Small Council also elected the Great, choosing only persons who supported the new order. Finally, the Small Council came to recruit both its own members and the heads of the guilds. The guilds themselves no longer had a part in the political process.

As in some other Swiss communities, the government in 1682 limited the list of burghers to those families then having a member holding office. The result was to limit full citizenship to thirty-four families.[100] The Small and Great Councils came to select the canton's officers, thus eliminating the last power of the old General Assembly. The Grand Council grew in importance, obtaining in 1721 the right to initiate legislation.

Conclusion

Although each is centralist in form, the eleven regimes just described are quite different in many other respects. They differ, for example, in the date at which a centralist regime came to power: in Austria, France, Portugal, Ireland, Scotland, and Lucerne it was long before the Reformation; in Solothurn only during the Reformation struggles. Some states were ruled by burghers, some by a nobility or a king. Some were great European powers; others small and isolated. In Ireland and Scotland the body politic consisted of groups of kinsmen headed by a chief who served as a governor. Beside these kin lived dependent populations. The body politic in France consisted of all free men born of French fathers regardless of wealth or of title of nobility; in Lucerne and Solothurn it consisted of all persons formally admitted to citizenship by the existing agencies of government. We have found that three governments retained important feudal elements, the governments of France, Spain, and Austria. In Bavaria and Portugal there were nobles and towns, but the major feudal obligations of lord to vassal and of vassal to lord had been suppressed before the Reformation. In some states the fate of the Reformation seemed largely dependent on internal developments. One of these, France, experienced a great civil war before it was clear that Protestantism was only a minority movement. In other states, Austria and Berg-Jülich, for example, the indigenous governor's powers were supported at a critical juncture by foreign allies, this apparently enabling him to consolidate a centralist regime.

The nobility of Castile contained many wealthy men and these were powers in their regions of the country. But the power they held had no formal status in the structure of government whether national or regional. By contrast, in Austria, in some areas of France and Spain, and in Berg and Jülich there were important bodies in addition to the governor exercising authority in jurisdictio. The Bavarian body politic was represented in exercising jurisdictio only by the Small Committee of the Estates. In Portugal, much of

France, the greater part of Spain, in Solothurn, Ireland, and the Scottish Highlands there were governors ruling alone in jurisdictio as in gubernaculum.

The interpretations in this book ignore these many differences and others. They depend rather upon the form in regimes of relations between agencies embodying the common interest and those embodying special interests. Regimes treated in this chapter are called centralist only because all of them had a governor and because he alone had formal authority in gubernaculum, this in the period when the Reformation crisis was resolved.

In retrospect, there appears little doubt that most of these ten regimes are properly classified. I have some important reservations only about Ireland and Scotland. The descriptions of the Irish and Scottish septs do indicate that the current chief exercised gubernaculum essentially on his own authority, but this may be an overstatement. Just as anthropologists have frequently found that what first seemed an absolute chieftain was only the spokesman for his community and a man who lacked significant independent powers, so a more detailed picture of the actual making of decisions within Irish and Scottish septs might lead one to judge their regimes commensal rather than centralist. But that possibility seems the only likely alternative to the designation I have given them and, given our hypotheses, it would lead to the same prediction: commensal as well as centralist regimes are expected to remain Catholic at the Reformation.

[V]

Limited Centralist Regimes

EVERY LIMITED CENTRALIST STATE adopted Protestantism by official decree and some were among the earliest in Europe to embrace Reformed doctrines: Prussia in 1525, Württemberg in 1535, Denmark and Sweden in 1536, Brandenburg and Saxony in 1539, England in the period from 1547 to 1553, and Hesse in 1605.

The regimes of these states were headed by a governor who at the center of government had sole authority in gubernaculum. His authority extended also to all applications of his policies in each local area of the state. It was his power actually to administer those policies in local areas that was limited. For one reason or another he and his principal officers had to cooperate in local administration with local authorities having important independent powers. Moreover this cooperation was not a transient temporizing with independent local notables, but instead a formalized procedure for adminstration.

Consider, for example, these details given in a recent sketch of the English regime:[1]

> In February 1589, Sir Thomas Mildmay and Robert Clark examined suspected robbers in their native county of Essex. In March, Thomas Fanshawe settled a dispute over title to some property in the town of Barking. In May, Edmund Pirton compounded the claims of a bankrupt merchant's creditors. In August, Fanshawe joined Thomas Powle and former sheriff Robert Wroth in special watches occasioned by bands of wandering soldiers. In December, Thomas Gen investigated the "decay of trade" in the town of Halstead. . . .
>
> These men were justices of the peace. In that office, they

dispensed the queen's justice and administered her laws on the local and county levels. . . .

. . . .

The justice of the peace is the most familiar example of the English monarchy's reliance on part-time, unpaid, nonprofessional officials for the administration of government on the county and local levels. . . .

The justices were crown appointees chosen from among the more substantial landowners of the county they were to administer. However, both formally and informally the appointive powers of the crown were limited:[2]

. . . The Lord Chancellor was officially responsible, but the King, privy councillors, judges of assize, or lords lieutenants might be involved in the naming of any given man. In most cases, however, "the initial nomination of a new justice came from some magnate in the county itself. . . . Government policy set limits to the choices county magnates could make. A minimum number of attorneys was required. A prelate or two were to be included. A great lord or a man who was powerful in national politics could not be kept off the commission if he wanted to be a justice. Some mayors or other urban officials were justices *ex officio*. Most justices, however—75 percent would be a reasonable estimate—held office for other reasons. They were first appointed because they had the requisite wealth, local reputation, and style of life, and because they were relatives, friends, or adherents of justices more powerful than they.

. . . Justices were one another's friends or rivals, business associates, neighbors, and kin. Of the Elizabethan justices in Essex (not counting peers, prelates, and high officers of state) whose family ties are known—some 60 percent of the total of 132— "about 30 percent were fathers of Essex justices, 8 percent were sons-in-law." . . . Of 108 local governors in Somerset under Charles I . . . 35 were linked by marriage in their own or in the preceding two or three generations. . . .

The method of selection also made it possible for justices to perpetuate themselves in office. Commissions of peace were issued at irregular intervals because any change in a county's list of justices voided the entire commission. Hence, tenure was not fixed. But most justices held office for several years. . . .

The crown's cooptation of the gentry led to dependence on privately owned means of administration. This dependence prevented central control of appointments and allowed for local initiative in the selection of candidates. . . .

The powers which justices gradually came to exercise were important and diverse. They:[3]

> . . . collected taxes, held elections to the House of Commons, dispensed poor relief, repaired roads and bridges, impressed conscripts, decided suits at law, punished crime, suppressed vice, harassed Catholics, established maximum wages, enforced labor contracts, drilled the militia, distributed pensions to veterans, and regulated the distribution of grain when the harvest was bad. . . .

There are several differences between local officials like these and the locally powerful notables in a feudal system. In a feudal system local notables have in their own right original jurisdiction over their subordinates; in a limited centralist regime their jurisdiction is delegated to them by the governor. In a feudal regime the subordinates of a local authority are that authority's personal vassals or property; in a limited centralist regime they are subordinates of the governor as well. Under feudal circumstances there is, in principle, no right of appeal to the governor by persons subordinate to a local authority. Limited centralist regimes provide a system of courts organized under the governor and independent of local authorities and, at least in some important cases, any member of the body politic may appeal to these for adjudication of his affairs. Finally, the governor in a feudal order has separate contractual relations with each of many notables in the state, these contracts being formed by means of his negotiations with each separately and questions in jurisdictio being handled by means of renewed separate negotiations. In a limited centralist state the governor's authority is held generally over the whole of the state, he having the right to define policies applying equally to all of its local subdivisions. If questions arise in jurisdictio, these are questions concerning the rights of all subdivisions taken together in relation to the governor rather than of rights peculiar to any particular subdivision. Thus the English kings had to work with Parliament in jurisdictio as issues arose affecting all the counties of England, but the rights of each county were essentially those of any other.

Government in the eight societies I call limited centralist seems to have had all of these characteristics whereas government in societies I call centralist lacked all or nearly all of them. I have followed the additional rule that the powers of local authorities in limited centralist regimes must be supported by institutionalized guarantees. Specifically:

1. The governor must employ independent and local constituent bodies (or agents designated by them) in the regime's local exercise of gubernaculum, or—

2. The governor is limited in his choice of agents for the regime's local exercise of gubernaculum to members of the body politic residing in the area they are to govern, *and,* representatives of the body politic residing in those areas constitute a national diet which must give its consent in the making of laws and/or the levying of taxes.

In some limited centralist regimes both of these guarantees are present.

At the Reformation, the Swedish regime met the first of these criteria: local officials elected by all free men, including the peasants, administered the king's authority over their constituents' affairs. The regimes in England and Württemberg met the second criterion. The regimes of all other limited centralist states met both criteria—at least at the time these states adopted Protestant doctrines.

The importance and independence of even discretionary power in local hands is clear in all cases, including England and Württemberg where, in this period, the governor's authority was greatest. Thus Elizabeth's royal council in London had detailed knowledge of work by individual justices in individual counties yet, if dissatisfied with their work it:[4]

. . . could usually do little more than complain and rebuke. "The tone of helpless exasperation which occasionally sounds through the reproving, exhorting, and insistent letters from council to justices, and the recognizable instances in which the latter's quiet unresponsiveness defeated the council's intentions, suggest no very sure command of central over local government."

The council's harshest sanction, dismissal from the commission of peace, was almost never applied. The crown was too dependent upon local worthies, and the government knew it. In 1621, Commons debated a proposal to penalize recreant justices by one year's suspension from office. The proposal was a danger to county government, the solicitor-general argued, because the disgrace of suspension would be so great that a former justice would "not be willing to come in again." . . . The pool of possible replacements was limited by local control of nominations and by the fact that a place on the commission of peace could be costly. So long as the government filled the commission with men who "already possessed local authority, and . . . were confirmed in it, rather than given it" by the authority of office, it had to rely on local initiative and hope for the best.

All societies that developed limited centralism did so in the fifteenth century or later. The earliest seems to have been Saxony, the essentials of its regime being established by 1425. In England, this form of regime emerged slowly between 1400 and 1485; in Brandenburg and Prussia between 1450 and 1520. Limited centralism was apparent in Denmark in 1460, in Hesse by 1500, in Württemberg by 1514, and in Sweden by 1536. Thus, as of 1490, four of these eight states were limited centralist. Two, Sweden and Württemberg, were centralist. Hesse did not then exist as an independent polity.

The local authorities important in these regimes varied in composition. In Württemberg they were primarily the burghers of towns, these men dominating broader administrative districts of which the towns were a part. In Brandenburg, Prussia, Hesse, and Saxony, local organizations of gentry or nobles were most important. Rural districts constituted by local landowners, or by all free men, were important in England and Sweden, the towns also being significant. In Denmark, the towns and local organizations of the nobility served as agents of the central regime.

These differences in locally important elites remind us that our classification is indifferent to them. It depends rather on the relations between a governor, whoever or whatever the governor may be, and local authorities who serve as his agents, whether those authorities be merchants, burghers, nobles, landowners, free peasants, or whatever.

Denmark

The century preceding the Reformation saw in Denmark a struggle for power between the king and the nobles, the burghers being only periodic participants. The nobles had the upper hand in the early fourteenth century, and so complete was their dominance and so separatist their view that the country was threatened with dissolution into a collection of independent principalities. From 1332 to 1340 Denmark was without a king, absolute rule in her lands being divided between the counts of Holstein. The severity of their demands on the inhabitants and the jealousy of the lower nobility brought their dominion to an end, and a new king, Waldemar IV, was elected by the nobles. He began the process of restoring the monarchy's powers. Although he managed to defeat revolts by the nobility, their power was great enough to compel Waldemar to rule through his vassals. The policy of strengthening the crown continued under successive rulers until, by 1513,

> . . . the result . . . was the decline of the political importance of the nobility. . . . a burgher class was rising that was able to reconquer the national independence. . . . In part leaning upon this burgher class, the royal power organized itself more firmly. . . .[5]

The climax of the struggle for power began with the accession of King Christian II in 1513.

The lands governed by Christian II (1513-23) had become his under diverse circumstances. Denmark was an elective monarchy and he had been chosen to succeed his father as its king. By contrast, he had inherited his position as Count of Schleswig and of Holstein. As Count of Holstein, a fief of the Holy Roman Empire, he was a vassal of the emperor. Since the late fourteenth century the Danish royal house had been heir to the throne of Norway. By election as king of Denmark, Christian also became Norway's ruler.

The king's powers varied considerably from one of these

territories to another and neither he nor his predecessors had developed central ministries to coordinate the dynasty's holdings. In reviewing his sources of authority it is convenient to begin with Schleswig and Holstein.

The Danish nobility had elected Count Christian of Schleswig and Holstein as their king in 1460. At that time the principal nobles of the two duchies had important privileges and were a great influence in the ducal diets. Indeed the diet of each duchy continued to meet and participate in government even after each duchy had been divided among various princely lines.[6] All of Schleswig was brought under the Danish king's personal rule in the 1700's. Although their rights were never denied in principle, the notables of the duchies gradually lost their political powers during the 1700's and by the nineteenth century were no longer exempt from taxation.[7]

Norway's crown came to Christian by election, but the Danes so controlled Norwegian affairs that their choice was decisive. Christian's accession in Norway was the last pretence at an election of a Norwegian sovereign for the next three hundred years.

Christian's position in Denmark itself was weaker than elsewhere in his lands. His chief competitors for sovereignty were the greater nobles.

The Danish nobility had emerged during the breakup of the ancient clan system, individuals gaining exceptional personal power by employing military or economic skills. Most free Danes were farmers tilling their own small lands. In each province these freeholders met regularly as a landsting to elect the king, decide on military campaigns, make laws, render justice, and discuss matters of common interest. Under Waldemar the Great, the laws of the several landstings were codified, but there was still no legal code for the whole realm. (A code for Denmark was first adopted in 1638.)[8]

Around 1260, the Danish king, supported by the greater nobles, was able to extend his own judicial authority over the country and largely replace that of the landstings.[9] To gain the nobility's military support the king exempted their tenants from taxation. This encouraged large numbers of free farmers to sell their lands and become tenants of a noble.

In 1282 the greater nobles forced the king to sign a charter guaranteeing that his Council would meet once a year and, with the king, constitute the realm's supreme legislative body. The Council was made up of the greater nobles. At this same time the king agreed that he would observe due process of law in all his actions and agreed that the law enforced by the royal courts would not be more severe than that of the landsting courts.

The kings sought to evade these limitations, but rarely succeeded for long. Danish conquests in Sweden and the inheritance of Norway further enhanced the power of the nobles who obtained large estates and lucrative, prestigious offices in these dependent territories.[10]

By the reign of Christian II, lords temporal and spiritual owned almost three-fourths of the kingdom's land and peasants. Twenty percent of the farmers were freeholders. The landstings were no longer of importance. Judicial authority was divided between royal officials and landowners, the latter controlling the lower jurisdiction in their domains. In Zealand and other central Danish islands, many peasants had become serfs.[11]

The provinces were governed by lords-lieutenant, these being local landowners appointed by the king and owing him only a fixed amount of the provincial revenues while retaining the remainder for themselves.[12] These officials had civil and military authority over their districts.[13] The royal courts were organized by province, the king having to appoint judges for a province from its nobility and every freeman having the right to be judged in his province and by its laws.[14]

Like his predecessors, Christian II was crowned only after agreeing to govern with the advice, and, on certain matters such as taxation, war, and peace, with the consent of his Council. He also pledged, as had his father, that any person might have the right to rise against him if he, Christian, did not abide by the Council's decisions concerning settlements of major acts of violence.[15]

Christian II's reign is notable for his efforts to establish legal and commercial policies favorable to the urban merchants and with them to strengthen the powers of the crown. This policy, coupled with his loss of Sweden, produced a revolt of the nobles who drove him into exile.

His uncle, Frederick I (1523-33), reaffirmed the nobles' powers. Their representative acted as manager of the royal demesnes, head of the fleet, and dispenser of funds in the treasury. The king lost the power to name the members of his Council, agreeing that the nobility from a deceased councilman's province could present the king with a list of six candidates from which he would choose one.[16]

On Frederick's death, the lesser nobles of Jutland forced the Council to elect the current Count of Holstein as Christian III (1534-59).[17] In his reign the Reformation was adopted and Norway was declared a province of the Danish state.

Lutheran ideas reached Denmark in the reign of Christian II. In 1526 the Council was opposed to religious changes. In 1527, however, the Estates decreed that Lutherans should be recognized on equal terms with Catholics. This reflects the greater adherence to Lutheranism among the lesser nobility, the clergy, and the representatives of the towns. The king himself adopted Lutheranism. In 1530, the Estates approved the adoption of a Lutheran confession for the church.[18]

Christian III had established the Reformation in Schleswig and Holstein even before his election to the Danish throne. He was, therefore, unacceptable to many Catholic Danish nobles and required military assistance from Sweden to gain the crown from other contenders. When the Estates met in 1536 Christian was personally in a stronger position than many of his predecessors and a Protestant majority was at hand. At this meeting were represented nobles, clergy, burghers, and peasants. Roman Catholicism was abolished and replaced by a state church subscribing to

Melancthonian Lutheranism. The crown was made hereditary in Holstein's Oldenburg line, the Estates still to elect the individual from that line who would reign.[19]

Both crown and nobles benefited from the expropriation of the church's land, the crown's revenues increasing threefold. At this time, a small clique of nobles began to identify their own future with the increase of royal power and became a nucleus of strength on which succeeding monarchs were to draw.[20]

The kings who immediately followed Christian III governed a country constantly embroiled in great foreign wars and disturbed internally by efforts of crown, nobles, and burghers to control the state. On the average, the nobility continued dominant, but the foundations of their power were steadily weakened. The collapse came in 1660.

Frederick III (1648-70) had agreed at his accession that a council representing the three Estates would have the right to levy taxes. The major nobles were guaranteed great autonomy in the government of their estates and an exclusive right to the posts of lords-lieutenant, that is to the posts of royal governor in the provinces. They, however, then deserted the other Estates in dealings with the king and began to quarrel among themselves. Their two principal leaders were discredited when an audit showed they had mismanaged public funds. Faced with a dynamic and aggressive Swedish state, many nobles having domains in former Swedish lands, and some in Sweden itself, were of divided loyalty. The nobility as a whole panicked and deserted the crown when Sweden's Charles X marched his forces across the frozen waters of the straits, invaded Lolland and Zealand, and forced a Danish capitulation. In 1659 the Swedes again appeared in Zealand and laid Copenhagen under siege by land and sea. Once again the nobles and their peasant militia failed to save the state. At this point, Frederick made a pact with the burghers of Copenhagen agreeing that in return for their continued resistance he would make the capital a free city and transit center and grant them the same privileges with respect to status, taxation, and participation in government that the nobles then possessed. The garrison at Copenhagen held out and a Swedish withdrawal was forced by the arrival of allied armies from Poland and Brandenburg-Prussia.

When the Danish Estates met in 1660 the country was in ruins.[21] The greatest of Denmark's provinces, Scania, was lost to Sweden. The nobility was divided and discredited. Large areas of farmland were derelict. The burghers were too few and too poor to lead the state. The national resources were largely unavailable to aid recovery, half the soil and peasants being held by a tax-free noble oligarchy of about 150 families who also had no obligation to render military service and who monopolized the state's administration. However, even these great families were impoverished from years of war and defeat.

An alliance of the crown (including its generals and their German mercenaries) with the burghers, the clergy, and some of the nobility broke the powers of the greater nobles. The throne was made hereditary in the male and female lines of the Oldenburg dynasty. The king was given all executive, legislative, and judicial powers. In the Royal Law of 1660, this was interpreted to mean that the monarch was restrained only by these limitations: he must abide by the Augsburg Confession; he must not alienate the kingdom's lands nor change the rules of succession to the throne; he must not breach existing rights of private property nor withdraw existing exemptions from taxes.[22]

In implementing the crown's new authority, Frederick and his successor, Christian V (1670-99) laid down a system of government which persisted without essential change until 1848. The old Council was abolished and a royal privy council consisting of advisers chosen by the king was put in its place. Burghers and men from the king's German lands took over most of the important posts in the central government, subject always, however, to the king's will. The greater part of the crown lands were sold to Danish burghers and to German civil servants to pay for the Swedish wars. These new owners sought a quick return on their investment and exploited the peasants with great ruthlessness.

The old nobility was stripped of its independent right of participation in the central government. The old office of lord-lieutenant was abolished, the country was divided into royal administrative districts, and new royal governors were appointed—governors having very limited powers and sharing provincial administration with a series of boards all responsible to the king.[23] By these means the monarch established an effective control of local administration. The whole country was resurveyed and a new general land tax introduced.

Partly to console the old nobility for its loss of political authority and partly to reward the new servants of the state, Christian V introduced a series of high noble titles: those of count and baron. By a law of 1672 holders of these titles gained important privileges: rights of high and low justice on their estates; freedom from imprisonment for debt; the right to remain in residence on their lands until criminal cases against them were decided by the royal courts; the dignity of having only the new supreme court of the kingdom act as a court of appeal from sentences given in their private courts; the right to transmit their fiefs to male heirs.[24] Very few of the old Danish nobility accepted the new titles, most holders of countships and baronies being Holsteiners and other foreigners.

Under Christian VI (1730-46) and Frederick V (1746-66) Danish policies were in the hands of immigrant German statesmen.[25] Rationality, benevolence, and centralization were the qualities of this Danish government most remarked upon by visitors from abroad.[26]

England

The England of which Henry VII (1485-1509) became king after his victory at Bosworth had for two centuries been a mixed polity in which the crown, local authorities, and Parliament exercised important and independent powers. It had, at most times since William the Conqueror, been ruled by strong central institutions and, perhaps from an even earlier time, its institutions had evolved without radical breaks and disruptions.[27] With the granting of *Magna*

Carta (1215) there were formalized two principles: that the king was bound by the customs and laws of the realm and might be punished for breaking them; that the greater nobles—the baronage, acting as a corporate body—had the duty of seeing that the king obeyed the law.[28] Of equal importance, from that time the barons sought to support the monarchy's executive functions but to reserve for themselves an important role in legislation and judicial proceedings. Taxation became legitimate only with the barons' consent.

By the time of Henry IV (1399-1413), the landed gentry and urban merchants were formed as a corporate legislative body, the Commons, and that house had gained two important privileges: all money bills had to originate there, and the king promised to make no important changes in the wording of the Commons' petitions if he decided to enact them into law. Parliament's laws were defined in principle as legislative actions taken jointly by the king together with his lords and Commons. Parliament had also gained the right, by proceedings of impeachment or acts of attainder, to accuse, and force the dismissal of, unpopular royal ministers.[29]

Modern historical opinion sees the reigns of the Tudors not as introducing a royal absolutism but as strengthening the crown, the agency among the major elements of government that had been greatly weakened by the regime's failures in the Hundred Years' War and in the Wars of the Roses. It is notable, moreover, that the Tudors' reigns also saw the reinvigoration of the courts and of Parliament.[30]

The nobles, boroughs, and gentry were woven into the structure of government and were influential upon it in many ways. First, all were represented in Parliament: each peer receiving a personal summons and, in each county, the boroughs and those freeholders having incomes above a stated minimum being represented by men they elected. In part because all were subject to taxation (as were the clergy), all had an incentive to employ their legislative rights.[31] England was, moreover, a state in which all administration was conceived as the application of law and any servant of the king was accountable for his administrative actions before an ordinary court of law.[32] Not only did lords and Commons participate in the making of law, but their members presided in the local courts in which most cases were heard.[33]

From the reign of Edward III (1327-77) the central government had extended its rule over local areas by developing the office of Justice of the Peace. The counties, and the towns taken out of them by charters of incorporation, were recognized as the only legitimate territorial divisions of the kingdom for purposes of royal government. The justices were to be men holding land in the county over which the king appointed them his administrators and justices. Henry VII, like his predecessors, exercised the right of reappointment each year. By his reign the office of royal sheriff had become of little importance as had the seignorial courts and the traditional courts of freemen—the hundreds and shires. Indeed, courts of honour held by lords for those enfeoffed under them had done little business (and that was concerned with only minor cases) since the twelfth or thirteenth centuries.[34] The decline of these agencies gave more importance to the justices of the peace.

At the King's instance, the Lord Chancellor appointed from among each county's major landowners approximately fifty justices. Each had the judicial powers of all, those powers covering the whole range of criminal law with the exception of treason and some other great crimes.[35] Under this system:[36]

> Local jurisdiction and administration were committed to amateur and unpaid officials whose main obligation was to fulfill the law rather than the orders of the central government and whose affinities were strongest with the Common Law courts and with Parliament. . . .

In each county the justices sat quarterly, exercising concurrent jurisdiction with the king's judges in criminal cases and gradually developing an independent jurisdiction over civil offenses. In criminal cases, a jury was required.

Under Edward III and his successors the justices came to be given responsibility for executing and administering the law and royal ordinances. Most of the common duties of local government, as, for example, collection of taxes, establishment and control of local police, and construction and repair of roads and public facilities were in their hands. They appointed and supervised the overseers of the poor. Their expenses were paid by the crown, but no salary was attached to the office.

The Tudors met little opposition from their justices, but it was clear that the justices and juries tempered or even ignored the royal law when it ran counter to strong local feelings. The Tudor laws against enclosures went unenforced and in Catholic Lancashire the recusancy laws of Elizabeth were readily flouted. On the other hand, decisions of local justices could always be appealed to higher royal courts.[37]

The common people of England were not peasants or serfs. In England, as contrasted with France or Germany, it was illegal from 1290 for a person holding a fee simple (that is a right to property inheritable by primogeniture) to alienate his right to a tenant by subinfeudation. Tenants were, in such cases, to be created rather by "substitution," that is by the owner's substituting the tenant in his own place in the feudal pyramid.

> . . . the Crown had everything to gain through the enactment of the statute. No new tenures could be created, although in the inevitable course of events many old tenures became extinct, escheated to the lord above, or were forfeited to the Crown. The Crown was therefore gradually becoming less separated by intermediate tenures from the tenant in demesne.

As a consequence, the king was able to exercise a more direct authority over the holders of rights in land.

The use of land slowly changed. In no country was agrarian change influenced so powerfully by "industrial" interests as in England where the rural wool trade and the cloth industry formed a union. Enclosures spread, affecting the Midlands far more than the rest of the country. Free farmers were by far the most suitable agricultural workers under this system and their operation of farms on an entrepreneurial basis replaced the feudal and traditional order. Trade, industry, and colonization absorbed the large number

of agricultural workers made unemployed by the enclosures.[38]

The aristocracy gradually absorbed many of the new
leaders of commerce and industry. The English aristocracy had traditionally been open to accessions to its ranks
from the gentry and other elite groups and it remained so.[39]

The Reformation entered England only slowly. Henry
VIII had written a polemic against Lutheranism and apparently believed that the Act of Supremacy (1534) which
declared him supreme head of the Church of England
could be implemented, and that the dissolution of the
monasteries (1535-40) could be enforced, without altering
the doctrine and worship of the English Church. He saw
supremacy as restoring to the king ancient prerogatives
wrested from the crown by the Papacy and, of course, as a
solution to his diplomatic and dynastic problems. He saw
the monasteries as supplying money and land needed by the
royal treasury and the nobility. The clergy and laity were
toying with Protestant doctrines, but the king and government took no significant steps to disallow Catholic orthodoxy.
It was rather under Henry's successor Edward VI (1547-53)
that the doctrinal reformation occurred. Communion under
both kinds was permitted the laity, the clergy were allowed
to marry and were ordered to practice as ministers of the
Word in the Protestant manner rather than as priests. Only
baptism and communion were retained among the sacraments, the Eucharist being conceived in a manner midway
between the traditional mass and the mere commemorative
service of Zwingli's persuasion.[40] The Forty-two Articles
established in 1553 and the Thirty-nine Articles of 1563 provided a doctrine and government for the Church which, although definitely Protestant, were sufficiently vague on
crucial matters such as the nature of the sacraments to
compromise differences among Catholics and Calvinists.

Protestantism spread most rapidly in the country's eastern
coastal cities and in the Midlands, the latter being the heartland of English agriculture.[41] In 1570, a decade after Catholicism was outlawed in England, the Pope excommunicated
Elizabeth I. In a long arc beginning in the Scottish border-

lands and swinging westward and thence along the southern counties, recusancy flourished and sporadic rebellions in favor of Catholicism broke out.[42] However, by 1590 it was clear that the considerable preponderance of the population had accepted the new Church of England, the more violent Puritan objections to its structure were for the moment stilled, and the Catholic powers of Europe had failed to defeat this new Protestant state.

The later story of English government is too well known to need recounting: the brief and unsuccessful efforts of the later Stuart kings to gain a greater supremacy over Parliament, the steady growth of Parliamentary authority culminating in the late seventeenth and the eighteenth centuries when it gained legislative supremacy and gradually replaced the old royal privy council with a ministerial body responsible to Parliament. The final step in Parliament's rise was its defeat in the reign of George III of the crown's last effort to regain lost authority. There were struggles against possible royal absolutism in England, but no approach to absolute royal government.

Saxony and Württemberg[43]

This pair of duchies is distinguished from other German states by the relatively even balance of political power among duke, nobles, and burghers that emerged early in the fifteenth century and continued until the revolutions of 1830 brought an even more liberal constitution.

The Saxon lands had originally been frontier marches. Agriculture flourished and, although most towns remained small, three of them, Magdeburg, Leipzig, and Freiberg, were important centers of trade and industry. The country was also rich in minerals. In contrast with many other German rulers, the Wettin dynasty grew wealthier in the fifteenth and sixteenth centuries. Nonetheless, wars and (up to 1425) divisions of territory among hostile brothers forced the margraves to ask the towns, church, and nobles for financial aid.

The diet for the whole territory began meeting in the late fourteenth century. The nobles then as later held the lower jurisdiction on their estates, with the higher jurisdiction reserved to the margrave. The lesser nobility were always subject to the jurisdiction of the margrave's local officials. The Wettins were able to protect the peasants against any extension of their services to the nobles and peasant farming rather than demesne agriculture remained the predominant form of production.

Wealthy burghers bought up agricultural lands and there was no legislation reserving lands only to nobles. The peasants were encouraged to complain to the ducal courts against burgher or noble landlords.

The diet gained in power all during the fifteenth century. At that time it established principles it never lost: it alone could grant taxes; it had by right an important role in supervising the collection and expenditure of revenues; its consent was necessary for changes in the law or in the privileges of individuals or corporate bodies or in the organization of the courts. When the prince introduced the Reformation in 1539 without consulting the diet, he agreed not to use force against anyone with respect to religion. In the course of the sixteenth century the Estates became a corporation favoring orthodox Lutheranism and having a well-defined membership, definite rules of procedure, and regular dates for meeting. They were influential in the administration of foreign relations, finances, and religion.

At the local level, the county assemblies of nobles and other free men and the several towns each exercised important administrative powers, these being shared, however, with ducal appointees. Thus locally as well as centrally the Saxon regime was one of collaboration between ruler and people. In the middle of the seventeenth century, each county assembly of nobles and the local burghers elected deputies, these to meet with deputies from other counties and towns and to discuss matters connected with the diet and other important affairs. In this period the major towns formed a directorate responsible for preparing all documents for the diet. The elector did not possess a right to confirm members of these committees or members of the diet's own committees.

The exact powers of the Saxon Estates varied somewhat from time to time and they and their prince never ceased to seek greater powers from one another, but the duchy's law and its political realities almost always reflected a balance of control between these two major forces in the polity. Within the Estates there continued to be a balance of strength between the nobles and the towns.

Württemberg occupied a large area which played an important part in the politics of central Europe. Gradually extended, its boundaries became stable from the fifteenth to the end of the eighteenth centuries. The ruler was an Imperial count and leader of the Swabian Circle, the loose confederation of independent and neighboring principalities, cities, and monasteries. The land was divided only once (1442-82) and then reunited. In 1495 the Emperor Maximilian elevated the territory to a duchy inheritable by primogeniture. The Stuttgart line of the ruling house remained dominant uninterruptedly until November 1918.

Württemberg was a country of small towns and villages. There were no natural barriers to internal travel and no great sources of riches. Intensive agriculture provided the main income. By 1514 the manorial system had disintegrated, and every subject was constitutionally free to leave the country. The towns were represented directly in the diet. The towns, not the nobles, shared control of the government together with the duke. Most of the nobles had withdrawn from the diet early in the sixteenth century when they obtained the status of free Imperial Knights of the Holy Roman Empire. The nobility did not possess rights of patrimonial jurisdiction on their lands. Throughout the duchy it was the urban leaders who comprised the upper class from whom ducal officials were usually drawn.

In contrast to most German states, sharp social conflicts were absent in Württemberg. The ducal administrative districts, the amter, were self-governing corporations and voluntary associations dominated by the urban authorities who also represented the towns and districts in the diet. The diet itself was a unicameral body composed of fourteen prelates and fifty burgher representatives elected by their

respective towns. By the Treaty of Tübingen (1514) between the Estates and the duke, natives were to be preferred
for all important governmental appointments, major wars
were to be undertaken only with the advice and knowledge
of the Estates, the ducal lands might not be alienated, taxes
and aids were to be levied only with the Estates' agreement,
and the Estates obtained the right to administer the collection and expenditure of revenues obtained. These terms,
breached in various degrees by Duke Ulrich (1515-19, 1534-
50) became the foundation of the duchy's constitution which
persisted until the early 1800's.

During Ulrich's reign, the duchy was invaded by French,
Bavarian, and Austrian armies and the religious question
remained unsettled. Ulrich himself was converted to Lutheranism and introduced it in 1535 without consulting the diet.
After being expelled by Hapsburg troops. Ulrich returned in
1547 and Catholicism was reestablished. However, in the
reign of his son Christopher (1550-68), and especially after
the defeat of Emperor Charles V by Maurice of Saxony in
1552, Catholic priests and prelates were gradually replaced
by Lutheran clergymen, usually sons of burghers. The Confessions of Augsburg and Württemberg were accepted by
the Estates.

As in Saxony, duke and Estates quarreled frequently and
sometimes fiercely about their respective rights and for considerable periods one or the other was predominant. The
weaker party, usually the Estates, was able in time to muster
support, sometimes from foreign powers, in order to restore
its role in government. Thus neither dukes nor Estates ever
became supine before the other. The dukes retained their
power to confirm appointees to the Estates' administrative
committees and to appoint their own advisers and administrators and the Estates retained their many prerogatives. When possible, dukes avoided convening the Estates,
but recurrent financial or military problems forced them to
deal with the diet's administrative committees which met
frequently and which compelled them eventually to consult
with the diet itself.

Brandenburg and Prussia[44]

These lands were independent territories until united in 1618 through the person of their ruler, a member of the Hohenzollern dynasty. Each regime must be considered separately up to the time when it and the other territories of this dynasty were finally welded into a single state. Even when all were united, two Hohenzollern lands, Cleves and Mark, retained political institutions that distinguished them from the rest.

The nobles and towns of Brandenburg did not readily acquiesce in 1411 to the rule of their first Hohenzollern margrave. He managed to break their resistance and he and his successors gradually strengthened the central administration. The powers of individual nobles were confined to their own estates. Castles of robber barons were destroyed. The rulers set about regaining powers lost by earlier governors. Previous dynasties had pawned or sold to nobles and the towns many domain lands and many rights of government. In the latter half of the fifteenth century, and with support from the nobility, the margraves seized on any convenient excuse to dominate the towns. In each, they established military control, effected an alliance with the towns' patricians against the guilds, and greatly increased the towns' contributions to the territorial government. They resumed earlier rights to appoint town officials and withdrew, from any town that had it, the right of higher jurisdiction— that is of jurisdiction in "life and limb." By the time of the Reformation, the towns were paying two-thirds of the taxes received by the central state.

The dynasty was successful also in activating its own courts, the margrave's privy council sitting as a court of last appeal. (Since the granting of the Golden Bull in 1346, the supreme judiciary of Brandenburg had had final jurisdiction over cases arising among its people.) From 1473 the Hohenzollerns defined Brandenburg as chief among their possessions, initiating the policy of not dividing the territory and of bequeathing it on most occasions to a decedent ruler's eldest son. These several developments were consolidated just before the Reformation under Joachim I (1499-1535).

As the central organs of the state were gradually strengthened under the reigns of successive margraves, the powers of the nobility in local administration and in jurisdictio also increased. Throughout the fifteenth and early sixteenth centuries the rulers were forced by financial exigencies to pawn or sell their properties again and again, native nobles usually being the beneficiaries. In the fourteenth century the rulers of Brandenburg had sold or pawned the higher jurisdiction in a third of their domains west of the Oder. East of that river many noble families gained this jurisdiction as a hereditary right. In the fifteenth century, the rulers gradually lost to the nobility higher jurisdiction over most of Brandenburg.

The decline of the towns was economic as well as political and, as they declined, they no longer served as a serious counterweight to the nobles' powers in the state. Simultaneously there occurred a steady erosion of the independence of the Brandenburg peasantry. Brandenburg, like Prussia and Pomerania, had been a German frontier. The settlement of free peasants had been encouraged through generous privileges by which a man could own land, participate in local government, and, even as a tenant, receive a considerable protection of his rights from the margrave's courts. In the fifteenth century, however, these privileges were whittled away. The nobles' new control over the higher jurisdiction enabled them to curb peasant rights more fully. Simultaneously the nobles found increasing incentive to obtain large tracts of land and to practice demesne agriculture. The sandy soil of Brandenburg was profitable to those who could undertake large-scale production of corn, a crop much sought by purchasers in western Europe.[45] Nobles' estates were extended by an often barely legal encroachment on peasants' holdings and the freedom of peasants to leave a noble's land was restricted.

Estates had appeared early in Brandenburg, exercising through their diet an important role in jurisdictio. Under the Elector Joachim II (1535-71) this role was further strengthened. In return for the Estates' assuming his debts,

Joachim agreed in 1540 to the establishment of a financial administration under the exclusive control of a committee of the diet. The diet's agents collected taxes and paid the elector's creditors. To the elector were left the domain revenues, feudal dues, and such grants of money as the diet saw fit to make to him. The elector was compelled to promise "not to undertake or conclude any weighty matter touching the weal or woe of the land, or to enter into any alliance, without the previous knowledge and advice of the Estates." It should be clear, however, that this pledge concerned the Estates' rights in jurisdictio. Earlier rulers of Brandenburg had given similar pledges. They were more significant in Joachim's administration because his financial straits forced him to observe his agreements.

Joachim was also persuaded to increase the nobility's local powers. Up to his reign, and despite the nobles' possession of the higher jurisdiction on their estates, the ruler's courts were available for appeals by peasants. Now the right of appeal was restricted: no peasant could bring suit against his lord in the court of the elector as a court of first instance; and he could not bring suit there at all except on the grounds of a denial of justice by his lord. To make these constraints even more effective, the elector agreed to imprison peasants who attempted to bring to his courts annoying and baseless suits against their masters.

Regional assemblies or dietines of landowners existed in Brandenburg all through the fifteenth and sixteenth centuries. They apportioned taxes to which the central diet consented and sometimes elected the knights' representatives to that diet. They also had great influence in the elector's appointment of the provincial governors and judges, these men generally being local residents and more devoted to their districts than to the central administration.

The majority of the Brandenburg nobility had turned to Lutheranism by the time Joachim II began his rule. It was only slowly that the elector himself publicly accepted the new doctrines, the definitive change not occurring until 1539. Even then he sought a compromise with Catholicism, retaining much of the Catholic form of worship while adopting Lutheran views of the sacraments and clergy. The adoption of Calvinism by the Elector John Sigismund in 1613 led to its acceptance in Brandenburg as a tolerated religion and, after his accession in Prussia in 1618, to its legal acceptance there as well.

In Prussia the Hohenzollern's fortunes were at first somewhat different but came later to resemble those experienced in Brandenburg. Conquered and administered by the Teutonic knights, Prussia first developed as a country of peasants and small landowners, a land in which the nobility was less important and regarded with less prestige than elsewhere, a country in which strong groups of freeholders living directly under the ruling knights stood between the nobility and the peasantry.

Military defeats by the Poles and a spreading agricultural depression weakened the knights' control. Their ruling oligarchy of four hundred or fewer men had exercised absolutist powers. Now it appeared unable to defend its own borders. It was in part to strengthen the knights' position against Poland that they chose as Grand Master a younger son of a German territorial prince, electing Albert of Hohenzollern in 1511. In April of 1525 the Teutonic Order was dissolved in Prussia and the Lutheran Reformation, already widely spread as popular doctrine, was officially introduced. Albert became Prussia's first hereditary duke and a liegeman of the King of Poland.

In Prussia, the wealth and power of the knights prevented the rise of local Estates. The military and economic crises of the fifteenth century first brought the towns and nobility into the political affairs of the state, giving them control over taxation and other matters. Supported by the Polish crown, the Estates were entrusted with supervising the knights' agreement to treaties of peace. The nobles gained the right of local control including the higher jurisdiction over their peasants and, again with Polish support, the right to rebel against rulers who violated their privileges. Most peasants became the subjects of private landlords.

With the Reformation, Duke Albert became dependent upon the Estates for financial support. In return, the Prussian nobility acquired the right to approve foreign alliances, to rebel against ducal orders that infringed their privileges, and to force the exclusion of commoners from all ducal offices. The towns were of even less political significance than in Brandenburg, the leading towns having been ceded to Poland in 1466. Those that remained suffered an economic decline.

During the Thirty Years' War (1618-48), the Hohenzollerns' effective powers shrank. Brandenburg and Prussia were now united under a common ruler, but, especially in Brandenburg, the chaos of invasion and counterattack made difficult any sustained exercise of the elector's authority. The ruler was often out of the country. His finances were desperately strained. In Brandenburg the Estates controlled the levying, training, financing, and employment of the army operating in its territories. In Prussia, local independence was even more pronounced. The four chief officers of the state had come to hold their positions by hereditary right. One of them, the chancellor, could refuse to affix the duchy's seal to decrees of the duke, thus depriving them of the force of law. Local officials controlled the ducal privy purse and domains as well as the public funds.

Relations between the rulers and the diets of their several northern territories continued in this fashion to the middle of the seventeenth century. Then, in 1653, while granting his Brandenburg Estates new privileges, the elector obtained from them a six-year grant that enabled him to raise a small standing army. Thanks to this preparation, Frederick William was able to play a decisive part in the war of 1655-60 between Sweden and Poland. When the Estates of his several territories refused funds to support him in that war, he raised monies without their consent. In his triumph, he had gained a standing army capable of breaking any resistance against the collection of taxes required for its maintenance. No general diet was held in Brandenburg after 1652.

The Prussian Estates granted money to maintain a small army in peacetime, and against this army their privileges were of little avail. In 1674 the prince directed the army to occupy Königsberg and burgher opposition to him vanished. To the Hohenzollerns, the standing army was indispensable as the means for consolidating, administering, and protecting their scattered possessions.[46]

Founded on the privy council of Brandenburg, there grew from 1651 a new government uniting all the dynasty's lands in a single system of taxation, tax collection, and military organization. The Estates of most of these provinces met rarely if at all. Across the whole extended a new public law established beside the older codes and grounded solely on the will of the prince. Taxes were levied at the dynast's desire.

But this growth of a new, central authority was not unlimited. Beginning with the very concessions for which the Brandenburg Estates provided a standing army in 1653, the Hohenzollerns developed an alliance with their nobility which provided the princely house with the support it needed and brought the nobility into the general government while preserving their independent political powers. Serfdom was affirmed wherever it was in use. As we have seen, the nobles of Brandenburg and Prussia had come to exercise even the higher jurisdiction on their private estates and this the prince guaranteed to them. He forbade merchants or other commoners to buy nobles' land and provided financial help for nobles pressed to retain their estates. He reserved to the nobility the highest offices in the civil government and the army. Perhaps most important of all, he was forced to incorporate in the general government's administration of the counties the nobles' courts, assemblies, and administrative apparatus and also the noble-controlled courts of the provinces themselves.[47]

Perhaps the height of Hohenzollern "absolutism" occurred during the reign of Frederick William I (1713-40). (His practices were appreciably moderated beginning with the reign of Frederick the Great (1740-86).) What was the organization of the Brandenburg-Prussian polity in this period of strictest centralization?

The Estates no longer met as deliberative or legislative bodies. At the "county" (circle) level, public affairs were discussed by the nobles in a representative assembly or dietine and relations with the central authority were maintained through a rural councilor or landrat who was almost always a noble and was chosen by the dietine as its representative rather than as the king's.[48] (On occasion Frederick William I disciplined a dietine by refusing to allow it to present a candidate for the post of landrat.)[49] The circle itself was, by law, a seignorial corporation lacking judicial functions but otherwise having functions much like those of English justices of the peace: administering national policies on the local level, and communicating local problems and proposals to the central government.[50]

The growing central government established courts and administrative agencies in the provinces but these tended to deal with the newer functions of the state and with only a part of those. Thus the local offices of the war commissars were general agencies of the central administration with special responsibilities for the recruitment and support of troops and they served as intermediary agents for the collection of the new taxes.[51] But the nobles themselves were the immediate collectors of the main direct tax, the kontribution, a tax levied on their peasants but from which the nobility was exempt.[52] In addition, the old established courts of law at the local and provincial levels continued to administer the traditional law which encompassed most suits between private persons and these courts administered the customary criminal law.[53] They were strongholds of the squirearchy.

At the center of the new, unified state, the kings retained final authority but the most distinguished posts of government were set aside for nobles of old lineage. In the army, the nobility gradually gained almost a complete monopoly of all posts from the rank of captain upward.[54]

Frederick William I had begun the creation of cadres of nobles loyal to the crown and occupying the major posts of the central bureaucracy. His son, Frederick the Great, presided over a new compromise with the landed nobility which remained the major local power. No further attempts were made to curb powers of the dietines. These assemblies and the landrats were paid partly by the national treasury and partly by the local Estates.[55] The service nobility organized by Frederick William I amalgamated with the more prestigious landed nobility to form a single social and administrative structure.[56] The pay for officers of the traditional courts was increased. The prime minister, Cocceji, pursued most of his policies in consultation and close cooperation with the spokesmen for the circles. From them he sought nominations for the more important judicial posts in each district. Noble judges were given superior authority, prestige, and pay. The traditional courts were granted the right to handle all cases in which a nobleman was involved, even if the crown was the plaintiff, thus securing for the nobility effective legal protection against arbitrary governmental action.[57] After 1740, the ministers of the crown's principal administrative committee (the general directory) and the presidents of the war and domain chambers were almost always nobles. On the other hand, all nobles who entered the civil service had to be graduates from one of the four national universities. They won their appointments by performance on examinations and underwent a period of careful technical preparation. There were few if any sinecures.[58]

These developments during the rise and consolidation of the Prussian state may be contrasted with those in the government of France under the eighteenth-century absolutism. In France the nobles had largely lost their independent jurisdictions in the villages and in the countryside.[59] The intendants who were the great power in local administration were usually chosen from noble families with local connections, but were selected by the central government and responsible to it.[60] More than this, it was possible from 1653, after the collapse of the French nobility's conspiracy against the crown, to exclude the old nobility of descent from the seats of administrative and political power for at least two generations.[61]

Hesse[62]

The possessions of the landgraves of Hesse were scattered widely throughout central Germany. Conflicts within the ruling family during the fifteenth century resulted in a division of the domains and a strengthening of the Estates which had met first in 1387. The leading towns of the area, Frankfurt and Wetzlar, were free Imperial cities, hence outside the jurisdiction of the margravate. The towns within Hesse—Cassel and Marburg being the major centers—were too weak to counterbalance the power of the nobles. It was the Estates, and particularly the nobles, which provided some unity among the warring factions of the dynasty, developing compromises and arbitrating grievances.

In 1500 the territories were finally reunited under William II. William was seriously ill, however, and a committee chosen by the Estates governed together with a regental committee of five nobles selected by the landgrave. This regime was in office from about 1506 until William's death in 1509 and thence during the minority of his heir until 1518. The Estates assembled on their own initiative. They demanded that the regents consult with them on important matters, and on lesser affairs with their standing committee. In 1509 the Estates were granted the power of the purse and their other demands on the regents were accepted. A diet was to be summoned every year, and the Estates were entitled to assemble on their own initiative. From 1513 to 1518, however, the nobles split into factions and, disunited, lost much of their effectiveness.

In 1518 the new ruler, Philip, came of age. He forbade the Estates to meet on their own initiative, rejected as difficult and unnecessary their petition for a diet, but agreed to meet with ten deputies chosen by him from a list of twenty-four submitted by the nobles. The new landgrave proceeded to develop an alliance with the towns; only they were summoned when he needed money. In 1523 he destroyed the castles and power of the independent Imperial Knights whose territories were scattered among his own. A full diet of the Estates was held in 1527 when the Lutheran Reformation was introduced, but under Philip only the towns were assembled thereafter. The landgrave introduced the religious changes on his own authority, assembling his Estates only to associate the country with his action and to devise an allocation of the monastic lands that would not alienate the nobility whose support he needed to effectuate the introduction of Protestantism.

The Estates never gained the right to legislate, but their consent was required for the levy of general taxes. Meetings concerned with taxation and issues of war and peace were held throughout the sixteenth century, every member of a noble family holding a fief having the right to be summoned. In 1594 and 1603 it was left to each noble family whether they would grant powers of representation to one of their number or whether they wished to appear in full strength. The urban representatives were usually officials of the towns, but the urban Commons often sent their own representatives to the diet. There continued to be a preponderance of native nobles among the higher officials and councilors of the landgrave. A committee of the Estates was elected to administer a new tax granted in 1532. Another committee was established to supervise the levying and administration of a new excise, but they had no voice in the allocation of the money. In the sixteenth century the nobles became liable to taxation, their opposition to it being crushed by the landgrave.

The Estates met often both before and during the Thirty Years' War and their powers waxed. After the war, the nobles and towns fell at odds and the landgrave took advantage of their disunion to establish what became the basic Hessian constitution from 1655 until about 1800: the diet would meet only with the landgrave's permission; full diets were required to decide on the levy of taxes applied to the whole of the country; in an emergency the landgrave was entitled to decree a tax for the army but afterward should seek the approval of a diet summoned "as soon as convenient."

By 1500 the Hessian towns commonly had considerable powers of self-government, these exercised by locally selected officers and a council. As in Württemberg, the representative to the central diet chosen by a town also represented the surrounding rural population, nobles and their subordinates excepted. The landgraves' officials carried out their work in these communes largely in collaboration with the local authorities, this partnership reinforced from the accession of Philip by the towns' support for the landgraves against the special privileges of the nobility. The burghers shared with central officials supervision over the levying and administration of taxes, the operation of the lower courts, the exercise of police power, and the implementation of the landgraves' ordinances.

In 1774 the ruling landgrave instituted a new type of regional office to stimulate the economic life of the communes. These new officials, the landräte, were chosen by the landgrave from a list drawn up by the Estates of each region. The landräte had additionally to prevent the absorption of peasant farms by noble landowners and to care for the operation of police and the supervision of taxation and military affairs. All landräte were, in turn, supervised by bureaus of the central government. This system continued to 1797 when the towns successfully argued for a return to previous practices.

Diets met frequently through the eighteenth century. Representatives were chosen by elections of the Estates in five administrative districts. The three Estates met separately. Within each house, decisions were taken by a majority, but all three houses—prelates, nobles, and towns—had to consent to a proposal, especially in matters of taxation. The Estates did not possess a treasury of their own and their right to supervise the levying and administration of taxes had disappeared. As in Brandenburg-Prussia, the nobles collected the taxes levied on their own lands.

Sweden

Sweden had experienced some degree of political unity from the tenth and eleventh centuries, but this was repeatedly disrupted by foreign invasion, especially from Denmark. Unity and independence were finally secured under Gustav

Vasa (1523-38). The constitutional structure of the Swedish state before and after this period has been described as follows:

> . . . Local self-government . . . has roots stretching down to the earliest days of State and Church. The democracy of the *ting*, the co-operation of all classes in the parochial council, are among the fundamental facts of Swedish history; and they proved strong enough in the seventeenth century to resist successfully the contradictory threats of the efficient centralizing officials of the monarchy, on the one hand, and those aristocratic tendencies towards social oppression of the type prevalent in Germany, on the other. Parliamentary self-government is much younger; but it is still of respectable antiquity. Before the end of the fourteenth century the *Riksdag* had begun to take shape; before the end of the fifteenth it had become an important element in the political life of the nation. It was of high significance that the Diet should have included, from an early date, a separate Estate of peasants. As with the English parliament, it was only gradually that the *Riksdag* took over the task of safeguarding the liberties of the nation, and no notion of that sort lay behind its early summonses. The constitutional opposition, the guardianship of the law, the check upon royal aggression, was at first the nobility, in Sweden as in England. They strove to keep the monarchy elective; they made the *råd* the watch-dog of the constitution.[63]

Gustav Vasa's success against the Danes was made possible by the support of nobles, burghers, and peasants. His efforts to establish an absolutist rule were thwarted by the nobles who, nevertheless, continued their traditional support for a strong state. The peasants, never subjected to the thorough-going feudal obligations and serfdom of the Continent proper, always contained a large proportion of freemen and were a potent political force at all periods. The parallels with England are many and striking.

The ancient desire of Swedish leaders for national unity has given rise to interesting speculations. Why was there no development of separatism such as appeared elsewhere on the Continent? Heckscher proposes:[64]

> First of all, the estates and fiefs of the landed nobility were scattered over many different provinces. This made for an interest in communications between the provinces and for a far stronger national orientation than would have been possible

had the holdings of the aristocracy been confined to individual provinces. . . . Another important factor is that enfeoffments in Sweden were never quite hereditary; consequently to preserve large landholdings intact from generation to generation was a difficult task. . . .

While these conditions might account for the interest in national unity, they do not explain how it was actually attained. To understand this one must consider the nature of Swedish communications. . . . the country possessed two methods of communication which were . . . difficult to block.

One was offered by the long coasts. Other countries with long coastal strips, like England, Norway, and Denmark, likewise succeeded in avoiding feudal disintegration. . . . the important trading centers along the Swedish coast are shielded by archipelagoes which make blockades extremely difficult. If anyone had attempted to collect a toll somewhere in one of the island groups, the small vessels of those times could easily have evaded it by slipping through the maze of sounds and straits.

Secondly there were the winter roads which had no counterpart in more southerly climes. The snow and ice offered a rather unique opportunity for easy transportation in spite of the extreme difficulties in constructing and maintaining ordinary highways. In winter, such small hauls as might be called for in the medieval economy were easily carried on sledges across land and water even without any ordinary roads. Should it occur to some lord to levy a toll along such a winter track, nothing could be simpler than to open up another one. . . . This mode of transportation is largely accountable for the absence of feudal disintegration in Sweden.

From the middle of the fourteenth century Swedish kings had been obliged to govern with the advice of their councils, these bodies being composed of the greater nobles. Gustav Vasa was freed from this bondage by the decimation of noble ranks which accompanied the struggles for liberation (and the discrediting of some of the greater nobility after their support of the Danes). He leaned instead on the diet, usually having no difficulty in obtaining its support. In 1544 the diet recognized the crown, long elective, as hereditary in Vasa's line.[65]

The diet then was only beginning to emerge as a body with an important constitutional role, growing from the national assemblies which, since 1319, had met to elect the king. Gustav Vasa had been so elected in 1523. But at almost no time after the diet's session in 1527 (at which it adopted the Reformation), was a major act of state conceivable with- out the diet's endorsement.[66]

The peasants were especially powerful in local govern- ment. In the later Middle Ages and for long thereafter the Swedish economy was almost totally agricultural, towns, commerce, and industry being of little importance.[67] Much of Swedish agriculture was controlled by the free peasants who were a power in the government of the state and in the local courts.[68]

Medieval Sweden was a union of various provinces which long retained their own laws and diets. To this union, the crown added a set of judicial districts in which elected law- men declared the law and dispensed justice at the meetings of the assembled freemen. From the fourteenth century, the lawman not only presided over the provincial diets, but began to go on circuit about his district, holding courts in each small political division—each "hundred."

The hundreds were presided over by an elected executive committee whose members served for life. This committee performed the functions of a jury and carried on much of the local administration. By the middle of the fourteenth cen- tury the committee's administrative functions had passed partly under the king's control and he then came to appoint the lawmen and the presidents of the hundreds' committees.

At the same period there was also a practice of granting to some great noble the right to administer a district on the king's behalf and to act as the crown's fiscal agent. No such position was hereditary and the holder had no right to priv- ate, as against royal, jurisdiction. Medieval Sweden was not a feudal country. Gustav Vasa reduced the number of such posts and replaced the nobles with royal bailiffs. After 1550 almost no noble performed this function.

The hundreds continued to have wide powers. Nobles often found that these meetings of freemen were dominated by their tenants. There never having been villeins or serfs in Sweden, all adult males were eligible for participation. The peasants' representatives to the national diet were chosen by the "hundreds" from among peasants who owned land.[69] The hundreds provided methods for the local assessment and collection of royal taxes. They and their committees had considerable autonomy over such local affairs as adjudicating disputes over property, building roads or fences or bridges, and establishing systems of charity. For such purposes they could levy taxes, establish and enforce laws, and pay local officials.

Smaller than the hundreds were the parishes and villages. Parish meetings, concerned with the local church, public morality, and charity, were even more democratic in operation than the hundreds.[70] Village communities had their own courts of neighbors who could judge cases by local custom with rights of appeal to the hundred. They could enforce uniformity of agricultural practice on their members, employing bailiffs to carry out their decisions.[71]

The political powers of the peasants were supported by their control of land. During Gustav Vasa's reign peasants owned half of Sweden's land, the crown held twenty-nine percent and the nobility twenty-one percent.[72] Even on lands held by the crown or nobility, peasants had personal liberty and the hundreds provided good protection against possible extortion or cruelty by the landlord.[73]

The nobility was not numerous, but together with the crown it was usually the most potent force in the national diet and in the central administrative organs of government. Each noble family sent one representative to the diet.[74] From 1525, the degree of a noble's obligation to aid his king in war was determined by the amount of income he could realize from his lands.[75]

In sum, Sweden at the Reformation was a land in which crown, nobles, and peasants were organized in a national system, each able to influence the polity in significant ways and each accommodated to the others. Of these three participants, the crown was clearly predominant and became vastly richer than any of its subjects through the dispersal of church lands.[76] The nature of the partners' relationship may be seen in the system of checks and balances among them: the highest officers of the state and the members of the Council were to be Swedish nobles as, normally, were all sheriffs. All officers normally held office for life, being subject to dismissal, however, if the king judged them guilty of misfeasance or malfeasance. No law could be made or modified without the consent of the Council and/or diet and no decree put into effect without the Council's advice and the consent of those affected by it. No war could be declared or peace concluded without the consent of the Council and diet. No man could be punished nor his property taken away without due process of law. The king normally had initiative in legislative matters.[77] The diet had no monopoly on legislation nor any right to initiate laws.

In 1527 a diet composed of the four Estates dispossessed the church of its lands; the confiscated property, and revenue greatly strengthening the crown.[78] Protestants were given religious freedom. In 1536 the breach with Rome was completed and the doctrines of Luther and Melancthon given equal weight in the new state Lutheran Church. The church itself was given great independence, being governed by the clergy and laity with the king exercising only a right of final approval of their policies. The new church also retained many of the sources of revenue of the old. Finland, then under Swedish rule, was reformed in the same manner.

We are told that outside Stockholm the Reformation depended little on a popular religious awakening, the king's attitude being of first importance. By the reign of Erik XIV (1560-68), however, Lutheran doctrines had become firmly rooted in the country's population.[79]

After the Reformation, short reigns, royal madness, and a disputed inheritance somewhat weakened the power of the crown relative to that of the nobles. The greater nobles again increased the powers of the Council. Then, under Gustavus Adolphus (1611-32), the Swedish government was modernized and the powers of the crown were enhanced as the king brought his nation to the status of a great power in Europe. Cycles of this sort with diet, crown, or Council preponderant occur repeatedly in subsequent years, with the long-run trend being toward the enhancement of the diet. But, equally important, there was no long period in which any one of the nation's major constitutional partners was strong enough to rule without the others.

Perhaps the closest approach to royal absolutism occurred during the reign of Charles XI (1672-97) and the early years of Charles XII's (1697-1718) administration.[80] Charles XI became ascendant in alliance with the peasants, clergy, and burgesses of the diet who sought to counterbalance the power of the greater nobles in the Council, that power having increased so greatly in the period after Gustavus Adolphus' death. In that period the nobles had come to own seventy-two percent of Sweden's land. The diet declared the king absolute sovereign in 1693, retaining for itself only the power of voting taxes in "normal" times. As the reign ended, the crown, nobles, and peasants had each come to control about a third of Swedish territory, crown finances were stabilized, and the threat from the nobles to the future independence of the peasants was averted. Charles XII continued the alliance against the nobility, but his allies, their objectives already won, showed increasing unrest in the diets of 1710 and 1713. After Charles' death in battle, the diet elected a queen to reign, adopted a new constitution giving all Estates an important role in government, and made quasi-absolutism a thing of the past.

Conclusion

Four of the eight states just described are at their Reformation settlements easily seen as meeting the requirements established for limited centralist regimes. These are England, Saxony, Sweden, and Württemberg. The four that remain, Brandenburg-Prussia, Denmark, and Hesse, had sufficiently chaotic histories in the period of the Reformation to require special care in classification.

Recent histories of Brandenburg and Prussia stress in the fifteenth and sixteenth centuries the loss of the governor's powers to the nobility. Many earlier histories pictured this period in Brandenburg as one of gradually increasing electoral power. Writers in earlier and in recent times agree that the diets of both territories assumed great powers during the Thirty Years' War. The following seems to me a reason-

able synopsis: the Hohenzollerns first acquired in Brandenburg a regime feudal and centralist in form and ineffective
in operation. In the fifteenth century they gradually established their hegemony. They were able to crush revolts
by the nobility but not to subjugate the nobles. They were
able with noble assistance to gain control of the towns.
Although forced to pawn or sell domains and rights in local
jurisdiction, they kept alive a central executive and judicial
authority and, in municipalities, even strengthened it. The
many occasions on which they convened a diet of their
Estates to ask for taxes resulted in the growth of the legislative institutions of those Estates and in administrative
institutions supervising for the Estates the monies granted
by them. On the other hand, the monies were granted for
the expenses of the electoral government and for purposes
defined by the elector. The rights gained by the Estates
in return for these grants constituted a regularization of
their involvement in jurisdictio, not participation in the
electors' central exercise of gubernaculum. Simultaneously,
however, the poverty of the electors enabled nobles to buy
greater jurisdiction over local affairs. Also the frequent calling of diets and the gradual growth of the central apparatus
of the state increased the importance of the regional dietines,
in which nobles living in a particular locality met to propose
to the elector, candidates for appointment as his local governors and judges and to plan the local administration of taxes
and programs to which the central diet had assented.

After the rationalistic, absolutist rule of the Teutonic
knights almost any late medieval government might seem
feeble. But the knights in Prussia had to reform their administration and finally to disband. The towns and nobles
had formed independent leagues and, in alliance with Poland, forced the knights to grant them important local
powers of government. In addition, as a Prussia-wide movement, they had formed a diet of Estates with which knights
and Poles had to deal. The knights had exercised all central
rights in gubernaculum and jurisdictio. Under the reformed
system, they had to share local application of gubernaculum
with individual nobles and with local assemblies of nobles

and they had to share the central exercise of jurisdictio with the organized Estates. It was this system that Albert of Hohenzollern acquired when he became duke and the Reformation was introduced.

During the Thirty Years' War, Brandenburg and Prussia certainly were neither centralist nor commensal states. If anything they developed temporarily some of the features of heterarchic or balanced regimes. These features vanished from 1651, limited centralism again being firmly institutionalized.

The problems of classifying the Danish regime are similar to those just described. I begin by considering whether Christian III, the Reformation king, was a governor. I conclude that he was. He was elected by the Estates, having life tenure. The greater nobles formed a council and this body shared with the king the exercise of jurisdictio. From 1260 the crown had extended its judicial authority over the whole country, the monarch appointing the judges and the major officers of the law. At the same time, the monarch had agreed that he too was under the law. Even in the period of greatest noble power, the king retained formal control over the higher jurisdiction. He appointed the lords-lieutenant who acted as royal governors of the provinces. Christian III's predecessor, Frederick I, lost the power to name the members of his council, but this should properly be seen as a strengthening of the nobles' formal machinery for exercising jurisdictio rather than a lessening of Frederick's authority in gubernaculum. More serious, however, was Frederick's loss of some important rights in gubernaculum: management of the royal demesnes and power to appoint the head of the fleet. These functions were now exercised by a representative of the Council. Christian III, however, coming to the throne with help from foreign allies and with much greater personal power, was able to regain the monarch's traditional role in gubernaculum. Even Frederick I would have qualified as a governor, but perhaps governor of a regime moving in the direction of the form I have called balanced: his central exercise of gubernaculum being shared in part with a representative of the body politic.

Christian III was able to nullify this qualification on the crown's authority.

This settled, the nature of the Danish regime is less difficult to interpret. Not only was the king himself under the law but he was required to appoint governors of provinces and judges in the royal courts from the nobility of the territory in which each served and every free man had the right to be judged in his own province and by its laws. Further, he had to appoint as members of his council, noblemen chosen from a list of only six candidates chosen by the nobility of the province from which a vacancy on the council had occurred. Requirements like these seem exactly to constitute the limitations on centralism described in this chapter.

In Hesse, as in Brandenburg-Prussia, the rulers finally brought powerful Estates under control. Unlike the Hohenzollerns, however, the Hessian rulers never fully succeeded in eliminating the diet of Estates and it retained important formal powers. At the local level, they had to employ, among the administrators of their policies, officials chosen by the towns or local Estates. It appears that the powers of these local authorities, although significant, were not as great as those of their counterparts in Brandenburg-Prussia.

[VI]

Balanced Regimes

AT THEIR FINAL REFORMATION SETTLEMENT, seven European states had balanced regimes: Bohemia, Cleves and Mark, Hungary, Transylvania, Scotland (the Lowlands), and the city-state of Geneva. All turned primarily to Calvinism. Their Reformation settlements occurred between 1536 and 1593: Geneva's in 1536, Hungary's in 1540, Transylvania's in 1557, Scotland's in 1560, Cleves's and Mark's in 1569, and Bohemia's in the period 1575 to 1593.

These states are called balanced because there was in each a governor and because that governor formally shared with constituent bodies the making of central policies in gubernaculum and not only the local application of those policies. The formal share of constituent bodies in shaping central policies was not merely nominal. In each state the governor had to work with constituent bodies or persons responsible to them in developing central policies or in the central administration of those policies or in both. Thus, as we saw in Chapter IV, where information about Cleves and Mark was first presented, the duke ruling as governor in these Rhenish territories had, at the Reformation, to rule in gubernaculum with the consent of his principal councilors. The Estates, organized as a diet, appointed twelve of their members as ducal councilors and these had, with the duke, to be cosigners of all important actions of government. The diet consisted of representatives from the thirteen principal towns and all legitimated members of the nobility. In addition, as in limited centralist states, the policies of the central government were applied in local areas by organized bodies of local citizens, these having considerable autonomous discretion in their conduct of affairs. This pattern of local government is not a defining characteristic of balanced states but it appears in all of them except possibly Geneva.

In all of these states except Geneva the governor was a king or nobleman. In Geneva the governor was the city's self-perpetuating Great Council. The constituent bodies sharing the governor's central exercise of gubernaculum were diets or their representatives in Cleves and Mark, Bohemia, Hungary, and Transylvania. In Geneva they were the town's burghers meeting as a General Assembly. In Scotland they varied by the area of central policy concerned: the regulation of domestic and foreign trade being shared by the king and his councilors with the Convention of the Royal Burghs; the central administration of fiscal, military, and judicial affairs being jointly in the hands of the king, of certain hereditary councilors, and of a self-perpetuating council known as the Lords of the Articles. The Scottish Parliament had, in principle, to approve the king's appointees to his privy council.

In all six of these states, the governor also shared important central powers in jurisdictio with constituent bodies. Those bodies were organized as diets or as other legislative agencies everywhere except in Geneva. In Geneva the Assembly of all burghers had the legislative role. Some central powers in jurisdictio were exercised in Scotland by the king jointly with the Convention of his burghs.

We found, in some limited centralist states, committees established by the Estates to apportion or collect taxes or to supervise the expenditure of taxes and aids. Why not count these committees as a participation by constituent bodies in the central exercise of gubernaculum? I thought it inappropriate because in this period of history the granting to a governor of taxes and aids is almost always defined as a power in jurisdictio and because the Estates' committees have only the power mechanically to implement agreements reached between the regime and the body politic. The importance of these committees is that, representing the body politic, they assure that the agreements will be kept. Unlike the constituent bodies ruling with a governor at the center of a balanced state, these committees in limited centralist polities have no authority to help determine the regime's objectives or the administrative procedures for attaining them; officers of the regime are not responsible to these committees, removable by them, or bound to hear their advice.

Bohemia

Bohemia became a kingdom in 1212 when the Holy Roman Emperor conferred a royal title on Otakar I. The country broke away from the Catholic Church early in the fifteenth century, and Hussite doctrine was then accepted by most of the notables. Huss's doctrine varied from Rome's in but two important respects: its declaration that Scripture prescribed the taking of communion in both kinds by laymen as well as clergy and its insistence that communion should be taken frequently.[1] Although the Roman Church had no settled dogma on these issues (until the determinations made by the Council of Trent), the Holy See resisted local reinterpretations contrary to its wishes, reinterpretations which inevitably carried a challenge to the Papal supremacy.

A less obvious challenge to Catholicism, but one which Luther was later to note in his appreciation of the work of John Huss, lay in the Hussites' demands that clergymen lead exemplary lives on pain of losing their posts, that they possess no great worldly possessions, and, in the phrase of the Compactata of 1437, that "The Word of the Lord is to be freely and truthfully preached by the priests of the Lord and by worthy deacons."[2] Such demands, although from one view merely urging the conduct which Catholic authorities usually desired of their clergy, involved the imposition by laity of a standard and discipline over the church, a prerogative which the Papacy held as belonging to Rome alone.

The kingdom had long had a mixed polity. From 1310 the diet had the right to grant or refuse taxes proposed by the king and the king was obliged to consult his diet before changing any law.[3] Most of the kings were elected by the diet. By 1500 the greater nobles had become the principal though not dominant force in the state, introducing a constitution which gave the diet power to vote taxes, regulate

the use of monies received, and to fix the number of effec-
tives necessary for the national defense. The king could dispose the army only in case of foreign attack. Under this
regime, provincial officials were elected by the diet and
took an oath to support the constitution. The king lost his
right of pardon. Members of the supreme court were made
irremovable and their verdicts irrevocable. In 1508 the
king's debts were assumed by the diet on condition that the
Estates manage his royal revenues.[4]

After the Hussite wars, the magnates made virtual serfs
of the large body of free peasants. No peasant might leave
his lord without the latter's consent. The lords turned to
large-scale agriculture of the kind found also in Prussia and
Hungary.

Bohemia had had no large and strong body of smaller
landholders or lesser nobility. The magnates had, however,
to contend with the towns. These were heavily German in
population, prosperous, and politically powerful. From 1446
their representatives composed one house of a tricameral
diet (the other houses being those of the magnates and of
the gentry). Legislation required a majority vote in all three
houses.[5] Excluded from the diet by the constitution of 1500,
the towns forced the magnates to readmit them in 1508.

For purposes of internal administration, Bohemia was
divided into twelve counties, each having a dietine—a local
assembly—of its nobility and each was administered by a
knight and a noble together with a small group of clerks.[6]
These dietines had some similarities to those in Poland but
were less powerful. They met only to elect members to the
national diet, to choose some local officials, and to provide
for the execution of national statutes.

Great as the magnates' powers had become, the crown
was not without resources. The king had a substantial
private income and a large royal income, the latter consisting of revenues from the cities, from the customs, and from
his monopoly on mining and salt. He shared the power of
legislation with the diet. An attempt in 1547 to give the
diet power to legislate without the king's assent failed of
passage.[7] The king could issue administrative orders on his

own authority, could summon, adjourn, and dissolve the diet and the assemblies in the counties, and could make treaties concerning his dynasty. He was assisted by certain institutions separate from others controlled by the diet. The king directed the activities of three of the great feudal courts (those of the treasury, fiefs, and appeals). The diet controlled the supreme court, the land tables, and part of the Chancellery as well as the courts of first instance on the estates of large landholders.

On the other hand, the great officials of the realm—the Chief Chamberlain, the Chief Justice, the Chief Chancellor, and others—were directed by the diet and chosen from its members. Together with the judges of the supreme court, the court of the land, these officials made up the king's Royal Council.[8]

The death at Mohács in 1526 of Louis, King of Bohemia and Hungary, was followed in that year by the election of Ferdinand of Hapsburg (1527-64) to the Bohemian throne. Capitalizing on disputes among the Bohemian nobility, Ferdinand obtained for his eldest son the right to inherit the Bohemian throne (but not to make it hereditary beyond that accession) and gained the diet's approval for his appointing royal officials without first obtaining the diet's consent. In 1531 Ferdinand was elected Holy Roman Emperor.[9]

The great Catholic victories led by his brother, Charles V, enabled Ferdinand to consolidate his control in Austria and Bohemia. Thus in 1547, after Charles' triumph at Mühlberg, Ferdinand curtailed the judicial and administrative autonomy of the Bohemian towns and appointed royal officials with administrative and judicial authority over the provincial towns and over Prague itself. No local council could meet without approval from these new stewards of the crown and into their hands was given power of veto over all actions of town governments. The Bohemian Brethren, a pietistic and evangelical wing of the Utraquist—the Hussite—Church, was outlawed, its leading men terrorized or executed, and the estates of certain nobles who supported the Brethren were confiscated in an act of exemplary punishment.[10]

But Charles' successes were only temporary and although Ferdinand strengthened his position and weakened the Brethren, he failed in the larger aim of combating both Utraquism and the rapid spread of Lutheran doctrines in Bohemia. As a result of the great remaining powers of his Bohemian subjects and his own constant preoccupation with the Turks and with the wars in the west, he was able only to introduce the Jesuits (in 1556) and bring comfort to Bohemian Catholics.[11] His successor, Maximilian II (1564-67) was, at best, an unenthusiastic Catholic. Plagued like his father with constant foreign wars and apparently a secret sympathizer with Protestant doctrines, Maximilian was confronted by Estates in Lower and Upper Austria which demanded the introduction of the Reformation. When he met the Bohemian Diet in 1575 the Czech Confession (Confessio Bohemica) was submitted for his approval. This confession contained the essentials of the Augsburg Confession but was Calvinist with respect to the Eucharist. Maximilian temporized, assuring the Protestants full liberty of worship and allowing the Lutherans to appoint fifteen defenders to manage their religious affairs.[12]

Maximilian was followed on the throne by Rudolf II (1576-1612), a devout Catholic but a negligent monarch. By 1593 it is likely that two-thirds of the Bohemian population had turned Protestant.[13] The ideological stresses of the Reformation, the Jesuits' success in reforming the Roman clergy, and internal weaknesses of the Utraquist Church had sent many Utraquists back to the Catholic fold.[14] Their successors at the head of church reform were the Lutherans and, to a lesser extent, the Bohemian Brethren and the Calvinists. In 1609 Rudolph was forced to sign a letter of majesty assuring free exercise of religion to all who professed the Czech Confession and giving the diet control of the government of the Utraquist Church and of the University of Prague, this last at the expense of the Jesuits. His heir, Matthias, confirmed this letter in 1617. When some of these pledges were ignored by royal officials, a crowd of Protestant nobles hurled the king's principal advisers from windows of the Castle of Prague. In that same year, 1618, the diet expelled the Jesuits from Bohemia.[15]

Matthias' successor, Ferdinand II (1619-37), was a passionate Catholic.[16] As Archduke of Styria he had quelled rebellious Estates and restored Catholicism in his domains. Bohemia went into open revolt at his accession. Ferdinand held firm even when a Bohemian army approached Vienna and he simultaneously denied the Estates of Austria their demand for full religious liberty. Vienna was saved by a combination of circumstances: the Bohemians' lack of the artillery necessary to breach the city's defenses, the disaffection of unpaid Bohemian troops, the approach of winter, and a Turkish invasion which forced the Bohemians' Hungarian allies to return to their homeland.

The Bohemian diet declared theirs an elective monarchy and chose as king Frederick V of the Palatinate who assumed the throne in 1619. (A strict Lutheran, Frederick was disturbed by the strong Calvinist direction now taken by the Reformation in Bohemia.)[17] After preparing for a year, Ferdinand struck the Bohemians at White Mountain near Prague. His force of Austrians, greatly augmented by troops from Spain, Poland, Italy, and Bavaria, won easily.

Under Ferdinand's direction, the Jesuits began to restore Catholicism, Protestantism was outlawed, the leaders of the rebellion were executed, and the crown was made hereditary in the Hapsburg line. The crown took over all powers of administration and assumed the right to revise or annul decisions of the courts. The diet continued to have the right to approve royal proposals for taxation but lost its other legislative prerogatives.[18] From this time the history of Bohemia merges with that of Austria.

Hungary and Transylvania

1. The United Realm:

Hungary's boundaries of the early sixteenth century had been established in their essentials since 1250. Hungary was a large and bountiful land, the western and central areas consisting of a vast fertile plain and the eastern third, Transylvania, being rich in forests, minerals, pasture lands, and in soils suited for raising grains and potatoes.[19] In about 900 A.D. the central areas of this land were conquered by a nomadic and pastoral people, the Magyars, who turned gradually to grain agriculture as their major source of food. The Magyars spread back east into Transylvania in the tenth and eleventh centuries where their settlements were principally on the grain lands. There they encountered and subdued a large population of Rumanians and a people of culture similar to their own, the Szekels, who now came to live beside, but not under, the Magyars.[20] All these territories came to be governed by the central Hungarian regime. By these steps, and unlike many European states, Hungary arose as an integral state, not a dynastic union.

The monarchy had arisen from efforts of the seven original Hungarian tribes to coordinate their military activities, effecting a political unification of the country under a single general government in St. Stephen's reign (997-1038). In that reign, by a process now obscure, the commonly owned tribal lands became the private property of the king, a standard coinage was introduced, and a written codification of the law begun.[21]

Military and economic crises in the reigns of Andrew II (1205-35) and Bela IV (1235-70) brought about a drastic reduction of the royal lands as the monarchs bought services and support from the greater landowners. This process sharply depleted the principal basis of the king's wealth, and, hence, his power, and produced a small group of great landowners who, under the exceptionally generous terms of the monarch's gifts, received their land in full ownership and with no obligations attached. To compensate in part for these losses, the king demanded higher taxes and debased the coinage. Although the lesser Magyar gentry compelled Andrew to sign a charter of rights, the Golden Bull, in 1222, neither this measure, vague and rarely enforced, or others in succeeding reigns were effective in again reducing the power of the magnates.

It was, however, to provide a counterweight to the power of the magnates and to strengthen the eastern frontiers that in 1224 Andrew granted German immigrants from Saxony a charter providing complete self-government for any towns they might establish. Most of these settlements were made in Transylvania. Under this charter, the Saxons were to be ruled by a count whom they would elect and who would hold his authority directly from the king. They were to have the right to elect their own judges and clergy without interference and to be the exclusive owners of property in territories assigned them. Their merchants were to be exempt from all tolls and dues in all parts of the kingdom. They were assigned certain military duties in peace and war. This special corporate existence was retained virtually unimpaired until 1868.[22] Other developments in Transylvania will be sketched after the Hungarian regime is described.

2. The Hungarian Regime:[23]

Apart from royal lands and taxes, neither being sufficient to support their activities, the Hungarian kings had only such financial resources as their own skill in exploiting their office could provide. The crown was elective, each noble having one vote.

In Hungary, all landowners were nobles. More exactly, as Otto Battaglia says of Poland and Bohemia, in Hungary:

The correct meaning of nobility . . . [was] simply that of full membership in the nation, a membership that is not mediated through landlord authority. . . .

The Hungarian nobles were organized by county, each county's assembly electing a court or permanent committee which performed local judicial, administrative, economic, and financial functions. The crown did not exercise control over local government through its own agents.

The national diet consisted of two houses, the upper composed of magnates and prelates and the lower of delegates elected in each county by the nobles' assembly. (Although they were of no political consequence, the diet also included representatives from the towns.) The king had had only loose control over the nobles' county organizations in the years preceding 1486, his representative, the lord-lieutenant, having control only in matters of tithes and coinage, but after 1486 the law required that the king obtain the nobles' consent to his choice of a lord-lieutenant prior to that officer's appointment. It was common that the magnates were chosen for this post and that they, in turn, were more interested in national than local affairs, leaving their county responsibilities to a deputy. In 1548 the nobles in each county gained the right to elect this deputy. Long before this time all other county officials had been popularly elected. Local officers supervised the collection of taxes, maintenance of public order, and means of communication, and registered persons liable to military service. They had a free hand in local taxation. They sent instructed delegates to the national diet, the king being required to indicate with his call for a diet the measures on which he wanted consideration. Delegates were bound to refer to their constituents in matters on which they had not received instructions. Only county authorities executed royal rescripts and ordinances and, if these seemed not in accord with law and custom, they could and did disregard them.

The limitation of the monarchy by the national diet can be seen clearly in the latter's growing control over the principal royal officers. Chief among these officials was the palatine who gradually acquired judicial powers not derived from his representation of the king and gained a new character as president of the diet in the king's absence. From 1231 the king had to remove unsatisfactory palatines at the request of the diet, from 1291 he was bound to ask the diet's advice before appointing a palatine. A law of 1397 gave the diet power to require palatines to account for their conduct and to impeach those whom they disapproved. In 1439 the palatine was declared elected by the diet to serve as a judge between the king and people in questions of rights and obligations, and as the king's guardian during the latter's minority, claiming, in that period, the obedience due a king. The palatine was made commander-in-chief of the national forces, becoming responsible for the security of the kingdom.

If the monarch were incompetent or misfeasant, the palatine could receive ambassadors and negotiate with them. From 1525 he could hold office for life.

The Chancellor's office developed in a similar manner as did also that of the treasurer. From St. Stephen's time, the king's representative in Transylvania, the voivode, held office on terms similar to those of the palatine.

The diet's great powers can be seen in other legislation. In 1404 it decreed that the king might make appointments to posts in the church and determine which Papal bulls and encyclical letters could be circulated. Between 1490 and 1516 the division in the population between nobles and non-nobles was made rigid and permanent; all peasants were declared in perpetual servitude and their obligations raised; the community of nobles was declared the seat of sovereignty and the crown identified as but that community's symbol. From 1504 both houses of the diet had to approve the imposition of taxes.

This recitation of noble privilege at local and national levels may obscure two important facts: during most of the fifteenth century and well before, the magnates, not the gentry, were the overwhelming important force in the country's economic structure, in county assemblies, in the diet, and in the king's own council. Second, the gentry being numerous and not adequately organized to conduct, develop, or implement a national policy, the king and magnates were usually in charge of national affairs. Central control was strengthened further by the necessity of defending the country against incessant Turkish attacks which increased in seriousness in the fourteenth and fifteenth centuries climaxing in the fall of Constantinople in 1453.

In the reign of Sigismund of Luxemburg (1387-1437) there were great increases in the magnates' power. Some twenty to thirty families, many of foreign origin, together owned estates more than five times as large as the king's. More than half of the country belonged to sixty families, their estates gained at the expense of the king and of nobles who had opposed him. This group "constituted, on the whole, a competent and devoted managerial class," serving the country and royal policy as long as it was consistent with their interests.[24]

The gentry had a friend in the Regent John Hunyadi (1446-52), himself the greatest of the magnates, but their support of Hunyadi gained them little power. Matthias Hunyadi Corvinus (1458-90) created a mercenary army to fight the Turks and taxed gentry and magnates alike, alienating both while protecting the country. He did remove the magnates from the royal council and from the county administrations, appointing civil servants chosen for competence.[25]

When Matthias died, the Estates were determined to elect as weak a king as possible and their choice fell upon Vladislas, King of Bohemia. With no means of his own, Vladislas (1490-1516) could not compete with the greater nobles who now regained their political importance and once again became the actual rulers of Hungary. These magnates abolished the special tax which supported the royal army. They looked toward the eventual enthronement in Hungary of Maximilian of Hapsburg whose armies had penetrated Hungary in 1491 and who was then bought off by being made Vladislas' successor, providing the latter died without a direct male heir. In return, Maximilian guaranteed to preserve the nobles' privileges. The Hungarian diet refused to validate this treaty in 1492, but the greater nobles supported the plan seeing for themselves careers and riches in Hapsburg service far superior to those offered in Hungary alone.

It was the lesser nobles who displayed a strong national feeling in opposition to the pro-Hapsburg policies of the magnates. Their leader was John Zápolyai, himself a magnate, whom Vladislas had made voivode of Transylvania in 1511. Slowly the lesser nobles gained concessions; sixteen of the twenty-four members of the royal council were to be selected from their ranks and the royal councilors were to be responsible to them as well as to the king. It was also decided that decrees issued by the king without consultation with his councilors were to be considered invalid. The diet of 1505 debarred foreign rulers from election as kings of Hungary, but Maximilian and Vladislas concluded a double bethrothal of their children with the effect that the Hapsburgs gained some further claim to the Hungarian throne.

The growing exploitation of the peasants produced a ferocious rebellion in 1514. This was crushed with great brutality, a task in which John Zápolyai showed distinction.

In this reign Hungarian customary law was codified. The division between nobles and non-nobles was made unalterable. The community of nobles was declared to be the seat of Hungarian sovereignty and the Crown but its symbol. This last was a great victory for the lesser nobles as was the ruling that the nobles had no obligation of military service except in case of a defensive war.[26]

Vladislas was succeeded by his young son Louis II (1516-26). The nobles quarreled violently among themselves; the economy was in chaos; from 1521 the Turks threatened. At last they came and the king and his small army were destroyed at Mohács in 1526.

As Vladislas and Maximilian had planned, this left Louis' brother-in-law, Ferdinand, Archduke of Austria, with a claim to the throne. Many of the barons and a majority of the lesser nobles favored Zápolyai and in 1526 the diet elected Zápolyai king. But a minority of the nobles met in rump session and elected Ferdinand, and, from that year, Hungary had two rulers.

Hapsburg troops swept over Hungary, driving Zápolyai from the country. Mustering foreign support, Zápolyai returned, and with French and Turkish aid conquered Transylvania and a large part of eastern Hungary. The opposing forces contested for the remainder of the country but reached a stalemate. As a result, the two rival kings signed an agreement in 1538 providing that on Zápolyai's death the country should elect either Ferdinand or Ferdinand's son to the throne. In 1540 with the news that he was father to a son, Zápolyai repudiated the agreement of 1538. In a few days he was dead.

The Turks recognized Zápolyai's son as rightful ruler and countered Ferdinand's effort to occupy Hungary by seizing all of the country they could. At the end of the campaign in 1541 the country was divided into three parts, the western edge remaining in Hapsburg hands, the center under Turkey, and the east—including Transylvania—held by supporters of Zápolyai's heir, John Sigismund. And so it was to remain through the seventeenth century, for the Turks were not driven out nor Hapsburg authority regained in Hungary until 1699. Transylvania continued to have a career separate from the motherland's until 1848. For our purposes, western Hungary now disappears under Austrian administration and the focus of attention can turn to Transylvania.

3. The Transylvanian Regime:

As we have seen, Transylvania was peopled by Saxons who had been invited into Transylvania in 1224 and granted broad rights of self-government, and by Rumanians, Szekels, and Magyars. The Szekels and Magyars, like the Saxons, had developed independent communal institutions and political organization.

The Szekels, perhaps a Turkic people, probably moved to Transylvania in the eleventh century or somewhat later to serve as border guards for the new Hungarian kingdom. They maintained their nomadic economy and primitive tribal organization far longer than the Hungarians, but eventually their social and economic development paralleled that of Hungary.[27] In the thirteenth and fourteenth centuries they began to settle in villages, these being based on the principle of communal ownership of property in which all shared equally. The dissolution of the royal domain in this part of Hungary freed land which became the basis for the rise of a wealthy stratum of Szekel landowners. From the early fifteenth century these new magnates strove to enserf the common people, and between 1506 and 1603 eight uprisings took place.[28] These were repressed, the people tied to the soil, and private land replaced communal holdings.

Szekel settlements were primarily in southeastern Transylvania. Like the Saxons, the Szekels were organized in seven, later eight, seats all under their own count who held authority directly from the crown. All Szekels were considered noble and therefore exempt from taxation.[29]

The Magyars were organized in seven counties, these being administered on the same lines found in the rest of Hungary, placing all political power in the hands of the nobles.[30]

Distant from the center of Hungarian government, Transylvania had tended increasingly to transact local business in its own diet—a body standing between the national diet on the one hand, and, on the other, the county assemblies of the Magyars and the "national" assemblies among the Szekels and Saxons. The nobles first met to consider military and financial matters in 1291 and many meetings followed in the fourteenth century.[31] All Magyar nobles attended but the Szekels and Saxons sent representatives.

The peasant revolts of 1437 crystallized the Transylvanian elites into three privileged "nations" united against the Turks and against the lower orders whether Rumanian or of their own ethnic stocks. (From the eleventh century, the mass of the Transylvanian population was of Rumanian origin and was held in bondage.) The breakdown of the Hungarian monarchy from 1490 onward helped touch off a fresh peasant revolt in 1514, this time mainly among the Magyar population. Once again it was suppressed by the three nations.

Upon the reconquest of Transylvania in 1541, the Transylvanian diet became a real parliament and the three nations undertook to share the burdens of defense and administration in equal proportions.[32] The prince was elected by the Estates. The Szekels lost their immunity from taxation and, by 1562, a portion of them were reduced to serfdom, while the more powerful were incorporated into the Magyar nobility. In all parts of Transylvanian society, the hold of elite families grew stronger.[33]

With one exception, Michael of Wallachia, the prince was chosen from the major Magyar noble families. It is significant that the ruler had the title "prince," not the title "king," thus reflecting the subordination of his lands to Hungary and Turkey and his nobles' hope for the reunion and freedom of the Hungarian kingdom.[34]

Whether as a result of constant external threats or because of indigenous conditions, the Transylvanian nobles were never as separatist or as autonomous within their counties as were the Magyars of western Hungary. Even in the fourteenth century, the voivodes, as governors of a border march, had had extraordinary personal authority granted by the king. They convoked the Transylvanian diet and they, not the king, chose the counts who represented the Hungarian central administration in the counties.[35] Unlike western Hungary, the counties' nobles did not elect their own subprefects, the voivode and later the prince giving that privilege to the counts themselves.[36]

In the sixteenth century, the prince was often very strong and was far wealthier than any of his nobles. His powers were a function of his wealth and not of ideology or constitutional right. He chose his own council. The diet met, but often assented to his proposals without debate. The prince had the right to declare war, conclude peace, accredit ambassadors, and dispose of the revenues and the army. He was commander in chief and chief justice. At the same time, however, the Tripartitum, the Hungarian code of nobles' rights as granted in the reign of Vladislas, continued to be the formal statement of Transylvanian policy.[37]

Transylvania's most powerful native ruler was Gabriel Bethlen (1613-29). In his reign, the diet continued to function, but the prince gained initiative in most matters affecting the state as a whole, establishing a patriarchal but enlightened regime. He developed mines and industry, nationalized foreign trade, kept a sumptuous court, conferred hereditary nobility on all Protestant pastors, forbade landlords to prevent the schooling of serfs' children, and sent students abroad to study at Protestant universities. The transiency of his power and its association with his person is indicated by the fact that when he died, the diet abolished most of his internal reforms.[38]

In 1658, after the disastrous failure of George Rákóczi II

(1648-60) against Poland, the diet put state revenues under control of a treasurer whom they elected. They also named the prince's council and required that their consent be obtained in matters of war and peace.[39]

From 1660, Transylvania was not her own master. The Turks intervened to control her foreign policies and name her prince. In 1664 the Austrian victory over the Turks brought control from Vienna, shaking princely power beyond recovery. Reunion with the Empire was completed in 1691. The Emperor Leopold confirmed all existing laws, rights, and privileges in Transylvania and gave the diet sovereignty in internal affairs, but Transylvania's external relations and military forces were put in the hands of a special chancellery in Vienna.[40]

4. The Reformation:

The Saxons in Transylvania and, after Mohács, the gentry in all of Hungary, began to accept Luther's doctrines.[41] Until 1540, however, it was exceptional for a Protestant to profess himself publicly. The Queen, an Erasmian, favored critical preaching and protected Protestant clergymen. George of Brandenburg, a Lutheran and the young King's ward, was a potent sponsor of Lutheranism at the royal court. The Roman Catholic hierarchy was too feeble to combat these heresies. Seven of its sixteen prelates were killed at Mohács and the rest fled Hungary when the Turks triumphed in 1547.[42]

The king felt constrained to ask the diet of 1548 to speak out against the Reform. It complied in such a way that it seemed to condemn only more radical Protestant ideas and not the Lutherans. Protestants were a majority in this diet.

Most Hungarian churches were conducting Protestant services by 1545. Many, perhaps most of the magnates embraced Protestantism, bringing over whole counties to the Reform. Calvinism was particularly attractive to the middle and lesser nobility. From 1551 it spread among all levels of the nobility in Transylvania with almost all of them becoming its adherents. By 1562 Calvinism was dominant among Transylvanian churches in number of adherents and ecclesiastical power. (Some of the Szeklers remained Catholic, some became Calvinist, and some, along with the native bourgeoisie of the cities, adopted Unitarian beliefs.)

In Hapsburg Hungary, the magnates were gradually re-won to Catholicism, the turning point usually being associated with the work of Archbishop Pázmány around 1613-16. Most of the gentry remained Protestant.[43]

The Diet of Torda (1557) established toleration of the four religions attractive to Transylvania's elites: Calvinism, Catholicism, Lutheranism, and Unitarianism. Even after Transylvania fell under Austrian domination in 1691, toleration continued in force and remained so after 1848 when Transylvania was once more a part of Hungary.

5. Hungary and Transylvania in the Eighteenth Century and Beyond:

Until its reunion with Hungary in 1848, Transylvania remained a political backwater. The power of the Austrian chancellery increased to the extent that it had to be obeyed. The diet met but was increasingly ineffective on most matters of state policy. The nobles continued in control of county government.

Yet, in part because the Austrian government was spending its energies on war in the west, the three nations were able to maintain the essentials of their social order against Vienna's control.[44] In 1731 and again in 1751, an attempt by Austria to restore former church lands to Catholicism and to overthrow the equality of the four religions in Transylvania met with such opposition that it had to be abandoned. (In 1766 the population contained 547,000 Rumanians, most of them of Orthodox faith, 140,000 Calvinists, 130,000 Lutherans, 93,000 Roman Catholics, and 28,000 Unitarians. Among the Rumanians there were 47,000 Uniate Catholics giving allegiance to Rome.) The Magyars' control continued to grow, and their relations with the Saxons deteriorated. In 1791 the vote in the diet was changed from a ballot by nations to a vote by persons, confirming for the state as a whole the control which the Magyars already exercised in most county administration. Indeed, by 1790, Vienna had been forced to abandon efforts to reform the local authority of the Magyar nobility and the latter had begun to turn toward an interest in a reunion with Hungary.

During the reign of Francis I (1811-34) the imperial administration repeatedly breached the Transylvanian constitution. But union with Hungary was in sight. In 1846 Magyar was made the official language in the provincial diet and extended to all governmental institutions of the Magyar and Szekel territories. In 1848 the Hungarian parliament passed an act of union with Transylvania that confirmed all those special laws and liberties of Transylvania which were favorable to national liberty and unity, the details to be worked out with the Transylvanian diet.[45]

In western Hungary, while the Turks still occupied the country's heartland, the great nobles were rewon to Catholicism and became loyal to the Hapsburgs. They were made a separate Estate as Ferdinand I (1526-64), introducing a practice previously unknown in Hungary, instituted hereditary titles of rank and created in the Hungarian diet an upper house made up of persons thus distinguished, together with the major officers of the crown and the higher prelates. Many nobles of western Hungary went into revolt when Austria refused to help the Transylvanians defeat a Turkish attack in 1657. They even sought to conspire with France, the Turks, and other foreign powers. This effort was crushed by Austrian troops and the Counter-Reformation was driven home. In 1673 the constitution was suspended and Protestantism forcibly crushed.[46]

The subsequent history of Hungary never finds that country again independent in foreign affairs, but displays wide variations in the ability of its diet and other governmental agencies to operate the internal administration. For the most part, local and internal control was maintained as before in noble hands and, from 1867 to the First World War, Hungary was constituted as a semi-autonomous member of the Austro-Hungarian Empire, Austria clearly being the senior partner.

Scotland: The Lowlands

Relative to the leading states of Europe, Scotland had always been economically poor and was more largely dependent on agriculture than on trade or manufacturing.[47] The towns, most of them strung along the eastern coast, had only a modest prosperity. Capital was in very short supply. Commercial life was limited in scope, the merchants being purveyors rather than processors of goods.

Scottish agriculture consisted primarily of small-scale subsistence farming. Famine was recurrent. The rate of economic growth was very slow. Like Scottish commerce, the country's farms shared in none of the high prosperity enjoyed in England during the sixteenth century.[48]

In the Lowlands, the king, the great nobles, and to a much lesser extent the gentry, church, and merchants had effective political power. They were generally united on certain fundamentals. In principle all land was held from the king and in 1426 Parliament had declared all Scotsmen subject to his laws. Since the early fourteenth century the gentry and clergy had supported the country's independence and the monarchy. At least from the reign of James III (1460-88) the great nobles had aimed their political struggles at gaining access to the crown's authority and not at dividing the country.[49]

The Scottish elites were also united by important but even less tangible bonds. Although the clans had not retained any power as a system of government or inheritance in the Lowlands, the great families were often bound to one another in ties of sentiment and heritage. Traditional forms of mutual aid between the senior and cadet branches of a family were reflected in joint celebrations of great occasions and in the greater ease among their members of financial and political cooperation. These important residues of times past have been too little studied for one to judge precisely the extent of their continued importance, but enough is known to establish them as a source of cohesion among the governing classes of Scotland.[50]

These residues seem, among other factors, a source of the

equalitarianism of Scottish life. There were great differences in power among families and individuals, but these seem not reflected in significant differences in respect. Titled men had no special rights if brought to trial or sentenced. Magnates and gentry and burghers intermingled socially and married readily into one another's families. The clergy, both Catholic and Protestant, was drawn largely from these same families. The lay elders of the Presbyterian system were usually of similar origin.[51]

There were, however, some points of serious alienation. To protect the country from England, the royal governments had long pursued a policy of close alliance with France. This policy often committed Scotland, the decidedly weaker partner, to wars that seemed only in the French interest. Indeed for this reason the Scottish armies had at first refused their king's order to attack the English at Flodden Edge (1513) and at Solway Moss (1542). Following the death of James V in 1542, first Mary of Guise, the Regent, and, later, Mary Stuart, James's heir, enlarged the crown's dependence on France. Mary Stuart was the wife of the French dauphin. French troops and officials were brought into Scotland, ostensibly to protect the country from England but, in the eyes of a growing number of the native elite, to remove Scots from participation in government, to introduce the French system of "absolute" monarchy, and to make Scotland a province of France.[52]

For many centuries, the integrity of the Scottish state had been threatened not only by English invasions but by the fact that some important nobles held land in England and were, in law and sentiment, vassals of the English crown. Other Scotsmen were found all too often in the pay of the English government, seeking to turn Scottish politics in directions favorable to England. After England broke with Rome, the minority of Scots then Protestant in persuasion looked to England for help against the influence of Catholic France. The crystallization of these religious concerns was evident at least from 1528.

When the Reformation was finally adopted in Scotland, it came only with English military aid. The Scottish Protestant nobles, united as the Lords of the Congregation, had been unable to defeat the French forces supporting the Regent. While the rest of the country's forces, Protestant and Catholic, stood aside, the Congregation and the English expelled the French troops. An outpouring of gentry and burghers then joined the magnates in the Parliament of 1560 which established the Reformation.

But, foreign influences to the side, what was the character of Scotland's indigenous government?[53] The resources immediately at hand for a king were substantial enough to make him the superior of his nobles, but modest in absolute amount. The principal sources of revenue under the Stuart monarchs were the royal lands, the customs, mercantile fees paid by the king's burghs, the profits of justice, and feudal casualties. The church's wealth was tapped for special needs. Immediately before the Reformation, demands on this wealth were heavy and continuous. In the reigns of James II, III, and IV, Parliament had on rare occasions imposed a special tax on the country at large, but collections were slow, difficult, and never completed.

The nobles opposed creation of a standing army and it never came into being.[54] Instead, the king depended for military support on his own armed retainers and on the service due him as monarch from all free men. In most actions, this service came from private armies supplied by magnates then allied with the king. These same forces engaged in the police actions which Scottish kings undertook periodically against the chiefs of the islands, highlands, and borders, and against magnates of other factions.

The monarchy never had power sufficient to enable rule without support from some large fraction of the greater nobles.[55] The kings generally regarded as strong were able with such support only to keep down the most violent of internal feuds and insure that violations of royal law were brought before the king's courts and punished. They were unable, however, to gain effective regulation of the administration of local government outside the towns or to quell the feuds and the constant invocation of private justice.

In the sixteenth century each noble of importance hoped

to be a member of the ruling faction. Feuds were frequent and bloody. The crown had almost no right to intervene between a tenant-in-chief and his dependents and the average tenant was loyal to his immediate superior, not to the king.[56] The officers of the crown were no match for the armed power of the lords. The root problem was the responsibility of the lords for the life and goods of all dependents.[57] Unavenged injuries to any person or thing was an insult to a lord and a derogation of his authority. His power depended on his ability to defend his dependents.

The actual administration of the kingdom had fallen largely to special groups. Thus private armies, enlarged from profits due the crown, served as police. There were no effective central courts to supervise the work of local courts and there was no rationalized or codified royal law to guide local judiciaries. Instead, the local courts went their independent ways and their determinations were of interest only to the parties concerned. In 1425 the authority of the king's sheriffs was reduced by giving them only concurrent jurisdiction with baronial courts in all cases except those involving treason. On the other hand, each baron and freeholder was required by law to answer at royal justice ayres for misdeeds by his own men upon his own land, and could be fined for his dependents' offenses.[58]

Foreign trade was administered with great independence by the royal burghs, they having a monopoly in this matter. They were organized together under a court or convention.[59] This agency had legislative, administrative, and judicial functions. It established and conducted the entrepôt in Flanders through which much, perhaps most, trade with the Continent was channeled. It was empowered by Parliament in 1487 to make rules and statutes for the conduct of trade and government within and between burghs. It consisted of delegates elected by burghal merchant guilds. It met annually; chose its own moderator; strove to protect the burghs from encroachments by magnates; fostered parliamentary legislation promotive of burghal interests, regulated the merchandise, manufactures, and shipping of the country; controlled the Scottish merchants on the Continent; sometimes defrayed expenses of Scottish ambassadors; allocated among the burghs their proportion of all imposts and taxes imposed by Parliament, selectively easing the allotments of towns suffering from local economic problems. The court adjudicated claims of towns to be admitted to the privileges of free burghs and checked weights and measures. Burgesses who attended Parliament or a General Council went as delegates of individual burghs and the whole convention. In the sixteenth century, the convention met to instruct its delegates before such sessions. It ruled that no burgh could raise any matter in Parliament or General Council without the convention's prior approval.

In local affairs the burghs also had considerable autonomy. Before 1469 they appear to have been relatively democratic and self-governing. Thereafter the existing burghal councils elected their successors. The old and new councils together with a representative elected from each craft guild were to choose the town's officers and magistrates. Merchants, not craftsmen, were eligible for office. The towns exercised the higher jurisdiction over their inhabitants.

Both Parliaments and General Councils were assemblies of Estates.[60] The membership of both was uncertain, although it appears that all nobles had the right to attend a Parliament. General Councils were called at the king's discretion and their membership set at his judgment. For important decisions, both assemblies usually included burgesses. Either a Parliament or a General Council could legislate and tax but only Parliament could sit as a court. In principle, Parliament had to approve the membership of the king's privy council.

Even the kings who desired their attendance had difficulty in getting the lesser nobles, freeholders, and clergy to Parliaments. From 1468 a smaller body, the Lords of the Articles, served as a semicontinuous body consulting with the king and privy council when Parliament was not in session and setting the agenda for Parliament.[61] It always included burghal representatives. Little is known of its composition other than that the lords spiritual chose the lay lords and vice versa, the burgesses choosing their own representatives. The Lords of the Articles are usually pictured as thoroughly controlled by strong rulers and as taking some initiative for central policy-making during regencies or during the reigns of feeble kings. They chose royal commissioners of shires and burghs. In the sixteenth century there seemed but a narrow distinction between the Lords of the Articles, the king's own privy council, and the General Council of Estates.

The reigns of James VI (1566-1625) and Charles I (1625-1649) come closer than others to royal control. Parliament, always feeble, was of little importance and the king had solid control over his privy council and the Lords of the Articles. On the other hand, the general administration of the country continued as before, under the control of burghs, nobles, and church (now the Reformed Church), and the king, as before, governed only with the support and consent of the magnates. Neither monarch was able, even with the powers each simultaneously exercised as King of England, to subdue the northern Highlands, or substantially to reduce the use by nobles of private armies to execute justice or pursue feuds. James sought but failed in 1587 to introduce a system of local administration more responsible to the crown and patterned on the English justices of the peace. His and Charles' efforts to enlarge the monarchy's powers and control the government of the Church and Charles' flirtations with Catholicism raised the hostility which led to the nobles' joining with English Parliamentary forces to overthrow the monarchy. From about 1640 the Scotttish Parliament, like that of England, was usually the principal political force in the realm. In 1707, it was united with the Parliament of England.

Geneva[62]

Geneva, long associated with Swiss affairs, did not formally enter the Confederation until 1814. It had been ruled by its bishop as an independent episcopal town and was surrounded by territories of larger powers. From about 1287 the surrounding area was part of the lands ruled from Turin by the House of Savoy, that dynasty holding the island castle in Geneva and exercising from it a lower jurisdiction in the town. Much of Genevan history before the Reformation concerns the town's struggles with its bishop and with the Dukes of Savoy who, from 1416, controlled the selection of new bishops for Geneva.

From the fourteenth century the chief magistracy of the city consisted of four syndics. Early in the fifteenth century these officers were nominated and elected by a General Assembly consisting of all burghers and all citizens (the distinction between bughers and citizens resting on length of residence in the city as free men).

The syndics were aided by a Small Council of twenty members, first formed in 1364 and elected by the burghal Assembly. In 1387 the bishop granted exercise of the higher jurisdiction to a court composed of the four syndics and four citizens elected by the Assembly.

In the fourteenth century the syndics were elected for terms of one year, rendering the Assembly an account of their services during and at the end of their work. They were required to submit grave decisions to the Assembly for its approval. In that period and in the fifteenth century the Assembly could revoke actions of the Small Council. Only the Assembly had the right to authorize the imposition of taxes or the making or obtaining of loans. As of 1491 it decreed syndics not eligible to succeed themselves in office for a period of six years.

Over time the Small Council became the major element in the city's daily government. Its composition also changed. Each syndic had asked two or three trusted men for advice. These advisers gradually came to be a part of the Council itself until, early in the fifteenth century, that body was legally declared to consist of the four syndics, of their four predecessors, and of eight councilors (two chosen by each current syndic), a treasurer, and a secretary.

While these changes were taking place in the Small Council, the Assembly created a second body, the Council of Fifty. It appears that this was done to provide an agency that could supervise the Small Council and be consulted by it, an agency that could be assembled easily and conduct its

affairs privately during the difficult years when open meetings of the Assembly were threatened by Savoy. In 1459
the Assembly gave the Small Council the right to choose
the Fifty, with the stipulation that equal numbers of members be chosen from each district of the city. The Fifty were
enlarged to Sixty in 1502.

Beginning in 1504 the House of Savoy attempted to assert
sovereignty in the city. The burghers were divided on this
issue, there being those who, for familial, commercial, or
ecclesiastical reasons, supported the party of the duke and
those who opposed him. The duke was at first victorious and
his partisans came to control the Small Council. His opponents, strengthened by an alliance with Bern, finally triumphed. In 1526 the supporters of Genevan independence
controlled the meeting of the Assembly. They arranged the
creation of a Great Council which would promote their
cause and would control the Small Council.[63] (Unfortunately
the manner in which members of this new body were chosen,
the means intended for their replacement, and the powers
given them are all unclear. The secretary responsible for
such matters seems to have made no record of what trans-
pired.)[64] At this same time the city's bishop gave all his
rights in civil government to the burghers.[65]

In 1530 the Great Council assumed the right to choose the
eight councilors of the Small Council; the syndics, secretary,
and treasurer still being selected by the Assembly. Simultaneously the Great Council gave the Small Council the
right to choose the former's members. This set of elections
occurred once each year.

The General Assembly continued in this period to consist
of all burghers and citizens. (It was not until after the Reformation that a substantial organization of trades and crafts
into guilds occurred in Geneva and, even then, these bodies
had no regularized part in the political life of the city.)[66]
As it had for many years, the Assembly elected the syndics
and other principal judicial and prosecutory officials, voted
on fiscal proposals and propositions concerning war and
peace and on the conclusion of alliances, and exercised a
general legislative power.

Thus, when the Assembly voted in 1536 to adopt the Reformation, Geneva had developed a balanced regime. The Small and Great Councils had come in considerable measure to be self-perpetuating and the principal agencies for gubernaculum. At the same time, the Assembly had a role in gubernaculum through its annual election of major officials of the commune and its right to examine the work of those officials at the close of their terms. Its elected officers were, as members of the Small Council, a part of the electorate which annually chose the members of the Great Council. Although the regime retained its character as a balanced order, the role of the Assembly in jurisdictio was gradually restricted over the subsequent two hundred years. The powers of the Great Council became defined and strengthened.

1537—The Great Council decided that henceforth any member elected by it to the Small Council would be replaced if opposed by twelve or more of the Great Council's two hundred members.

1539—The Great Council proposed, and the Assembly rejected, a procedure by which only measures first examined by it and the Small Council could come before the Assembly.

1543—The Assembly rejected a proposal that only two of the four syndics submit to reelection each year but accepted the limitation of its choice of syndics to a slate of eight presented by the Small and Great Councils. It also agreed to consider only those measures first examined by the two Councils. At about this same time, the Great Council limited its selections for the Small Council to choices from a list prepared by the latter. Limitations on terms of office for all officials were insensibly forgotten. Only one nominee was presented to the Assembly for vacancies in offices other than syndic.

1568—The Assembly ruled that close relatives (for example, brothers or fathers and sons) could not serve simultaneously on the Small Council.

1570—The Assembly was persuaded to give the Small Council full power to submit fiscal proposals to the Great and it approved in advance whatever disposition the Councils made of these matters. This action was taken only with many abstentions.

1584—There were debates in the Councils concerning the possible suppression of the Assembly. These failed of action.

1597—The Great Council decided to meet at its own initiative and at regular dates. It gave each of its members the right to initiate proposals. This was followed, in 1604, by a decision to strip the Small Council of ultimate judgment in civil cases.

As thus constituted, the Geneva regime continued with little change until, in the latter part of the eighteenth century, forces gathering for a hundred years forced the adoption of a more broadly based and democratic government.

Conclusion

There is a sharp contrast between the regimes in Geneva, Cleves, and Mark, and the regimes in Bohemia, Hungary, Transylvania, and Scotland. The first three governments were stable and effective; the last four were often faltering and weak. In Geneva, Cleves, and Mark many functions in gubernaculum were exercised by a council representing the population's elites and no significant part of that elite was left out of government. In the four kingdoms, however, a monarch was governor. Each kingdom's elites were divided among themselves, and their struggles served further to weaken the state.

These same conditions provide certain problems of classification. For example, should Cleves, Mark, and Hungary be thought heterarchic rather than balanced? Some case can be made that the dukes in Cleves and Mark had little or no control during the international wars that swept over their territories in the sixteenth and seventeenth centuries. The Diet of the Estates, and agencies formed by it, conducted most affairs of state. I decided, however, to call this regime balanced on the grounds that the chief parties concerned seemed still to regard the dukes as governors, although governors who at all times shared gubernaculum with the

Estates and who, because of current exigencies, were temporarily unable fully to play their roles.

The formal position of the last king of Hungary seems to have been even weaker. The monarch had been declared only the symbol of the nobility. Nonetheless even the weakest of Hungarian kings retained the appurtenances of a governor: initiative over the whole range of gubernaculum, sole formal control over some aspects of executive and judicial operations, and the disposition of the resources of the crown lands and income. Perhaps even these formal prerogatives would have been stripped away had the nobility had the leisure to continue their reconstruction of government. But Mohács intervened and we shall never know.

The Scottish regime presents different ambiguities. We see in Scotland a monarch struggling to put down the feuds among his nobles yet dependent upon their private armies for the enforcement of public order. Should we think of the Scottish regime as, in form, centralist and feudal? I conclude that it did not meet the criteria for a feudal order. In particular, all free men were defined as subjects of the king and under the protection of his laws. More than this, there was a system of royal courts to which any free man might appeal what he considered a serious miscarriage of justice. There was also the system of royal justice ayres for supervising the operation of local justice. The crown was often weak, but its negotiations with nobles and merchants were legitimately with these groups taken as a whole and not with particular members in terms of the special rights of each. The attachment of free men to local lords seems, in law, to have had only the force of a convenience to gain added personal protection rather than the force of vassal subordination. In short, the Scottish regime seems best described as balanced, this description at first made difficult by the crown's weakness and by the widespread growth of certain kinds of local authority which had superficial resemblances to feudal ties.

Finally, there is the case of Geneva. Should it be considered heterarchic rather than balanced, the Great and

Small Councils and the Assembly being partners in the state? Probably not. The General Assembly of burghers and citizens shared with the Great Council certain aspects of gubernaculum but, unlike the Great Council and its agents, did not by right have initiative with respect to all areas of gubernaculum. By contrast, the Council had all the attributes required of a governor.

One further point is important. Were each of these four cases coded incorrectly, the most likely alternative classification would lead, in every case but Scotland's, to the prediction of the adoption of Calvinist Protestantism. Were Scotland more appropriately described as a feudal order, one would have expected the retention of Catholicism.

[VII]

Commensal Regimes

WHEN EACH ACHIEVED its final Reformation settlement to 1700, ten of our 41 societies had commensal regimes. Eight of these societies remained Catholic, two—the Swiss cantons of Appenzell and Glarus—adopted Calvinist Protestantism.

We have already considered one commensal regime, that governing the city-state of Venice. In addition to Venice there were in Europe cities, rural cantons, and a few larger territories that had succeeded in freeing themselves from all higher authority and, in some of these, there emerged government by all members of the body politic. As in Venice, the ranks of the body politic were frequently much smaller than the territory's adult population, being limited to males or to heads of families or to persons meeting certain political or property qualifications. Whatever the case, the entire body politic dealt with all matters we have subsumed under gubernaculum, conducting its affairs either directly or in part through officials elected by and answerable to it. It performed all functions of a governor and exercised all rights of jurisdictio.

I call a regime "commensal" if it has two characteristics: if it lacks a governor and if the persons who exercise gubernaculum and jurisdictio do so only because they are members of the entire body politic or because, among such members, they are those judged to have certain skills needed by the regime. In no case do they come formally to exercise their powers in the service of personal interests or in the service of special groups which they represent.

We saw earlier that these two conditions were institutionalized in the Venetian regime by the right of all members of the body politic to participate equally in the regime and by certain formal restrictions against the regime's coming to speak for the interests within its membership. Several Swiss cantons were like Venice in that ultimate power in gubernaculum and jurisdictio was vested in an assembly of all adult male members of the body politic and in each canton, devices similar to the Venetian were employed to insure that their regime represented only the common interest. These cantons were Appenzell, Glarus, Schwyz, Unterwalden, Uri, and Zug.

Somewhat different mechanisms for operating a commensal order were found in the Italian city-state of Florence. In Florence, all members of the body politic belonged to one or more organizations. Officials of the city's regime were chosen by lot from lists of persons considered by those organizations as members in good standing and approved as acceptable by a commission consisting of representatives of all the organizations. Because many citizens belonged to more than one of the city's constituent organizations, a man's failure to be in good standing in one group did not preclude his being among another's nominees. The effect of this procedure was to produce a list of the city's men acceptable both to special groups in which they held membership and to most of the other parties to Florentine politics. Acceptance by the commission was thus endorsement of candidates as Florentines, not as members of particular groups within Florence. The final step, choice by lot, furthered the process of selection without regard to the representation of particular groups. In this polity it was a matter of indifference that, in choosing by lot, members from only one group or a few of the groups might occasionally be drawn.

At Fribourg in Switzerland, the regime was commensal to 1505, then shifted swiftly to the form of a centralist state —this being concluded by 1553. It regained a commensal character in 1627. Fribourg is here grouped with commensal states following the rule already stated that in societies little touched by the Reformation the regime would be described as it was in 1500-1550.

The last of these commensal states was the kingdom of

Poland. At its final Reformation settlement, Poland had become a commensal state, its king reduced almost to a figurehead and the whole of the Polish gentry and nobility required to be in agreement before any policy of government could be formulated or implemented. The principle of universal agreement was institutionalized as follows: the body politic consisted of all landowners. Poland was divided into districts, the landowners in each electing the officials of local government and the representatives to the national diet. At all levels, the practice grew of requiring unanimous consent to actions of government. In arriving at this state of affairs, Poland changed from a centralist state, a feudal monarchy, to a limited centralist and then to a balanced regime. As it did, the majority of members of the body politic embraced first Lutheranism and then Calvinism. With the establishment of a commensal order, almost all returned to Catholicism.

Schwyz, Unterwalden, and Uri[1]

Each of these "Forest" cantons was governed by an Assembly of all its adult, male citizens.

> . . . The primitive democratic assembly . . . was the sovereign, deciding upon peace and war, alliances, treaties, and laws; it elected the Chief Magistrate . . . and the other Cantonal officials. It consisted of all adult males who possessed rights of citizenship and who had not been deprived of these as dishonorable persons. Every year the men of the Canton, rich and poor, came together . . . for the principal Cantonal assembly, having not merely the right to attend this, but the duty to be present under a penalty; not infrequently they were also summoned to extraordinary assemblies; they all attended all in the proud consciousness that the highest authority of the State was vested in them in common.[2]

The men of each of these cantons were united in possessing a common land and in controlling, in common, certain tributary lands. Their assemblies, the landsgemeinde, not only determined taxes and decided as to proposed laws but also exercised judicial powers. Each man had one vote.

A chief magistrate, the landammann, was elected every year. Those who had held this office were then life members of their canton's Council. It was typical that a young man from a family of high social status would be elected by the Assembly to the post of cantonal secretary, a position requiring skill in writing. The office of secretary was a frequent stepping-stone to that of landammann. The Council, also elected by the Assembly, advised the cantonal officers. All were responsible to the Assembly.

Zug

Although Zug had the general form of a "landsgemeinde" canton until 1604, certain peculiarities should be noted.[3] The city of Zug and its environs were separated administratively from the Canton's three other communities, each, after many struggles, having gained autonomy in all matters except foreign and confederate affairs. The landsgemeinde of the whole canton chose the supreme magistrate. He, in turn, presided over a council of forty members, thirteen elected from Zug and nine from each of the three rural communes. The landsgemeinde also named a cantonal banneret, a "porte-drapeau," and other major officials. It had the executive, legislative, and judicial powers customary to a landsgemeinde except that its range of jurisdiction was restricted as previously described.

In 1604 the cantonal Council gained all legislative authority. It had, however, to get agreement from all four constituent communes for any important decision. Each commune was governed directly by its burghal Assembly or that Assembly's agents. In this way the regime at Zug continued its commensalistic form into the seventeenth century.

Fribourg[4]

Fribourg was founded by Berchthold IV of the Zaehringer dynasty and was intended as a military strongpoint and a center for trade. From the beginning, its composition was that of a military post, the town being divided into banners, each led by a banneret. The guilds that existed gained no substantial control over the economy and were of no importance in politics.

A ducal *Handfeste* of 1249 confirmed the many rights then possessed by burghers including the right to choose their own burgomaster, priest, council, bannerets, and other functionaries. The council was an administrative and judicial body of twenty-four men presided over by the burgomaster. Its judgments had the force of law. The community as a whole had the right to decide on matters of war and peace, to conduct foreign relations, acquire territory, choose the form of government it preferred, enact civil and criminal laws, name and dismiss its magistrates, levy taxes, and establish a coinage. A Great Council of two hundred members, also popularly elected, appeared in 1337. Ten years later the burghers created a Small Council consisting of sixty citizens elected by the bannerets, the latter choosing twenty men from each of the city's three banners.

Important constitutional changes occurred all during the fourteenth and fifteenth centuries, most of them tending to circumscribe the political role of the General Assembly of all burghers. Thus in 1344 the practice began of having each banneret choose twenty men of good judgment from his banner; the resulting body of sixty chose for one-year terms the Small and Great Councils and the Treasurer. The community continued to elect the burgomaster and the bannerets.

1373—The right to participate in general meetings of the community was restricted to those persons convened by the bannerets.

1387—Each banner was to elect its own banneret. The Sixty electors were abolished. The Great Council and General Assembly were to be convened at least four times a year to hear a review of communal affairs. It was declared that all elected functionaries could be dismissed and replaced at the burghers' pleasure.

1404—A year of great change. The bannerets were urged to act as watchdogs of the commune's rights in the councils and given power of veto over any act of the councils that infringed the burghers' rights. At the same time, each banneret came to choose six responsible men from the then four banners of the city and these, together with a revived

Council of Sixty, designated candidates for office to be presented to the burghers for election.

1469—By this date several developments had crystallized. The twenty-four associates of the bannerets had developed a corporate character and were designated the Secret Council. They had their own minutes. They proposed new laws to the other councils and the burghal Assembly. They had gained the power to name the members of the Sixty.

1505—The Great Council ruled that the bannerets could not present the burghal Assembly with any proposal not previously reviewed and sanctioned by the Small and Great Councils.

1553—The Great Council assumed the power to choose, remove, and replace bannerets. The Secret Council became a legal body that could convene the Great Council, that had exclusive power to convene the Sixty, and that was confirmed in the right to fill its own vacancies. The Assembly of burghers was removed from all political decisions.

1606—By this time the Secret Council had gained the power to name, confirm, or depose the Great Council's members. Its own members had tenure for life.

1627—Burgher privileges were made the exclusive property of members of the Great Council and their families, a ruling which gave full citizenship to only seventy-one families. In 1782 all burghers were declared ennobled.[5]

It seems correct to say that the regime at Fribourg was commensal at least to 1505. The new constitution of 1553 removed the mass of burghers from control over gubernaculum and jurisdictio and, soon after, with all powers falling to the Secret Council, Fribourg became a centralist state. Then, in 1627, burgher status was redefined and thereafter, on a far narrower base, Fribourg's was again a commensal regime. The Reformation made no serious inroads at Fribourg.[6]

Glarus[7]

During the fifteenth century and up to the outbreak of Reformation agitations, the political structure of Glarus maintained an essentially constant form. The landsgemeinde composed of all adult, male citizens met at least once a year. It elected the principal cantonal officials, determined the admittance of new citizens, decreed legislation or taxes, established administrative and judicial organs, acted as a supreme court of appeal in both civil and criminal cases, and decided questions concerning war and peace and the establishment of foreign alliances. The canton's continuing agency of government was a council composed of thirty members. Around 1500 this body was given permission to expand its numbers in proportion to the gravity of the business before it. It appears that each member of the council was elected by the citizens of the rural district in which he resided and each could now bring from one to three fellow-citizens to assist in the deliberations.[8] The Council exercised high justice, organized the police, hired mercenaries as needed, governed foreign relations, sat as a court for major offenses, and conducted the routine administration of the canton.

The first formal response to the Reformation was an action in 1528 by which the landsgemeinde gave each district of the canton the right to vote on whether it wished to become reformed and to appoint its own clerics. During the next few years it became clear that more than two-thirds of the citizens had adopted Protestant doctrines. Protestants and Catholics now struggled for control of the state, creating and re-creating institutions suited for the new divisions by religious community. Although the exact nature of those institutions was in flux from 1531 and well through the seventeenth century, their general form remained relatively stable. Each confession was to be represented at a fixed ratio (around three Protestants to two Catholics) in all cantonal agencies. The landsgemeinde continued to meet as before but its actions were restricted to decisions that would not upset the measures governing confessional balance in administration. Each confession developed certain new institutions (courts of marriage, for example) that regulated only its own members.

Appenzell[9]

Appenzell was the last of the thirteen original members of the Swiss Confederation, being admitted in 1513. It was divided into twelve communities (Rhoden). Since 1377 these had been united in a single landsgemeinde for the whole country and had elected a landammann and a council. Each of the Rhodes, a direct democracy in its own internal affairs, was administered by a council of twenty-four with a captain at its head.

The constitution of Appenzell as of 1513 continued in force until the canton was divided as a consequence of struggles during the Reformation.

> . . . At the foundation of all was of course the ancient Landsgemeinde. It assembled twice a year . . . and by it were chosen the Landammann, the Landschreiber (Land Clerk), and the Landweiber (Sheriff). Next to the Landsgemeinde in importance were the Rate or Councils. There were three of these— the Kleine Rat (Small, or Executive, Council), the Grosse Rat (Great Council), and the Zweifache Landrat (Double Land Council). The Small Council is rarely mentioned, but probably consisted . . . of the Landammann and other leading State officers. The Great Council consisted of the leading State officers and one hundred and forty-four members, twelve from each of the Rhodes. The Double Land Council consisted of the leading State officers and two hundred and eighty-eight members, twelve from the Small and twelve from the Great Council in each of the Rhodes. The organization of the Rhodes was much like that of the State. In each were a Small and Great Council, and an executive officer or Hauptmann.[10]

The several councils and the cantonal officers sat as courts of varying competence. The Great Council directed foreign affairs, and all local ordinances of the Rhodes were subject to the approval of officers that this Council appointed.[11]

The Zwinglian Reformation entered in 1518 and spread rapidly. At the Landsgemeinde of 1523 it was voted that priests teach only what was found in the Holy Scriptures. After this the Double Land Council decided that preaching should be allowed to Catholics and Protestants and, in 1524, the landsgemeinde declared religion to be a question each community might decide for itself. This last decision proved to have settled nothing. An overwhelming majority of the citizens of the six outer Rhodes became Protestant. The great majority of those in the six inner Rhodes remained Catholic. Because the outer Rhodes were considerably more populous than the inner, they dominated the cantonal landsgemeinde and soon Catholic candidates for office were never elected. (About three-fourths of the cantonal population was Protestant.)[12] Strife was continuous and, in 1597 with other cantons acting as mediators, Appenzell was split into two cantons. Each was to have independence in all matters except the government of those subject lands jointly held and in the exercise of Appenzell's single vote in the diet of the Swiss Confederation.

The histories I have been able to examine shed almost no light on the conditions, whatever they may have been, that led the inner Rhodes to remain Catholic. I will quote the one suggestion I have found, but it is only that—a possible lead for further study:[13]

> The town of Appenzell was the State capital, and it was situated in the midst of the Inner Rhodes. Here the Landsgemeinde, the Councils, and the courts held their sessions. As a result of the remoteness of Appenzell from the Outer Rhode communities the attendance of the Council members from these communities was both slight and irregular. Rarely were more than three from any one of the Outer Rhodes present at the Great Council or Double Land Council. This circumstance threw almost the whole power of government into the hands of the Council members from the Inner Rhodes. Besides, the piety of the people of the Inner Rhodes was of a sterner sort than that of their brethren in the outer communities, and church organization with them was, therefore, more thorough. A council existed called the *Kirchnore* (Church) *Rat*. It comprised the members of the Great and Double Land Councils. Now the members of the Church Council, being also members of the Councils of State, and as such being accustomed (by the habitual nonattendance of their colleagues from the Outer Rhodes) to wield entire power, gradually came to transact the public business to a large extent in the Church Council instead of in the State Councils. Thus the Church Council . . . waxed very powerful. It assumed to punish by imprisonment and banishment, and even to make alliances with foreign Powers. Hence, at the breaking out of the Reformation in

Appenzell, this Council was a potent instrumentality in behalf of the established faith. . . .

Italy

By 1500 and for long thereafter, much of Italy was under the direct control of France, Austria, or Spain and its history becomes a part of theirs. At Rome was the secular monarchy of the Papacy controlling the center of the peninsula. There remained on Italian soil only two independent powers of any significance: the city-states of Venice and Florence.

1. Venice:

The city apparently began as a colony of refugees fleeing the wars and chaos of the Italian mainland. In 1032 the rising merchants concluded a successful revolt against the doge, demoting him to the status of a salaried official and putting strict limits on his power. The financial needs of "a militant colonial and commercial policy . . . made the participation of the patriciate in administration unavoidable."[14] From 1268 doges were elected by the Great Council.

Membership on the Great Council had from early times been a right of Venice's major merchant families. By legislation in 1296-97 the size of the Great Council was made unrestricted and membership given to all who had been members in the preceding four years and to those whom an electoral commission determined to be citizens of substance. In 1319 a list of families was compiled all of whose adult male members were automatically members of the Great Council. These families, their names inscribed in the Golden Book, comprised the nobility of Venice until Napoleon's armies smashed the Republic in 1797.

By law, all important offices were filled by members of the Great Council. Indeed the major business of this body came to be that of electing persons to other agencies of the state and the approval of constitutional changes.[15] The Small Council (the Senate) was elected by the Great and had general oversight in matters of policy and administration. Terms in the Senate were for life. The Pien Collegio served as the state's executive. Elected by the Great Council, its officers could not have more than two successive terms, each of six-months' duration.[16]

The Venetian government was increasingly pressed to obtain enough service from a body of nobles fixed for all time and, as a consequence, diminishing in numbers as families died out for lack of male heirs. It enforced participation in government with the threat of heavy fines. Even so, in the early sixteenth century the approximately twenty-five hundred males eligible to participate were spread thinly through the upper echelons of state service and had to be supplemented by the services of a lesser bourgeois population of clerks and secretaries.

2. Florence:

The Venetian economy was founded on a vast network of transoceanic trade; that of Florence on industry, especially textile manufacture, and on international banking. Like many Italian city-states, Florence had to contend with feudal families and soldiers of fortune who, in the Italy of the twelfth century, resided in the towns, built strong houses and towers, conducted endless feuds with one another, and terrorized the community. At Florence, the nobles were severely curbed from 1282, and in 1295 were allowed to remain citizens with limited rights only if they took membership in one of the several recognized trade guilds into which the population was divided. Nobles were prohibited from ever holding office.[17] The constant flux and internal complexity of Florentine politics defies almost all generalizations. Nevertheless, certain features were usually characteristic of its laws and of practice in the period from the subjugation of the nobles to the republic's end in the sixteenth century:[18] The guilds of those merchants engaged in manufacture and in foreign trade usually held a dominant position in the state but had always to contend seriously with other guilds and with popular institutions; most major offices were held for periods of only a few months to a year; old agencies of government were rarely abolished, new structures being created beside them; the operations of the state itself came increasingly to be a source of profit for its burghers; military and economic crises were endemic and often overcome by the temporary installation of an individual or commission, a balia, with extraordinary powers.

The regime installed in 1282 was headed by a podesta and six priors and was controlled by twelve of the city's more than thirty guilds: the seven major guilds and the five middle guilds.[19] The office of podesta continued to be what it had been for many years before, a post of chief judge and commander-in-chief in war. Occupants of this position had to be foreigners and were appointed for one year only. (Many Italian cities of the period had developed this type of office and a number of men had careers as podestas, moving from one community to another.)

Under the rules adopted in 1282, the podesta was understood to be immediately responsible to the priors who were the new executive charged with initiating legislation and directing the commonwealth's policies. Six in number, the priors served for two months. Toward the close of their term their six successors were selected at a session of the incumbent priors together with the heads of the twelve ruling guilds and a number of wise men chosen at the guilds' and priors' pleasure from among the six wards of the city.

The priors' regime was protected by a militia organized by the twelve ruling guilds. This political militia was additional to the older and still existing militia of all citizens mobilized for war. The captain of the new militia was ranked as one of the heads of state and was provided with two advisory councils of guildsmen in good standing.[20]

By 1366 the number of priors had increased to eight, and it had become a requirement that other major officials charged with the administration of justice be foreigners.[21] The priors and podesta together comprised the Signoria, the keystone of the communal edifice. Their terms of office continued as before and their powers were further constrained by the scrutiny of a vigilant, suspicious citizenry ready to bring legal charges of malfeasance.[22]

It is critical for an understanding of Florentine politics to understand the exact procedure by which the names of those eligible for the priorate and other offices came to be placed in the bags from which final slates were drawn by lot. Thus in 1323, says Sismondi, the Florentines:[23]

> ordained that a general list of all the eligible citizens, Guelphs, and at least thirty years of age, should be formed by a majority of five independent magistracies, of which each represented a national interest: the priori, that of the government; the gonfalonier, that of the militia; the captains of the [Parte Guelfa], that of the Guelphs; the judges of commerce represented the merchants; and the consuls of the arts, industry. . . .

We have seen that the priors were the chief magistrates. Who were the others? The gonfalonier was one of the priors, specially commissioned to execute sentences passed by the podesta. The judges of commerce were officers elected by companies of merchants to promote their domestic and foreign activities. The consuls were the elected heads of the major and minor guilds, members of merchant companies usually belonging to one of the former. There remain the captains of the Parte Guelfa.

The Parte Guelfa arose sometime after 1250 as an association of Guelf nobles contending with the Ghibellines for control of the city. In the early fourteenth century its leadership was synonymous with the city's ruling elite. In 1343, however, an influx of new blood into the communal government turned the party toward more partisan interests. The newly powerful guilds and merchants of the commune forced the party to acknowledge the supremacy of the communal government. Its membership was broadened to include most families of status and substance without regard for their origins. It remained in outlook patrician, though not noble; standing for rule by the most powerful families, for support in Italian politics of the interests of the Church rather than those of the Holy Roman Empire, and for support in foreign affairs of powers sharing its views. The captains were a self-perpetuating elite within the Parte.[24]

The list of those eligible for office once prepared, it then went for scrutiny and possible revision to a balia:[25]

> . . . composed of the magistrates in office and the thirty-six deputies chosen by the six divisions of the town. The balia effaced from the list the names of all those whom it considered

incapable; and classed the others according as they appeared suitable to the different magistracies, to which they were finally raised by lot. Lastly, it divided the names by series; so that the destined purse from which to draw the signoria contained twenty-one tickets, on each of which was inscribed a gonfalonier and six priori; similar purses were prepared from which to draw by lot the names of the twelve *buon' uomini,* the nineteen gonfaloniers of the companies, and all the other magistrates of the republic. All this arrangement was to last only three years and a half, after which a new balia recommenced. . . .

Favorable action by the balia required a two-thirds majority.

The electoral process was complicated by further constraints and requirements. Thus there were rules limiting the frequency with which an individual or family could be represented in the executive office: a prior could not return to that post before three years had passed nor could any member of his family succeed him within a year of the expiration of his term of office.[26] In 1343 it was ordained that two of the then eight priors should be from the upper guilds, three from the middle guilds, and three from the minor guilds. More than this, two priors were to come from each of the four wards into which Florence was then divided. As a result of such provisions shopkeepers and craftsmen came to have a large role in the government.[27]

It was a characteristic of Florentine government to provide every individual or group having executive power with a body of advisers. Sismondi has introduced us to the Twelve Good Men and to the Captains of the Military Companies, the Sixteen gonfaloniers, elected as described. Each group had a corporate character as a College and each advised the priors.

From 1328 the podesta was given a council of 250 members (the Council of the Commune) with which to consult and the captain of the militia, the gonfalonier of justice, a council of three hundred (the Council of the *Popolo*). Both councils were elected by the Signoria and the Colleges for six-month terms which, in 1366, were reduced to four months. Neither assembly had authority to initiate legislation; the councils considering only those proposals which had previously been approved by the Signoria and the Colleges. A majority of two-thirds was required in each council for the passage of a provision, and the tabulated votes on these measures provided useful guides for ascertaining public opinion on important issues. That these assemblies played a vital, though passive, role in communal politics is proved by the large number of proposals which failed to gain their acceptance, even after being submitted two or three times.[28]

Although vastly more complex, the Florentine regime had striking similarities to that at Venice. Instead of a Golden Book there were the certified lists of citizens eligible for office. In Florence, current officeholders, chosen by lot from those lists, could add or delete names of persons possibly eligible for office. In both communities a considerable part of the population was kept from full citizenship but the vast majority of those who had such citizenship could expect to hold an office of one sort or another. Even under the Medici, who eventually ruled openly as heads of state, the commensal order was retained as the legitimate foundation of Florentine polity, the new rulers being defined as merely its agents —as but a new instance of the ancient balias.

The most serious threats to the Florentine regime came not from the noble families or the disenfranchised majority of artisans but from divisions within the elite. The great merchant guilds had considerable authority for the regulation of the production and sale of most commodities. The commune did insist that their officers be selected only with the Signoria's consent, but they were, nonetheless, a part of government.[29] It was from these struggles of the great merchants with one another, and of the greater guilds with the smaller and with the government, that the Medici gained their power.

The Medici, one of the great merchant families, came gradually to be the organizers of modifications in government and municipal finances in the interest of those of their kind. The military and economic crises which made this possible are many and complex and need not be enumerated here.[30] The outcome was the creation of new agencies, self-perpetuating and under Medici control which gradually assumed the legislative powers of the old councils in most matters of importance.[31] This process was completed in its essentials by 1480 and continued until the revolution of 1494 brought a brief return of the old regime. Florence fell to Hapsburg and Papal troops in 1530.[32]

Poland

Poland, like other European lands, had undergone periods of disintegration and unification during the Middle Ages. Under Casimir the Great (1333-70) the nation's integrity was restored and the powers of the monarch stabilized. But this was not to last.

> . . . During the fourteenth century, Poland was a homogeneous monarchy still based on a homogeneous ethnic foundation with the system of estates; it was transformed from what was more or less an ordinary State of West European medieval type into a polyglot empire, a complex union of many lands which withal preserved their particularism in many respects. . . .[33]

In the fifteenth and sixteenth centuries, Poland itself was but the central state of a union of countries bound by various legal and dynastic ties.[34] Since 1385 there had been a dynastic union with Lithuania which in 1413 became a loose "convention" of union between the states themselves and in 1569 a parliamentary but not an administrative union. Complete amalgamation did not occur until 1791, nineteen years after Poland was first partitioned. East Prussia and Mazovia, first linked to Poland as semi-independent territories, were fully incorporated only in 1525 and 1529. Livonia became a personal fief of the Polish king in 1562 and remained such until absorbed into the state in 1569.

The Polish heartland itself was rich and productive, especially in the south and west. There were large deposits of iron, lead, zinc, rock salt, and silver. In the east and in the Carpathians were great forests. The Polish Ukraine contained large areas of fertile soil. In contrast, the regions along the Baltic were always lands of poverty and low density of population, their light, sandy soil being unproductive except for extensive agriculture. Until trade was disrupted by the Turkish invasions, Polish cities throve as intermediary points linking Western Asia and Muscovy with Europe.[35]

The monarchy and peerage had grown, not from feudalism, but from alliances among indigenous clans of free peoples. By the late 1400's however, the Eldermen of clans, together with their families, had formed a higher class than the other members, and the mass of freemen, having lost their importance in time of war, became subordinated. Certain individuals from diverse clans found a new path to eminence in the warbands of princes and from these grew a class of magnates.

Clan sentiment, if not clan government, survived well into the sixteenth century. It united those members of the gentry stemming from the same clan but living in different provinces. The Polish armies that defeated the Teutonic Order in 1410 fought under clan banners. When, in 1413, Poland and Lithuania established a convention of union, the various noble clans, each with its own coat-of-arms and denomination, adopted as members the principal families of Lithuanian boyars.[36]

Whether a product of ancient clan organization, or arising from some other source, there was a strong tradition of election of elders, princes, and kings, and of seeking unanimous decisions in representative bodies. There was, further, a well-developed system of quite autonomous local government by representative bodies in Poland proper. The monarchy, although having considerable independent powers, could exercise them only in collaboration with these local agencies.

The history of Polish national government in early modern times was characterized by the continuation of a powerfully based monarchy gradually limited by local authorities in the exercise of its general powers. What did not emerge was a division of labor between the two in which, through stable, legitimate institutions, they could jointly make policy and administer the state. They were more like two separate regimes in alliance than a single national government.

Apart from his personal resources and the powers traditionally assigned him, a Polish monarch's strength came in large measure from his position as the principal point of union among Poland's disparate territories. Lithuania was of special importance in this regard. Although the Polish kingship was elective, the elective principle had, since 1386, been limited for practical purposes by the requirement that the king also be Grand Duke of Lithuania. The ducal throne was, in turn, hereditary in the Jagellonian dynasty of Lithuania. Until 1569 when the Treaty of Lublin revised this system, the right of the Polish diet to elect its king provided it no great discretion.

Of even more importance was the king's power in Lithuania and, hence, in Poland. Lithuania was, in this period, a large and powerful state. Its gentry had limited authority in government. There were no local dietines. Through the reign of Sigmund August (1548-72) a Polish monarch's position in Lithuania was the final guarantee of his independent power.[37]

By the end of the fifteenth century, a national Polish diet had become well established as a continuing institution of government. Prior to that time, the king had called occasional national diets and had often dealt directly with the dietines, the provincial assemblies of the gentry. Thus in 1404 he convoked the dietines to obtain the extraordinary taxes needed to buy Dobrzyn province from the Teutonic Order. In 1454, in return for their consent to call up the levy of the whole kingdom to resist the Order, the king granted each of the several provinces a charter of liberties, these charters differing in considerable detail from one province to another but each containing the provision that no general levy should henceforth be summoned and no new legislation be introduced without the dietines' consent. Since the dietines consisted of all landowners holding in a province, however small their possessions, the effect was greatly to increase the political strength of the small gentry, the szlachta, and to weaken the powers that the magnates had come to exercise. The king thereby gained an ally against the magnates while the large numbers and disunity of the szlachta and their ignorance of foreign affairs gave him a freer hand in foreign policy.[38]

As of 1493 the national diet consisted of three parts: the king, the Senate, and the Chamber of Deputies. All three had to agree before an action could be taken. The Senate consisted of the Catholic prelates and the high officers of state appointed by the king with the diet's approval. The Chamber consisted of delegates elected by the dietines and bound to follow their constituents' instructions concerning national legislation. Burghers had not been included since 1467 when they were prohibited from owning land. The king could impose new taxes or declare war only with the diet's consent.

The growth of the diet's prerogatives, and through it the lesser gentry's, is reflected in major legislation.[39]

1497—Something close to hereditary serfdom was imposed on the peasants.

1496-1511—Self-government of villages abolished and appeal to royal courts from patrimonial justice greatly restricted. Members of the Senate were exempted from the jurisdiction of the royal courts. The diet gained control of the mint, previously an important source of royal revenue, and decreed that the king could not mortgage the royal estates without the unanimous consent of the Senate. The king's council came to consist of twenty-four Senators, these to serve in rotas of six for terms of six months. The Senate, in turn, consisted of men appointed by the king for life or for the period of his reign, their appointments being irrevocable. (These officials included two archbishops, fifteen bishops, thirty-three palatines—governors of provinces —and eighty-five castellans—commanders of fortresses and royal cities.) The Grand Chancellor and Vice Chancellor could be appointed only with the Senate's consent.

1501—The king's right of conferring local offices and his control over eldermen of clans was greatly restricted and the possibility was admitted that gentry might refuse to obey royal decisions that violated law or custom. (Particular dietines could, and sometimes did, refuse to administer even the diet's laws as inapplicable under the special provisions of their own royal charters.)

1505—It was reaffirmed that no royal legislative proposal could be put into effect without the consent of the Senate and Chamber. The king's council was now restricted to advising the monarch, its legislative functions being eliminated.

1515—Pope Leo agreed to the diet's demand that only men of purely noble descent should be made canons or prebendaries. This principle was extended in 1538 to abbots and priors.

1518—The right of peasants to appeal to royal courts was almost abandoned.

1520's—The diet took within its original jurisdiction the levying of troops, the collection of taxes, and the direction of the law courts. In all these matters the king was only their deputy.

1564-65—The internal administration of Lithuania was restructured to be like that of Poland with a concomitant increase of the Lithuanian gentry's powers.

1569—Lithuania and Poland were united under one king and diet, but Lithuania in internal affairs was still administered autonomously.

1573—All gentry individually were given a vote for the king, thus placing the gentry in overwhelming control of his election.

Even this record does not fully catch the growth of the gentry's powers and the extent of local control over national policy. Early in the sixteenth century it became the diet's right to be convened at least once every two years and the constitutional duration of a session was set at six weeks. It became a practice to seek unanimous decisions in the Chamber. Delegates could require that debate be reopened and continued until unanimity was reached and, if no passive or overt consensus was achieved in six weeks, an issue could go undecided until the next session. In the sixteenth century such cases were rare and no group or individual dared hold up decisions on important matters, but pressures in that direction were strong from 1572 and the power to prevent decision became frequent after the adoption of the *liberum veto* in 1652. From that date, foreign powers found it easy to paralyze the Polish government, bribing deputies when otherwise none sympathetic to their interests could be found. This situation, leading to internal anarchy, continued until Poland was partitioned by her neighbors. As a consequence, there was no period of royal absolutism in Polish history.

The Reformation:[40]

The Lutheran Reformation entered Poland at Danzig in 1518 and spread rapidly among the German merchants in the towns. It was followed around 1540 by Calvinism which proved even more popular among the native Poles. Protestants dominated all meetings of the diet from 1552 to 1565, invariably electing one of their number as president of the Chamber. The diet granted religious toleration to all Christians in 1555 and, after 1573, it became a constitutional principle that no Christian should be persecuted or punished for holding a particular view of the faith. Of lay members at the Senate meeting in 1569, fifty-eight were Protestant, fifty-five Catholic, and two were Greek Orthodox. We are told that, apart from German traders, Lutheranism found favor among the magnates of Great Poland who also embraced doctrines of the Bohemian Brethren. Calvinism was especially popular among the szlachta of Little Poland and the aristocracy of Lithuania.

The decline of the Polish Reformation was as phenomenal as its rise. There is general agreement on the following facts:

1. The Reformation in Poland had its support from townspeople and the great nobles. It did not penetrate the peasantry or the lesser gentry. Those of the middle and lesser gentry who showed an interest in Protestantism fell away from it when the secular power of the clergy was lost.

2. The continued support of Catholicism by the monarchs who, after the sixteenth century, excluded Protestants from the preferment for political office and supported the activities of the Counter-Reformation, placed increasing pressure on those whose Protestantism was but an uncertain faith.

3. Much of the return to Catholicism occurred without great coercion or force, the sons of Protestant nobles returning almost voluntarily to Catholic beliefs.

4. The association of the Protestants with the futile revolt against Sigismund III in 1606-7, led to their political eclipse.

The middle and lower gentry, predominantly Catholic, supported the king, but not to the detriment of their own prerogatives.

What we find emerging in Poland is not heterarchy, but pure democracy among the politically active parts of the population. There is not, as in Germany, a system of large princely states almost sovereign in their actions, but instead a body of landowners, many but little removed from peasants, whose individual power was slight, but whose collective power was superior to any other force in the state. The gentry, when the whole class is included, were estimated to embrace about ten percent of the population. Organized into regional diets at which national affairs were discussed by all local members of the class and from which instructed delegates were sent to the Chamber of Deputies, the gentry sought to institutionalize full consensus as the basis of government. At the same time, they were not separatists. Instead they supported the institutions of national unity. Theirs was the strength that defeated the rebellion by Protestants and others in 1606.

The Reformation made greatest headway among the merchants and burgesses in the towns, many of whom were German, and among the greater nobility. We know that, among the latter, the conception of the state as a kind of aristocratic federalism was common. These great magnates had, as individuals, the land and resources to take an independent course in national affairs. These tendencies were crushed decisively by the weight of the crown and the mass of the gentry. It was probably the prevailing order of unity through consensual, pure democracy that accounts for the strength of Catholicism in the country and the rapid, non-violent reconversion of Protestant families in the seventeenth century. One may imagine that the persistent support of Catholicism by the kings and the activities of the Jesuits would have failed but for the consistency with their efforts of the environing political situation.

The Reformation is said to have spent its force by 1573. That is the year in which the whole body of Polish landowners came fully to power. It is the year after the death of King Sigmund August, the last member of the Jagellonian dynasty and hence the last hereditary Grand Duke of Lithuania. At his death, candidature to the throne was at last fully elective and the king's special powers previously derived from his base in Lithuania were no more.

Conclusion

Among commensal societies, Florence and Poland presented the greatest problems of classification. Should Florence under the Medici be counted a centralist state? Should Poland be considered a balanced state?

The situation in Florence under the stronger Medici rulers was that of a regime in which the forms were commensal and the actualities frequently centralist. But the Medici did keep the ancient forms and on many occasions did find it necessary to observe them in practice, in order to prevent public disorders. Perhaps, however, one should give greater weight than I have to the Medici's effective domination of the state. If one did, he would count the regime as centralist and, as before, expect the continued support of Catholicism.

In Poland there were present for a time strong features of a balanced state. In that period a majority of the greater nobles favored Calvinism. But the form of the state, and, for most purposes, its practice came to be commensal, the crown being actually as well as figuratively the symbol and agent of the Polish landowners. The crown's resources were thereafter primarily at the landowners' collective disposal, an added power when needed for the implementation of their collective policy. In contrast with the situation in Hungary, the landowners of Poland were organized as a commensal whole rather than merely as representatives of the counties. In further contrast, the Polish king had had his independent powers in gubernaculum taken from him. He no longer met the minimal criteria required of a governor.

[VIII]

Heterarchic Regimes

FIVE EUROPEAN GOVERNMENTS were like commensal regimes in all crucial respects but one: ultimate authority in gubernaculum was vested in persons only as representatives of constituent bodies in the political community. Those bodies might be of any sort: guilds, aristocratic corporations, military companies, the peasants living in a region, a county-based organization of landowners or nobles. The particular interests represented are not important for our classification. What is important is that there be no governor and that gubernaculum be ultimately exercised by representatives of constituent bodies.

I want specifically to rule inappropriate for regimes called heterarchic certain practices employed in commensal systems. In a heterarchic regime there should not be, as in Florence, a system in which persons representative of the community as a whole must approve candidates nominated by constituent bodies before they can be considered acceptable as participants in gubernaculum. Similarly I want to consider as not heterarchic those regimes in which important decisions were commonly possible only if supported by all or the vast majority of representatives of constituent bodies. Such a procedure applied in Florence and Poland. I want finally to make inappropriate in a heterarchic system the holding of elections in any manner (as, for example, the drawing of names by lot from lists of all members of the body politic) that makes officials having ultimate control of gubernaculum representative of the community at large rather than of special groups within it. All of these devices make regimes without governors into commensal orders. They place overwhelming weight in decision upon what their constituent bodies have in common, not upon the points at which they differ.

All but one of the five heterarchic regimes appeared in a Swiss canton: the cantons of Basel, Bern, Schaffhausen, and Zurich. The fifth was the regime of the United Provinces. All five adopted the Reformed doctrines of Zwingli, of Calvin, or both: Zurich in 1525, Basel and Bern in 1528, Schaffhausen in 1530, and the United Provinces in 1579.

Zurich, Basel, and Schaffhausen[1]

Each of these cantons was dominated by a city, the latter governed by representatives of its guilds. Of these, Zurich holds special interest as the site of Zwingli's Reformation (1519-31).

Zurich had been one of the early allies of the Forest Cantons and Lucerne. Situated to the north and commanding major routes for north-south trade, the city prospered as a commercial center. The chief local industry was the manufacture of silk cloth. There were also significant developments in the weaving of linen and wool.

The inner Swiss cantons were almost as dependent economically on Zurich as on Lucerne (although Zurich, in its turn, was not completely tied economically to them). It was especially important for Lucerne and the Forest Cantons to obtain the cereal grains imported through Zurich which they themselves could not raise. (Thus when Zurich closed her markets to the Forest Cantons in 1531 they were forced to declare war at once for there was not a single field of wheat in Uri and Schwyz either then or until the latter part of the eighteenth century.)[2]

These strong but unequal dependencies, together with Zurich's size and prosperity and her need for policies that would promote her commerce with northern Europe, led to frictions with her allies. Sometimes Zurich sought to impose her policies on her allies, sometimes they theirs on her. Affairs reached a crisis when the Austrians induced Zurich to secede from the Swiss Confederation and become a Hapsburg ally. Both were defeated by the Forest Cantons and Lucerne in 1444. This was a major turning point in Zurich's internal development. The economies of Zurich and her conquerors were ruined. Neither party was strong enough to destroy or rule the other. The silk industry did not revive until the 1540's, and then as a result of a great influx of Italian Protestant refugees skilled in that work. However, Zurich's former Swiss allies were no less exhausted morally and economically. It was at this time, in an economically ruined country, that large numbers of Swiss from the Forest Cantons took up careers in foreign military service.[3]

One consequence of the military and economic debacle of 1444 was the overthrow in Zurich of the powers of the greater merchants.

> . . . This was a radical *caesura* in Zurich's development; by 1500 the economy had been set upon another basis. Zurich was now a city whose wealth derived primarily from trade; it took iron ore from the north-east of Switzerland and exchanged this for salt, grain and manufactured goods obtained via Basel—and for wine, imported and home grown. The most important local industry of the new period was that of the smiths: weapons were in demand. Further, cotton wool was being produced in the city for export. . . .[4]

Beginning in the Middle Ages the members of the twelve burgher guilds elected their guild masters who, in turn, constituted half the city's Small Council.[5] The economic changes before 1519 gave greater prestige and power to guilds of artisans and to merchants in the new lines of work.[6] The older patrician groups were constitutionally curbed.[7]

> . . . the City Council . . . consisted of a Large Council, its members elected for life by the gilds, and a Small Council, half designated by the Large Council from its own ranks and half named by the gilds. (The patricians in the Konstaffel were, in both places, allocated a special if limited number of seats.) The Small Council served for a year; when the Large Council met, as it did to decide important questions, it sat with the former. Finally, there was a Secret Council, which consisted of the two mayors (life councillors who led the Small Council), four gild representatives with watching briefs, two treasurers and the administrator of the city's cloister estates. Life memberships in the Large Council, the frequent renewal of membership in the Small Council, the reservation of election rights within the gilds to officers, appointments to state offices from a limited circle, all suggest that the government of Zurich was oligarchic. . . .[8]

The Councils supported Zwingli and broke with Roman authority in 1521-23, finally abolishing the Mass in 1525. "The dogmatic foundation of Zwingli's . . . reforms was his denial of the scriptural warrant for the efficacy of the Sacraments: the Spirit spoke only to the Spirit and the sole aim of Divine Service was the preaching of the Word."[9]

Although Basel and Schaffhausen did not experience similar economic upheavals, the structure of their governments strongly resembled that of Zurich.[10] In Basel, however, election to the city's councils was in the hands of the guilds' presidents rather than their members. The members nominated six candidates for every vacant council post and the presidents chose new councilmen by lot.[11]

Bern

Bern, founded in 1191 by feudal lords as a military stronghold, was long of little economic importance. Gradually a population of burghers became established outside the walls and later within. In 1350 most municipal authority passed from the feudal nobles to the burghers, with ultimate authority held by a General Assembly of all the burghers.[12]

At the end of the fifteenth century Bern was militarily the most powerful Swiss state. Powers formerly exercised by the Assembly were now held by a Great Council of about two hundred members. There was also a Small Council called the Senate, a Secret Council, and a roster of administrative officers headed by two chief magistrates, the avoyers. The system of access to office was complex, and, for our purposes, must be disentangled.[13]

Although guilds as such had not been of political importance in Bern, every burgher was enrolled in one of twelve abbeys, each having the name of a trade. These abbeys were military-political associations of the laity developed, as in many medieval cities, to provide a militia. (Although it is not certain, it may be that in Bern with its history of knightly founders, the abbeys arose as a transitional organization between the earlier feudal ties uniting the city's elite and its later structure as an association of burghers.) Four abbeys were of more importance than the others: the tanners, butchers, bakers, and smiths. These had surveillance over the four quarters of the city, each direct- ing in one of the quarters the conduct of police activity, the organization of armed citizens for public defense, and the extension of public assistance to the needy. In time the four major abbeys obtained what became their principal func- tion, that of administering the state's finances.

Until the revolutionary changes of the eighteenth century, the root of Bern's electoral process lay in the abbeys and in an electoral commission, the Sixteen, chosen by them. (The Sixteen had, in addition to electoral powers, the right to censure public officials guilty of official misbehavior.) Each of the four major abbeys chose two electors, and each of the eight other abbeys chose one. Those eligible for the post of elector were members of an abbey who had not been members of the city's Small Council and whose fathers and brothers had not held such membership. Once a list of such persons was established, each abbey chose its elector or electors by lot.

From the late fourteenth century the abbeys furnished a list of persons eligible for membership on the Great Council. These lists consisted of all adult male citizens "of good character." All the names submitted by all the abbeys were numbered and cards bearing the numbers were placed in a sack and thoroughly scrambled. The Sixteen together with the Small Council sat as an electoral commission of forty- three members. As a teller drew a name at random from the sack, and declared the name of the man so nominated, the commission would vote to accept or reject the nominee for one of the vacancies on the Great Council, continuing until all names were voted upon, those receiving the greatest majorities being declared elected.

However, by the mid-sixteenth century, abuses appeared which gradually gained the force of law. Each member of the commission gained the right to name a candidate for a vacancy; this nominee was then almost always elected by the commission. About sixty percent of the vacancies were filled in this manner. Even the remaining places became sub- ject to the commission's control, with the result that if a member had a close relative to recommend for such a vacancy, his election was almost assured. Young men who had sponsors on the commission would pay present members of the Great Council to resign their posts, thus creating a post to be filled by the sponsor.

In law, almost all administrative officers together with members of the Great and Small Councils were up for re-election annually. This requirement was met, but as an automatic reinstatement, the Electoral Commission (which included the Small Council) reinstating the Great Council which then reinstated the majority of the Small Council's members (but not the avoyers) who then were within its power of appointment.

The Great Council usually met three times a month to consider proposals put before it by the Small Council. The Great Council lacked the right to initiate proposals. (However, it was the Great Council which forced a reluctant Small Council to introduce Calvinism in 1528.)

The Small Council consisted of twenty-seven members including the cantonal officers. Something should be said of its functions and of the method by which its members were elected.

The Small Council was in charge of all the administrative details of the state. Its members spoke first on any issue before the Great Council. In the seventeenth and eighteenth centuries one of its subcommittees, the Secret Council, became the most potent organ of Bernese government. Consisting of the seven principal cantonal officers and the two Secrets of the Great Council (to be described), it handled the more important matters of policing, state security, and the conduct of war. It acted as the canton's foreign office, and advised the Small Council.

The Secrets of the Great Council were two of its members chosen to sit with the Small Council and, when appropriate vacancies occurred in that body, to act as replacements. As official heirs to the most important posts in the state, the Secrets sat with the Small Council, had some rights of participation in its deliberations, though not a vote, and provided a liaison with the Great Council. They could stop the Small Council's work if they thought it threatened the constitution.

The Secrets were chosen by a special commission of nine (three from the Small Council, six from the Great) whose members were selected by lot. This commission prepared a list of at least six candidates. The Great Council then narrowed the list to four by vote. Two of the four remaining candidates were eliminated by lot. The Great Council then chose between the two nominees, but only after a third of the Council's members had, by lot, been eliminated as voters on this issue. By this elaborate means intrigue and jealousies were minimized.

The most important of the cantonal officers were the two chief magistrates (the avoyers) and the heads of the four major abbeys (the bannerets). The two magistrates had, in earlier times, been ineligible for immediate reelection and the Great Council had, at all times, the power to remove them for malfeasance. By the seventeenth century, however, theirs became a lifetime post. When necessary, an avoyer was elected by the Great Council from a list drawn up by the bannerets—a list to which the Great Council could, but rarely did, add names. In alternate years, one avoyer was regarded as supreme, the other as of lesser rank. The ruling avoyer presided at the Great and Small Councils and cast a deciding vote to break ties.

The bannerets were elected by the Great Council for terms of four years. If at the time of his term's expiration, a banneret was his abbey's only member on the Small Council, he would almost certainly be reelected. If his abbey then had other members on the Small Council, the Great Council would select his successor from among all members of the abbey including the retiring banneret.

The elaborate checks and balances of Bernese government produced a regime of exceptional power and stability. Foreign visitors routinely noted the high morale of its elites, the equitable and considered quality of its decisions, the stability and orderliness of its administration, and the dullness of life in the capital.

Every member of the Great Council had the right to hold

an official post and the resultant income provided him a fortune.

In principle, all burghers could enter the Great Council. In fact, given the methods of nomination, membership in the Great Council, the Small Council, and in the posts of chief magistrate was customarily filled by members of certain prominent families and a young man from one of those households could obtain credits from domestic and foreign lenders on the strength of his financial prospects. Families sent members into government on a system of primogeniture to youngest sons.

In 1785 the Great Council abolished all titles of nobility held from the early feudal period and granted the prefix *von* to all members of the 283 families then eligible to participate in the government. Although, in that period, about three-fourths of these families were not participants in government, efforts to formalize that situation legally were never approved by the Councils.[14]

The United Provinces

The story of what later became the Netherlands is tied to that of Belgium during most of the Middle Ages and up to the formation of the United Provinces (in 1579) under William of Orange. In the beginning, the Low Countries lacked geographical, linguistic, or political unity.[15] The north and east were under German control, the southwest under French domination. In the far south, Walloon was spoken. In the center and north, Germanic dialects predominated. From the twelfth century until the fall of Napoleon, Flanders was usually dominated by France or Spain or Austria.

Lying at the point of confluence of the Rhine, Meuse, and Scheldt rivers, the Low Countries became great centers of trade and of industry. Economic development was reflected in general prosperity, in the growth of market and industrial towns in the provinces of Flanders, Brabant, Liege, Holland, and parts of Hainault. The industrialization of the cloth and metal industries was extensive enough to produce not only a bourgeoisie of merchant-entrepreneurs but a far more numerous class of artisans and apprentices. Struggles among the merchants, artisans, and apprentices occurred in the thirteenth century and afterward. The great merchants and guild masters were forced to call upon the strength of the local prince to control their workers.

The towns, although extremely powerful, did not acheive the position of free towns.

> . . . The explanation . . . must . . . be found in the attitude of the territorial princes in the Low Countries. These, as a general rule, were careful to avoid refusing the towns the autonomy which was indispensable to their development, and were satisfied with maintaining their own right of oversight which meant little real interference. The social conflicts of the fourteenth century, in which they were forced to intervene, strengthened rather than diminished their authority by identifying it with the cause of the anti-revolutionary elements in the ranks of the *bourgeoisie*.[16]

Beginning in 1384, with the accession of Flanders to the Burgundian dukes, the whole of the Low Countries came under Burgundian control. Everywhere but in Liege the new rulers were accepted by the people. The dukes managed to keep their lands at peace during the last phase of the Hundred Years' War. They gave minimal affront to the local loyalties of each province by governing each as its own lord rather than as rulers of the entire Netherlands. Their sovereignty was further assured by the migration of the revolutionary working classes following a decline of the cloth industry in the second half of the fourteenth century and in the fifteenth century. The bourgeoisie and the nobility looked upon the Burgundian rulers as indispensable for the continuation of political and social peace.

Stimulated by the dukes and by political union, a single coinage was developed, shipping underwent steady progress, and the lands enjoyed great prosperity. A common coinage was established in 1433. Centralizing institutions were founded—treasuries, courts, and a council.[17] Of special importance was the establishment, in 1430, of the Order of the Golden Fleece through which the local nobles were attached to the duke and, in 1463, the formation of an Estates General which represented the Estates of the several

provinces. The Estates General was an institution of consequence, having control over the raising of taxes.

Out of these experiences in unified action came a sense of
the unity of Netherlandish life.[18] But this sense proved to be
fragile, plagued by strong provincial loyalties and interests.

Protestant ideas found welcome in many parts of the Low
Countries. Baptist and Calvinist groups, especially the latter,
were growing with great rapidity in the reign of the Emperor Charles V, but it was under his son, Philip II of
Spain, that the crisis of the Roman Church and the Protestants reached its climax. In the events that follow, six
facts seem of salient importance:

1. The majority of the great nobles lived in what now is
Belgium, and these remained loyal to the Spanish Hapsburgs and Catholicism.[19]

> The magnates owed their rise and position to the Bur-
> gundian-Hapsburg monarchy, so that each one's broad lands
> lay spread over several provinces. . . . [Apart from Orange
> and Mansfeldt]. . . , the great nobles mostly belonged to
> Walloon families. . . . These men kept a truly princely state.
> . . . From their youth onwards these men were employed
> in the service of the monarch for the most important military,
> diplomatic, and political missions.[20]

So powerful was the control of the dukes of Brabant over
much of Belgium that a class of free farmers never developed.

2. Protestants and Catholics alike opposed the harsh
measures of the Austrian and Spanish Hapsburg governments in stamping out Protestant beliefs and in trying to
weld the Low Countries into a tool of Spanish dynastic
policies. Under the Emperors Maximilian and Charles V,
absolutism was, for all practical purposes, triumphant.[21]

3. Protestantism, whether Baptist, Lutheran, Zwinglian, or
Calvinist, seems to have had as strong support in Flanders
and Brabant to the south as in Holland and Zeeland to the
north.

4. The lands north of the Scheldt estuary were defensible
against the Spanish, while those to the south, lacking strong

natural lines of defense, were constantly under Spanish domination.[22]

5. In the northern provinces, the county of Holland itself was the overwhelmingly dominant partner. That county, in turn, was controlled by the oligarchy of the great merchants.

6. The political power of the towns in the south had been weakened by the decline of the textile industry.

The actual use of armed force against the Hapsburg rule came in the first instance as an effort to force mitigation of the Inquisition and retention of the traditional rights of the provinces. It quickly developed into full-scale revolt, with the southern leaders, still trying to placate Philip and the north, under the control of Protestants, now seeking full independence in religious belief.

Indeed the problem was at least as much political as religious. Philip sought to curb the powers Charles V had allowed the provinces and Estates. The Estates sought independence in foreign policy. They questioned the king's right to have concluded his recent concordat with the Pope concerning the support and reorganization of dioceses in the Low Countries. They rejected the king's incorporation into the Estates General of some of the bishops newly appointed by him.[23] After Philip's success in crushing the revolt of workers in western Flanders in 1566, he did what was unheard of—appointed a foreigner, the Duke of Alva, as governor of the Netherlands.[24]

> At first sight the Protestantization of Holland is an amazing spectacle. There can be no doubt that the Reformed constituted a minority, and even a small minority, and this continued to be so for a long time to come, for generations in fact. As late as 1587 they were estimated at one-tenth of the population of the province. . . . How was it that in the long run they even succeeded in winning the majority over to their side? This phenomenon became intelligible only through the state of war, a condition under which detestation of the enemy can cause a society to submit to harsh but purposeful leadership against its real inclinations.[25]

In 1568, while the southern nobility capitulated to Philip II, William of Orange, richest of the native nobles and royal lieutenant of Holland, Zeeland, and Utrecht and Marquis of Antwerp, returned from exile in Germany to lead a rebellion against Spain. Despite some French and German support, William's forces were driven back to the north where the counties of Holland and Zeeland became the seats of his power and where his resources came almost completely from grants by the Estates of Holland.[26]

It was Holland and Zeeland which continued to lead the new United Provinces after their triumph over Spain, shaping the general government which came to order the country's affairs. Holland and Zeeland themselves contained more than half the Dutch population. Their assemblies were completely dominated by magistrates elected by their burghers; their economies by commerce operated by urban merchants.[27] There were nobles in the county of Holland, possessing seigneurial rights in the villages, but those rights were limited to levying a head tax on descendants of former bondsmen, to income from tolls, fishing and hunting rights—taxes and tolls set at a low traditional sum. The nobles' lands were small, their power not sufficient to become oppressive. The burghers, gentry, and peasants lived in close social relations with one another.

Generally and traditionally within each province that entered the new Dutch state, government was conducted by a union of towns and rural districts, each represented in a provincial assembly. The assemblies developed into regular institutions with their own officials and funds and had great autonomy in the conduct of local affairs.[28]

Throughout the Republic the nobility formed an absolutely closed caste, but it wielded great political power only in the landward provinces. In these, save in towns of Utrecht and Groningen, town magistrates commanded but slight prestige. The towns were relatively small and . . . economically backward. . . . among the representatives of these provinces only the nobles cut any figure at The Hague in the general political life of the Republic. In Holland and Zeeland, on the other hand, it was the middle-class town regents who had the real power in their hands and played the leading role on the national stage. The Holland nobility, numerically weak as it was, allied itself as little with the great burgher families as did that of the more agrarian and feudal provinces of the East.[29]

The Union of Utrecht (1579), which established the new nation, was a union among provinces which had become sovereign after their disaffection from the Hapsburgs. These provinces, like the Swiss cantons, agreed to have a single foreign policy but to retain independence in local affairs. There was no national administration of any consequence, committees of the Estates General performing such coordinating work as was necessary for the conduct of foreign affairs. The delegates to the Estates General had no authority to act. They had, rather, to receive instructions from their respective provincial assemblies. All decisions of the national Estates had to be unanimous. This system of government continued for two centuries, though not without internal struggles. At times the Estates and their committees governed alone, but more often the administration was shared with the current leader of the Estates of the county of Holland or with a Stadholder (governor) of the House of Orange. There was no break, however, with the Estates' strong participation in administration as well as their monopoly over legislation. Even when, in 1815, the Netherlands became a hereditary kingdom, there was no growth of absolute government.

Conclusion

The constituent bodies essential to these five heterarchic regimes were not identical. In Holland and Zeeland they were the towns and, occasionally, individual nobles. In Basel, Schaffhausen, and Zurich they were guilds. In Bern they were military-political subdivisions of the population, bearing names conventional to guilds but including occupationally diverse populations.

There seems little doubt that the regimes of Basel, Schaffhausen, the United Provinces, and Zurich meet the criteria for a heterarchic system. Bern is not as clear an instance.

Under the Bernese system the Great Council had final authority in most affairs and the electoral process provided that each representative of an "abbey" could select one or more persons to fill vacancies on the Great Council. These Sixteen electors representing the abbeys also had the right to censure malfeasant officials. On the other hand, a majority of the electoral commission (about sixty percent of its membership) consisted of persons elected by the existing Great Council itself, consisted, that is, of the members of the Small Council. Thus a majority of new members of the Great Council would be choices of Small Councilors.

The procedures by which the Great Council chose the members of the Small Council varied, the bannerets and avoyers being selected by a vote of all members under the rules that a banneret had to be chosen from members held in good standing by his abbey, that each of the four major abbeys was entitled to a banneret chosen from its membership, and that neither bannerets or avoyers could be closely related to their predecessors in office. Most of the other members of the Small Council were chosen by an elaborate mixture of voting and selection by lot.

Thus we find in Bern councils that are not self-perpetuating but councils that change only slowly in composition and that have indirect control over the selection of a majority of their new members. The remaining vacancies, those filled by the Sixteen, were nonetheless a substantial fraction of the total and the practice in the Great Council of taking action on important matters only by large majorities assured that the views of this minority had to be taken seriously into account. This council structure has, thus, some properties of a balanced regime and, in the choice of bannerets, of limited centralism.

One can say with confidence that the regime at Bern was not centralist or commensal. Its major features were those of a heterarchic or a balanced regime with some hint of limited centralism. In sum one would judge that Bern had a regime congenial to Protestantism and, most likely, to Zwinglian or Calvinist rather than to Lutheran doctrines.

Religion and Regime, 1490 to 1780

CATHOLICISM SURVIVED THE REFORMATION in countries that had commensal or centralist regimes. Lutheranism or Anglicanism became the dominant faith in limited centralist states. With two exceptions, Calvinist or Zwinglian beliefs became the chief doctrines only under heterarchic and balanced governments. (The exceptions: a considerable majority of people in the Swiss cantons of Appenzell and Glarus adopted Zwinglian and, later, Calvinist theology. Each canton apparently had a commensal regime.) These exceptions aside, Protestantism was adopted by European societies only after there was a change from a commensal or centralist regime to a balanced, limited centralist, or heterarchic regime.

Those conclusions are the principal results of our historical survey. This short chapter reviews other results. Some of them are based upon tabulations contained in Table I at the end of this chapter. The column numbers that appear below refer to information in that table.

1. (Columns VII, IX, and X): I classified regimes according to the presence or absence of governors and according to the role in gubernaculum played by governors and by constituent bodies. I took no notice of the sort of person or group that served as a governor or as a member of the body politic. I also paid no attention in classification to the exact means by which constituent bodies shared in the exercise of gubernaculum. The historical record shows that councils, groups of kinsmen, and individuals acted as governors. Some were elected and others were hereditary or appointed officials. The membership of the bodies politic of these societies varied greatly. In one or more cases they included guilds, towns, magnates, gentry, nobles, knights,

peasants, royalty, burghers, or all free men. When constituent bodies had a share in gubernaculum they exercised their rights by a variety of means: by means of a popular assembly, courts of law, diets, councils, or committees. As Table I indicates, the spread of Protestantism is related only to the presence or absence of a governor and the involvement of constituent bodies in gubernaculum. It is not related to the many other differences among these regimes as just enumerated.

2. (Columns IV and V): By 1490 and even by 1450 a great many of these societies had acquired the form of regime in power at the Reformation. In all cases, however, the regimes in power in the first half of the fifteenth century were centralist or commensal.

3. (Column XIII): My classification of regimes depends in part upon the role of constituent bodies in gubernaculum but takes no account of their role in jurisdictio. There are considerable variations among societies within each type of regime: variations in whether, and by what means, members of the body politic share in exercising jurisdictio and whether their share entails power at the central or local levels of government. The acceptance of Protestantism is not directly related to these variations. This finding is consistent with a judgment discussed in Chapter II: the judgment that powers in gubernaculum rather than powers in jurisdictio best define the powers distinctive to a central government.

4. In view of the common disposition to associate Calvinism with the outlook only of merchants, the fact of its adoption largely at the instance of nobles in Lowland Scotland, in Bohemia, and in Hungary and Transylvania is of special interest. The findings from these countries can be supplemented by the data from Poland.

We have seen that, early in the sixteenth century, the centralist regime of Poland faltered. Merchants and artisans were excluded legally and almost totally from participation in provincial and central government. Nobles alone shared the crown's authority. The government was modified first to a limited centralist structure and then to the form of a balanced regime. Our survey of Polish history shows that a considerable majority of the nobility supported Lutheranism during the first of these changes in regime and Calvinism during the second. The form of the nobles' growing control over the state took final shape as a commensal regime —this from 1572—and, from about that date, the Polish nobility drifted back to Catholicism.

5. (Columns III and VI): Between the time their Reformation regimes were established and 1780, a number of societies experienced major political change. Some changes, although drastic, were of only short duration. Some societies simply disappeared as independent entities.

Of the societies still independent in 1780, only a few had changed to types of regime different from those in power at the Reformation. The Swiss cantons of Lucerne and Solothurn had changed from centralist to commensal regimes. England, originally limited centralist, was moving toward the pattern of a balanced polity. Denmark moved from limited centralism to centralism. None of these instances involves a Catholic society's changing to a type of regime congenial to Protestantism. In only one instance, that of Denmark, does it appear that a Protestant society adopted a "Catholic" style of polity. More important, the stability of relationship between religious outlook and type of regime as reflected in this comparison of only two points in time seems consistent with the picture one gets from a fuller inspection of the data. Thus, were one to estimate the type of regime each country had had for two-thirds or three-fourths of the years between the Reformation and 1780, he would obtain essentially the picture given by the simpler means just employed.

6. (Column VI): After the accomplishment of their Reformation settlements as determined by indigenous conditions, Bohemia, Ireland, Hungary, the Scottish Highlands, and Transylvania were conquered by foreign powers that had polities and official religious creeds other than their own. Each case presents its own complexities, but two tentative generalizations seem justified: (a) The indigenous religious faith disappeared if the occupying power set about

to extirpate it as a public profession and as a private belief. (b) When local elites were given status and privileges in the new political order before the time of their religious conversion, that conversion occurred more smoothly and rapidly than was otherwise the case.

The Austrian conquerors of Bohemia and Hungary refused to tolerate Protestantism and it seemingly disappeared in both territories. In Bohemia, but not in Hungary the Hapsburgs stripped away the natives' rights of participation in gubernaculum. (The action of the Calvinist government at Edinburgh in dealing with the Catholics of the Scottish Highlands was similarly intolerant of native doctrine and government and had similar results.) Protestantism survived in Transylvania where the triumphant Hapsburgs were forced to tolerate both it and the essential political structure established before their conquest.

In Ireland the English government followed a mixed policy toward native religion and polity. There had not been a formal central or provincial government founded on native institutions. As we have seen, the heart of native rule had lain in the ancient septs, ruling families of kinsmen under an elected chief. The English curbed this system of native government only insofar as it hindered their rule. In most periods they gave tacit toleration to the private profession of Catholicism and often to its expression in public worship—providing the latter remained inconspicuous and providing the people gave financial support to the Established Church, attended its services on required occasions, and publicly pledged their loyalty to the regime. Under these conditions Catholicism and much of the old system of government survived in Ireland under English rule.

The central Scottish government in extending its rule over the Highlands, and the Hapsburgs in ruling Hungary, gave native elites a significant part in government. In Scotland local representatives from the Highlands were included in the national Parliament and among the crown's local Justices. The Hungarian nobility were given positions and honors and opportunities in the Hapsburg's imperial system. In both cases this participation in the state was granted without first making a close examination of the religious beliefs of appointees and in both cases opponents of the regime's religion came gradually to accept the doctrines in religion that the regime preferred.[1] (On the other hand, the English in Ireland largely supplanted the indigenous Irish elite with foreigners, and religious conversion was required of natives as a precondition of participation in the new political order. As we have noted, there were relatively few conversions from Catholicism in Ireland.)

7. In summary, the historical evidence seems generally consistent with the explanation proposed for the spread and limitations of the Reformation. Special future attention must be given, however, to events in the Swiss cantons of Appenzell and Glarus which provided the exceptions to our interpretation. It appears that a majority of each of these canton's people adopted Zwinglian or Calvinist beliefs. About a third of the population in each remained Catholic. Religious conflicts persisted throughout the sixteenth century and, finally, most functions of government in each canton were given equally to each of the separate governments that arose to serve the two religious communities. The local histories do not provide material that I have found helpful in distinguishing the polities of these two areas of Appenzell or of Glarus either before or after the Reformation. More adequate data may suggest that Appenzell and Glarus are clear exceptions to my expectations. At present it is best to regard them so and to see whether data relevant for a more conclusive judgment can be had. Cantonal histories, although not sufficiently detailed, do suggest that Glarus and Appenzell were distinguished from Switzerland's rural Catholic cantons by the relatively circumscribed powers of the formers' general assemblies of all citizens and by the greater scope of powers exercised by their councils of representatives, these councils being chosen by localities within each canton. It is likely that only a fresh look at the primary sources will provide the clarifications needed.

Similarly, if we are to assess its implications, Protestant

Denmark's adoption of a centralist regime in 1660 requires a closer inspection than I have been able to give it. In this case the role of constituent bodies in local administration is at issue. The sources I have consulted (written in English, French, and German—but not those written in Danish) make it clear that the old nobility was deprived of such a role after being discredited in two wars. What is not clear is the role given the new nobility, those coming to control large areas of rural Denmark under a renascent monarchy. I have chosen to indicate for the present what the sources least favorable to my expectations declare, namely that from 1660 the monarch alone had independent jurisdiction in the local as in the central exercise of gubernaculum.

8. Is it possible that the associations drawn in Table I between changes in regime and changes in religion may be only associations; that rather than political changes being a "cause" of new religious beliefs, both they and the Reformation were produced by some third, presently unknown, forces? No conceivable empirical finding can eliminate that possibility. It may be that behind all our observations stands some unsuspected cause of this repeated association between polity and theology, the structure of government adapting to that causal condition more rapidly and visibly than the pattern of religious conceptions but the polity not producing those conceptions.

It is also possible that religious changes do follow those in politics but in no simple fashion. Indeed this is probable. I have proposed only that religious conceptions symbolize men's experiences with the collective procedures by which their society reaches decisions. I have assumed that most members of a society's body politic will experience changes in the structure, power, and moral force of such collective processes and that they will together seek in a theology to define the source of their new experiences in order more adequately to cope with these basic changes in their world. This assumption thus implies that a process of collective discussion and collective search must intervene between the rise of basic political novelties and the emergence and acceptance of a theological interpretation appropriate to them. That interpretation must be consistent not only with the changed polity but with a society's other institutions. How such developments occur or in what sequence is unknown. We can, however, be reasonably certain that some sequence of development must take place; that fresh, coherent, and acceptable theological schemes do not spring up immediately as people experience newly developed systems of government.

A finding that the Reformation was related to broad political currents does not imply that all of any society's people will be homogeneous in religious outlook. Just as members of different occupational strata understandably differ in their views of the economic system in which all strata participate, so one should expect that any condition providing men a special view of basic features of their society's polity will be productive of special religious conceptions. If sociologists of religion have documented any point, it is that religious ideas frequently vary in a society by age, sex, education, rural or urban residence, occupation, and the like.

But all of these qualifications and cautionary statements should not obscure the finding of a strong association at the Reformation and afterward between political and religious positions. Together with the finding of such an association in my earlier studies of primitive peoples, this observation at the Reformation suggests that the association is no mere happenstance nor a correlation peculiar merely to European events.

It also seems clear that, at the Reformation, political changes preceded religious changes. This is particularly striking in such countries as Poland and Austria in which each of several rapid changes in governmental structure were followed, as our hypotheses would predict, by the acceptance of specific changes in religious doctrine. These observations preclude any argument that the reverse sequence occurred, religious beliefs producing the political novelties of the early Reformation era.

Key to Table I

I. Nature of final Reformation settlement before 1700

    A.   Roman Catholic
    B.   Lutheran or Anglican
    C.   Calvinist or Zwinglian
    D.* B or C
    E.* A, B, or C
    F.* A, B, C, or specified others

        *Where 60 percent or more of body politic is of one faith, that faith is indicated in parentheses

II. Date of final Reformation settlement before 1700
    X.   Reformation made no serious inroads in society

III. Nature of regime in power at time of final Reformation settlement before 1700. Regimes of societies in which the Reformation made no serious inroads are described as of the period 1500-1550.

    A.   Commensal
    B.   Centralist
    C.   Limited centralist
    D.   Balanced
    E.   Heterarchic

The formal criteria for classifying regimes are given in earlier chapters. Certain of those criteria are embodied in this table as follows:

Centralist regimes: Only a governor is entered in Column VIII *and* an X or Z is recorded in Columns XI and XIV. *None* of the following notations appears in Column XII: A.1,3; B.1,2,3,4.

Limited centralist regimes: Only a governor is noted in Column VIII *and* there is *either* of the following:

      i. A notation of A.1 in column XIV
     ii. A notation of *one* of the following in Column XIV: A.2,3,4,5. Under XIII.A any two of the following are noted:

1,2,3,4. XIII.B contains either a 1#
or a 5#.

Balanced regimes: A governor and at least one
other agency are noted in Column VIII.
Column IX contains a notation of W and
Column XII a notation of B.1.

IV. Approximate date by which regime was established
which held power at the time of the final Reformation settlement before 1700

V. Nature of regime in 1490 (For a code, see III)
  X.   State did not exist in 1490

VI. Nature of regime in 1780 (For a code see V)
(Sections VII through XIV all refer to regime coded
under III)

VII. Scope of regime's authority

  A.   All free men
  B.   Governments of constituent bodies, these having
autonomous powers within their several domains to determine one or more of the following:
    1. The judicial structure and procedures em-
ployed
    2. The taxes that are levied and the units which
pay them
    3. The laws and ordinances that may be published
and enforced

VIII. Authorities having independent and original jurisdiction over some aspects of the regime's central
exercise of gubernaculum (governors are indicated
by an asterisk)

  A.   Assembly of all members of the body politic
  B.   A group of kinsmen
  C.   A diet (that is, one or more houses of Estates)
  D.   One or more councils
  E.   An individual

IX. Agencies by which constituent bodies share in the regime's central exercise of gubernaculum

    A.   Assembly of all members of the body politic

    B.   Diet

    C.   One or more councils or committees

    W.   Agencies are one or more of authorities specified under VIII above

    X.   None ascertained

X. Constituent bodies sharing in the regime's central exercise of gubernaculum by means of the agencies specified in IX above:

    A.   All members of the body politic

    B.   Towns

    C.   Rural districts—all free inhabitants and/or all landowners

    D.   Local organizations of nobles and/or gentry

    E.   Greater noble families

    F.   Nobles and/or gentry

    G.   Guilds

    H.   Administrative units (for example, quarters, amts) other than the above

    X.   None ascertained

XI. Constituent bodies sharing in the regime's local exercise of gubernaculum (the agencies by means of which this power is exercised being the constituent bodies themselves or one of those listed under IX above)

    Z.   There seem not to be any such local jurisdictions to be exercised

XII. Powers of constituent bodies sharing in the regime's central exercise of gubernaculum

    A.   Maintaining the regime

        1. Elect governor

        2. Share in exercise of regencies

        3. Right as an assemblage of constituent bodies to rebel against governor who breaches their privileges

          4. Right as individual constituent bodies to rebel against governor who breaches their privileges

B. Control over administrative staffing
    1. Name some or all major officials, these then being responsible in some measure to the constituent bodies
    2. Remove major officials who breach the law
    3. Name some or all major officials
    4. Nominate a slate of candidates for some or all major official posts, governor making appointments from this slate
    5. Consent to the accession to office of major officials named by governor

C. Supervision of administrative operations
    1. Supervise the collection and/or expenditure of taxes and aids
    2. Supervise trade and commerce
    3. Establish and/or maintain armies, militia, or fortifications
    4. Determine the uses made of armies or militia
    5. Consent to the establishing or revocation of alliances

(Constituent bodies listed under VIII or IX above)

W. Select or comprise authorities having independent and original jurisidiction in regime

X. None ascertained

XIII. Powers of constituent bodies sharing in the regime's central exercise of jurisdictio

A. Organization to exercise these powers
    1. Established rights of participation
    2. Established rules of procedure in deliberative sessions
    3. Established dates for meetings or right of participants to convene sessions as desired
    4. Established apparatus to pursue the legislature's work when that body is not in session

B. Decisions for which consent of constituent bodies may be sought (If their consent is required in principle, type of decision involved is followed by a cross-hatch (#))

1. Make or change laws
2. Codify laws
3. Exercise of highest judicial functions (for example, decisions in cases of treason, rebellion, lese-majesty)
4. Declare war or conclude treaties of peace
5. Levy or renew taxes; obtain or make loans

W. Constituent bodies listed under VIII above also undertake the regime's central exercise of jurisdictio

X. None ascertained

XIV. Powers of constituent bodies sharing in the regime's local exercise of gubernaculum

A. Control over staffing of local units of national administrative structure
   1. Name some or all major local officials, these then being responsible in some measure to the constituent bodies
   2. Name some or all major local officials
   3. Consent to major local officials named by governor
   4. Nominate a slate of candidates for major local official posts, governor making appointments from this slate
   5. Governor must choose major local officials from among that locality's inhabitants

B. Control over operation of local units of national administrative structure
   1. Control all or a large share of the local administration of the national system of justice and general administration
   2. Right to subject local administration by national officials to judicial review

X. None ascertained

Z. There seem not to be any such local jurisdictions to be exercised

TABLE I

Societies by type of regime
at their Reformation settlement

Societies	I	II	III	IV	V	VI	VII
Appenzell	E(C)	1524	A	1513	X	X	A
Florence	A	X	A	1282– 1366	A	X	A
Fribourg	A	X	A	1469	A	A	A
Glarus	E(C)	1532	A	1387– 1450	A	A	A
Poland	A	1607	A	1490– 1573	A	A	A,B.1,2
Schwyz	A	X	A	1353	A	A	A
Unterwalden	A	X	A	Before 1400	A	A	A
Uri	A	X	A	1373	A	A	A
Venice	A	X	A	1297	A	A	A
Zug	A	X	A	1415	A	A	A,B.1,2
Austria	A	1620	B	1521	D	B	B.1,2,3
Bavaria	A	1564	B	1505	B	B	A
Berg-Jülich	A	1614	B	1423	B	B	A
France	A	1685	B	1460	B	B	A,B.2
Ireland	A	X	B	1350	B	X	A
Lucerne	A	X	B	1424	B	A	A
Portugal	A	X	B	1490	B	B	A
Scotland (Highlands)	A	X	B	Before 1400	B	X	A
Solothurn	A	1533	B	1533	E	A	A
Spain	A	X	B	1492	B	B	B.1,2,3

TABLE I—*Continued*

VIII	IX	X	XI	XII	XIII	XIV
A	W	A	A	W	X	A.1
						B.1
D	W	G,H	Z	W	W	Z
A	W	A	Z	W	W	Z
A	W	A	Z	W	W	Z
C	W	D	D	W	W	A.1
						B.1
A	W	A	Z	W	W	Z
A	W	A	Z	W	W	Z
A	W	A	Z	W	W	Z
A	W	A	Z	W	W	Z
A	W	A	Z	W	W	Z
E*	X	X	X	X	A.1,2,4	X
					B.1,5#	
E*	B	B,F	X	C.1	A.4	X
					B.2,5	
E*	B	B,F	X	X	A.1,3	X
					B.4	
E*	B	B,F	X	X	B.1,2,	X
					3,4,5	
B*	X	X	Z	X	X	Z
D*	A	A	Z	C.5	A.1	Z
					B.4#5#	
E*	B	B,F	X	X	B.1	X
B*	X	X	Z	X	X	Z
D*	A	A	Z	B.5	X	Z
E*	B	B,F	X	X	B.1	X

TABLE I—*Continued*

Societies	I	II	III	IV	V	VI	VII
Brandenburg–Prussia	D(B)	1613	C	1450–1500	C	C	A
Denmark	B	1536	C	1460	C	B	A
England	B	1547–53	C	1400–1485	C	D	A
Hesse	D(B)	1605	C	1500	X	C	A
Saxony	B	1539	C	1425	C	C	A
Sweden	B	1536	C	1523	B	C	A
Württemberg	D(B)	1535	C	1514	B	C	A
Bohemia	C	1575–93	D	1500	B.1	X	A
Cleves-Mark	D(C)	1569	E	1480–90	E	X	A
Geneva	C	1536	D	1530	A.1	D	A
Hungary	E(C)	1540	D	1500	B.1	X	B.1,2
Scotland (Lowlands)	C	1560	D	1470–90	B.1	X	A
Transylvania	F(C)	1557	D	1541	X	X	B.1,2
Basel	C	1528	E	1521	E	E	A
Bern	X	1528	E	1500	A.2	E	A
Schaffhausen	C	1530	E	1411	E	E	A
United Provinces	F(C)	1579	E	1579	X	E	B.2
Zurich	C	1525	E	1444–1519	E	E	A

TABLE I—*Continued*

VIII	IX	X	XI	XII	XIII	XIV
E*	B	F	D	A.3 C.1,3,4	A.1 B.4,5#	A.1 B.1
E*	C	E	B,D	A.3 B.4	A.1,2,3 B.1,3#4,5	A.5
E*	B	B,F	B,C	B.2	A.1,2,3 B.1#5#	A.5 B.2
E*	B	B,F	B,D	A.2.B.4	A.1,2,3 B.4#5#	A.2,3
E*	B	B,F	H	A.2 C.1,3	A.1,2,4 B.1#5#	A.2
E*	B	B,C,F	B,C	A.1	A.1 B.1,3,4	A.1 B.1
E*	B	B	H	C.1	A.1,4 B.4,5#	A.5 B.1
C,E*	W	B,F	B,F	A.1.B.1 C.1,3,4	A.1,5 B.3#	A.2
B	W	B	B,C,F	W	W	A.1
A,D*	W	A	Z	B.1	B.1,4,5#	Z
C,E*	W	D	D	A.1.B.1,5 C.3	A.1,4 B.1#5	A.1,3
D,E*	W	B,E,F	B,E	B.1,5 C.1,2	A.1,2,3,4 B.1,5	A.2 B.1
C,E*	W	B,D	B,D	A.1,3 B.1	A.1 B.1,5	A.1 B.1
B	W	G	Z	W	W	Z
B	W	H	Z	W	W	Z
B	W	G	Z	W	W	Z
D	W	C	B,C,F	W	W	A.1 B.1
B	W	G	Z	W	W	A

[X]

A Wider View

NOW WE CAN LOOK BEYOND the Reformation and back upon it. What wider significance has our interpretation of Protestantism? In this chapter I discuss six questions, each addressed to some facet of this problem:[1]

1. Does the interpretation account for the immanence of high gods in societies outside western Europe?
2. Why did the political changes necessary for the Reformation occur in so many countries at about the same time?
3. How should we interpret the relation between Protestantism and rationalized capitalism?
4. What explanation can be offered for the Protestant stress upon predestination and upon the soul's corruption?
5. Why did individual Protestants conclude that they personally were corrupt?
6. What is the place of immanence as a topic for sociological concern?

The Immanence of Other High Gods

Does the interpretation given for the Reformation account for the immanence of high gods in societies outside western Europe? Without examining a sample of cases one cannot be certain. I have the impression, however, that this interpretation of immanence is fully consistent with data from only some of the other complex societies.[2] (It should be noted as possibly important for further research that, with the exception of Muscovy and Byzantium, none of these non-Western societies had reached the "evolutionary" level of those in early modern Catholic Europe. None had, for example, attained as clear a separation between religious and political institutions.)

We found (in Chapter I) that the great gods of classic civilizations in India, China, and Japan were far more immanental than is God as conceived by Jews and Christians. As we have seen, the major religions of Southern Asia and East Asia contained large elements of pantheism, the universe being therefore only an aspect of the divine nature rather than separated from it. The regimes of these societies were centralist. Moreover they were centralist in a degree unknown in the West. The continuing disputes over the source of "oriental despotism" should not conceal from us the lack of dispute over its existence in the Far East.[3] As in the West, centralist governments were not always strong, the word "despotism" referring rather to the form of the state. Among the features of this type of centralism were a lack of clear organizational separation between the political regime and religious institutions; the absence, in principle and practice, of participation by local authorities in the local or central exercise of jurisdictio; the division of local populations into arbitrary units (in China, for example, of five families), these units being creations of the central state and the bodies through which its administration regulated local life; the absence, locally or centrally, of legal practices, codes, and institutions significantly independent of the governor's will.

We have seen that the religions of ancient Greece and Rome contained many immanental features. The governments of those states vary from one period to another but they appear to be primarily commensal, centralist, or in the process of shifting between these two types of regime. But these cases are not absolutely clear. When republics, both Rome and Athens exhibited a curious mixture of commensalism and heterarchy, this requiring further study.

Eastern Orthodox forms of Christianity share all Roman Catholic beliefs concerning God's immanence. The states in which the Eastern rite took root were uniformly centralist: Orthodoxy's greatest centers being the Byzantine Empire and the Muscovite grand duchy.

Weber observed that in Judaism the scope of God's immanence was conceived as more restricted than in the great religions of Central and East Asia.[4] Pre-Reformation Christianity and Islam seem like Judaism in this respect. (Protestantism moves further from immanental beliefs than any of these.) The various regimes of the ancient Hebrews and of most Islamic states were centralist or, as in Athens and Rome, were mixed polities combining commensal or centralist structures with heterarchic structures. Thus we again have cases only sometimes consistent with the hypotheses here advanced concerning immanence and regime.

A next important step is to decide whether these and other religions can be sensibly arranged on some scale of the pervasiveness, within each, of immanental doctrine and whether differences among these several regimes will explain those doctrinal variations. That step will require further research. It is certain that I have examined only some cases from the array of societies and religions. Among the religious beliefs that need special consideration may be doctrines that had only a brief day in history: doctrines like those of the mystery religions of Hellenic civilization, of the Hussite and Anabaptist movements, and of the smaller cults of Islam. By means of comparisons among their delicate variations on the conception of immanence, and by examining the situations in which they arose, we may be able to specify more precisely the conditions which determine experiences of immanence and those which determine experiences of transcendence as well.

It is quite possible that the account of immanence I have given is limited in presently unknown ways by the two instances I have considered at length: primitives' beliefs in immanence of the soul and the problem of immanence at the Reformation. My account may distinguish properties irrelevant for some manifestations of immanence and it may omit distinctions crucial for other manifestations. In associating declining beliefs in immanence with certain complexities of social organization, I am sensitive to the common judgment that Christianity is itself sometimes explained as a response to declining ethnic differentiation and, simultaneously, to cultural and political unification in the Roman world.[5] And Christianity is distinguished by special doctrines. As compared with other religions existing at the time of its origin, it is a monotheism. It is universal in scope and ethical and salvationary in emphasis. It is also exclusivist, requiring not the addition of God to existing pantheons of deities but an acceptance of him as the only deity. It sponsors a great missionary movement to convert the world. It proposes as fact the mystery of incarnation in which God, fully divine and transcendent, became fully historical as well. Existing studies provide no convincing explanation for the rise of these beliefs or for their relations to immanence and transcendence.

Why Did the Political Changes Necessary for the Reformation Occur in So Many Countries at About the Same Time?

It is striking that a continent filled with centralist and commensal regimes saw the rise within a particular half century of several heterarchic, balanced, and limited centralist regimes, each of these soon adopting Protestantism. I know of no well-documented explanation for these events, but can suggest where the explanation may lie.

Between the late fourteenth century and the early part of the fifteenth a great many European regimes showed signs of faltering. Many feudal lands and populations had been greatly enlarged by dynastic inheritance, by success in war, or by the settling of vast tracts of wasteland. In these lands, the power of the general government was severely overtaxed. These governments were further weakened by continuous wars among the states of Europe, wars that usually sprang both from the conditions that had produced the expansion of Europe's several nations and from that expansion itself. These wars drained from governments the energies and resources that might otherwise have gone into creating institutions capable of handling the enlarged tasks of administration. As a result, we find kingdom after kingdom, each having once been unified and strong, collapsing into what some historians have called a neofeudal state, a state in which cities and greater nobles established their own armies and exercised gubernaculum almost at will. In some countries this process continued well through the eighteenth century.

The outcome of this collapse varied, although for reasons as yet unknown. In Poland and Hungary fragmentation continued, producing at the end regimes far too weak to govern their large territories or to protect themselves against avaricious neighbors. In such countries as Spain, France, Portugal, and Austria, centralist regimes became absolutist or were greatly strengthened by the development of new bureaucratic institutions for administration. In still other states, as for example in Scandinavia, Germany, and England, the administrative apparatus of central governments was augmented and, at the same time, those governments continued to use local authorities as their agents in the conduct of affairs.[6] Finally, in Switzerland and some of the smaller German states, matters took still another turn. The ebbing power of overlords, whether secular or ecclesiastic, removed foreign control over an indigenous polity with the result that local powers were free to shape the newly independent states. The degree of organized heterogeneity in the populations of those states seems to have determined the character of the governments which then developed.

I am suggesting, in short, that political conditions in early modern Europe made it possible for regimes to survive only if they developed modes of governing which were effective for territories, populations, and problems of a size and complexity previously unknown, and further, that under the direct influence of these emergent political conditions, or as a result of changes they forced on other states, new types of regime proliferated.

In this connection, one cannot help being struck by the persistence in many European regimes to our own day of those characteristics related to immanence and established in each state at the Reformation. As Lipset and others observe, Europe's strong parliamentary democracies—heterarchic or balanced regimes in each case—are now found only in traditionally Protestant states. It is tempting to follow other observers in seeing the "totalitarian democracy" of France from Rousseau to De Gaulle as a persist-

ence of secular and religious doctrines strongly immanental
in character and of regimes embodying either commensal
or centralist principles.[7] It is apparent that Fascism and
Leninism, each a secular doctrine that conceives values and
the ultimately valuable as immanent in history, took root in
lands where strongly centralist and even absolutist polities
provided the prevailing tradition. And, some writers note,
it was in Austria and Bavaria, both traditionally Catholic
and absolutist, that the Nazis found acceptance for the more
immanental features of their doctrine—the spermy mystique
of blood and soil.

Let us suppose that these gross continuities are valid.
They might be explained as follows: once there is established a mode of governing that is capable of dealing with
administrative problems approaching contemporary magni-
tudes, changes are unlikely in the most abstract characteristics which define that mode of government. Such an
argument has been made in specific cases. It is said, for
example, that the French revolutionaries were so shaped by
the more general characteristics of the Old Regime and so
pressed to govern effectively from the moment they came
to power that, both by preference and necessity, they continued the existing pattern of centralized government.[8] It
has likewise been argued that only a conquering foreign
power already possessing a basically different regime and
the resources and determination to impose it on the van-
quished can break this pattern of indigenous development.
I cite these observations only to suggest that, should they
have merit, there then follows the task of defining those
more abstract qualities of regimes that are most likely to
persist. The characteristics here associated with immanence
may be among them.

On the Relation Between Protestantism and
Rationalized Capitalism

I confine my remarks to the most important attempt to
establish such a relation, that of Max Weber.[9] Weber was
not the first to note an association between the prior establishment in a country of Protestantism and the early and

successful establishment there of modern commerce and industry. What distinguished his contribution was an effort to identify some of the more general characteristics of Protestant doctrine (he wrote particularly of its inner-worldly activism) and of modern economic enterprise (he stressed particularly its "rationality"). He then showed by means of comparative studies that no religion or economy with quite these properties had appeared at any other place or time in history. Despite his uncommon scholarship and his exceptional understanding of societies and economies, Weber's criteria for a religion's economic consequences were rather vague and his results inconclusive.

I also have no firm answer to questions about the relation between Protestantism and capitalism, but I have data relevant for answers:

1. England, certain Swiss cities, the German principalities of Cleves, Mark, and Saxony, and the United Provinces are usually given as among the sites at which capitalism first exhibited its modern characteristics, this occurring in the seventeenth century and later. (No Catholic state, except France, is among those commonly listed as among the first to undergo economic modernization.) Apart from France, each of these societies which early experienced modernization was already Protestant. Cleves, Mark, and the United Provinces were Calvinist. So were the more economically advanced of the Swiss cantons. Saxony was a Lutheran state. England, by the time of its economic modernization, was officially Anglican but provided legal toleration for a variety of Calvinist churches. In all of these societies, native merchants had gained strong participation in heterarchic, balanced, or limited-centralist regimes well before each regime adopted the Reformation. In England, merchants further increased their participation, especially from 1688.

2. In the states which Weber's critics like most to cite against him, the commercial cities of Italy, merchants, artisans, or both, operated commensal regimes and Catholicism remained secure.[10]

3. As Weber pointed out, Protestantism alone, or even Calvinism, was not a sufficient precondition for the estab-

lishment of modern capitalism. It is interesting, however, that Protestantism, whether Lutheran or Calvinist, was associated with early modernization of the economy *only* in countries where merchants or artisans and not merely nobles, participated in heterarchic, balanced, or limited centralist regimes. On the other hand, there were countries in which merchants had an important role in one of these types of regime but economic modernization occurred only slowly. Scotland is a case in point.

4. If Protestantism had any role in connection with the organization of the economy, one may ask whether this was a function of religious doctrine, of the forms of governmental regime so closely associated with a Protestant ascendancy, of both, or of factors connected to both but different from either. This clearly is an empirical problem and one not yet well explored. Pending studies that allow a firm answer, I lean toward the following line of explanation: modern economic enterprise, in the sense of endeavors designed and pursued with little attention to any considerations other than those bearing on the continuous maximization of wealth, could arise only if (a) such enterprise was legitimated, (b) social forces strongly competitive with such enterprise were minimized, and (c) there already existed persons having the knowledge, motives, and resources to capitalize on these conditions. In early modern times only merchants or artisans were likely to have such knowledge, motivation, and resources. Their interests and perspectives were legitimated to the extent they had a significant share in the exercise of gubernaculum.

In commensal regimes, even those controlled by merchants and artisans, the legitimation for maximizing wealth was more limited. On the one hand, great commercial and industrial wealth was usually produced in this period by individuals and firms, not by the social whole; by private enterprise and only in small measure by assistance from central planners. On the other hand, participation in gubernaculum was available to people in commensal regimes not as individuals with special interests and talents but as equal members of a single body politic. I suggest that these considerations legitimize private economic undertakings but not their pursuit to the extent that they threaten to subvert the equality of participants in the regime. In this way a commensal regime provides conditions strongly competitive with the single-minded maximization of wealth.

By contrast, merchants and artisans who participate in heterarchic, balanced, or limited centralist regimes have their enterprises thereby legitimized and, because they participate in a regime as constituent bodies which have special economic interests, they gain legitimation for the pursuit of their special interests as well. I recognize, of course, that there are always conditions that limit the single-minded pursuit of wealth. I suggest only that the kinds of regime associated with Protestantism, when coupled with the strong participation by merchants and artisans in the affairs of such regimes, provided in early modern times fewer restrictions to the full development of economic activity.

5. One must distinguish the conditions under which economic modernization first became established and those which fueled its further elaboration and expansion. Weber proposed an explanation he then quietly abandoned: the argument that modern capitalism's continuous elaboration was due to the activism of Calvinist entrepreneurs, these entrepreneurs ever seeking through economic success the reassurance that they were predestined to be among God's Elect. (It was fortunate that he dropped this argument because, as he fleetingly acknowledged, many of the Protestant sectaries he chose as epitomes of the "Protestant ethic" were doctrinally opposed to Calvin's notions about predestination, among those sectaries being the Methodists, Mennonites, Moravians, Quakers, most Pietists, and many Baptists.)[11] Unhappily, Weber did not offer an aspect of Protestant doctrine to replace this notion. He did suggest, however, that capitalist development continued not so much in the hands of the elites who first undertook its establishment as in those of upwardly mobile citizens fighting for wealth and power.

If this is so, and it seems consistent with what is known,

one may be able to abandon not only predestination but all of Weber's search for a master religious doctrine motivating economic growth across generations of descendants of the same families. One may find that the role of merchants in government was the key to economic growth. One may find that Protestant entrepreneurs, like the great merchants of Catholic lands, were generally content with their gains and that the whole economy was moved forward by efforts of the still disadvantaged men of rising classes. One may find, however, that the rising classes in Protestant countries had the special advantage of being upwardly mobile in a society that legitimized the individual pursuit of economic gain.

6. In recent years the study of economic development in the new nations has led to a fresh search for "functional equivalents" of Protestant doctrine, this on the assumption that some features of that doctrine facilitated economic growth in the West. I have raised some questions about the importance of the doctrine whether taken by itself or in combination with other variables. I note, however, that current efforts to find its equivalents seek these as driving and predisposing motives whereas my proposals would give them a different role.

Thus David McClelland's recent cross-cultural studies seem to show that "inner-worldly activism" or something very like it has appeared in certain primitive societies, in ancient and classic societies of both East and West, and in Catholic societies as well as Protestant.[12] He has shown that there were great fluctuations of emphasis on such activism within each society he studied. If this "equivalent" of Protestantism is to be taken seriously as important for economic development one must now specify the further conditions under which men will spend themselves on rationalized economic enterprise rather than on other objectives. The highly provisional account I have given for early modern economic development suggests that the motive to achieve in this sphere may arise coeval with collective legitimation and opportunity for economic entrepreneurship rather than being its necessary predecessor. This makes of the achievement motive more an evaluation of an existential situation than its source or motive. I grant, of course, that without the rise of some such evaluation it is hard to imagine the possibilities of the political and economic situation being exploited to the full. But a judgment that activism is coeval with development rather than its source indicates different priorities for economic planners.

Corruption and Predestination

Early in our discussion we concluded that there were two great clusters of ideas that distinguished Protestants from Catholics, the denial of immanence being fundamental to the first cluster and the Reformers' beliefs in predestination and the irremediable corruption of the soul underlying the second. Can the conditions that seem to explain a denial of God's immanence also account for the second cluster of Protestant beliefs?

For generations, apologetic writers have represented the formula "justification by faith alone" as the essence of Protestant doctrine.[13] Certainly these words expressed for Luther the essential insight gained when the Gospel's inner meaning suddenly opened before his eyes. They describe the road to salvation for Christians who find the soul's essence irremediably incompatible with God's will.

If human nature is perdurably corrupt, neither it nor its acts can be worthy of God. Yet the Scriptures say that some men are saved. This, Luther argued, must be a consequence of God's action, not man's. He must accept men as righteous despite their corruption.

God's goodness toward irremediably sinful men and his acceptance of them can be reasonable only if interpreted as an act of love. Because so extraordinary an act of love is beyond human reason, knowledge of it, and a willingness to accept it as true, must also be a gift from God.

In the Protestant economy of salvation, the faith these divine gifts engender is *fiducia*, that is, a trust that God will never impute to man the punishment and degradation his transgressions deserve. True faith, said Luther, is this confidence mixed with awe, humility, shame, and gratitude.

The fruit of this faith is an answering love for God which invariably shows itself in good works. God esteems good works, but works as such are irrelevant for a man's justification. What is relevant is the establishment of a relation of love between God and man.

If the doctrine of justification by faith is itself rooted in the notion that human nature is essentially corrupt, how can one explain the rise of that conception of human nature? Such a belief might have a variety of sources. I find it plausible to think that, at the Reformation, the important conditions were the same as those that produced a denial of God's immanence. I suggest that the Protestants' conception of human nature is consistent with the involvement of constituent bodies in heterarchic, balanced, and limited centralist regimes. The involvement of constituent bodies in such a regime embodies an ineradicable self-interest in the very institutions of the state.

The source and justification for any regime is the "common interest" in the body politic. But each member of the body politic, each constituent body, seeks his own welfare. The welfare of each is a special or selfish interest in two senses: (a) it is a personal gratification, not the common good, that ultimately is the aim in view and (b) the attainment by some constituent bodies of personal gratification prevents others from doing likewise. As we have seen, the structure of centralist and commensal regimes allows constituent bodies to participate legitimately in gubernaculum only as creatures or agents of the regime, hence as servants of the common interest. As we have also seen, constituent bodies in heterarchic, balanced, and limited centralist regimes may legitimately serve their own interests as well as the common interest. The structure of these latter regimes indicates that, in them, service to special interests is an ineradicable condition of government, the existence of special interests, their persistence, and their independent powers being a premise for the development of any viable government.

It also seems to me that these same political conditions are a likely source of the Protestant emphasis on predestination. Actually, the notion of predestination was held in similar form by Protestants and Catholics. It was the belief that God had from eternity declared and known the course of history and of every individual's life career. If one accepted the Catholic view that human nature is compatible with God's will and the Catholic doctrine that Christ is immanent in the Church, one could see God's eternal purpose as encompassing the salvation of most of the faithful. Human nature and an immanent, omnipotent Christ would assure it. If, however, one accepted the Protestant view of human nature and the Church, the likelihood of a man's salvation was appreciably lessened. Human nature was inherently in revolt against God and, although the visible Church honored God, it imparted to believers no puissant sacramental grace. For these reasons, we may consider Protestant concerns with predestination as grounded in whatever conditions produced the Reformed notions about human nature and immanence.

Calvin's special position on predestination differed from Luther's primarily in degree, Calvin believing that only a very few men would be saved. This difference may be due to Calvinism's association with heterarchic or balanced regimes. Those regimes provide a greater role in gubernaculum for the durable "selfish" interests of constituent bodies than do the limited centralist regimes in which Lutheranism arose.

I have stressed the seemingly common roots of (a) doctrines concerning immanence and (b) doctrines of human nature and of predestination. One should, however, note a point of difference. Rather soon after the Reformation settlements, the Protestant doctrines concerning human nature and predestination began to be modified and qualified whereas those immediately concerned with immanence have continued to our time as the core of a Protestant outlook. An exploration of the reasons for the difference is beyond the scope of our present interest, but I suggest one seek those reasons in the development, in heterarchic, balanced, and limited centralist regimes, of new institutions which reduced the impact on gubernaculum of the "selfishness" in constituent bodies, thus permitting a more optimistic view of human nature and of the likelihood of salvation for the faithful.

Feelings of Personal Corruption

Even if some regimes are penetrated by ineradicable interests that are both special and selfish, why should men conclude that they personally are ineradicably selfish? An answer to this question also requires further research, but suggestions toward an answer can be given. The case is easiest to state for members of a society's body politic. In some types of regime these people do participate, whether directly or through representatives, as special and selfish interests. To that degree they compromise the common interest. To the extent that the common interest comprises the broadest system of intelligent and intelligible order within which they live, it is both the apex and the ground of their careers and is likely to be considered as of ultimate or even consummate value. To view oneself as participating in the subversion of the ultimately valuable is to judge oneself essentially corrupt. Because the pursuit and enjoyment of the ultimately valuable provides coherence and order for the whole of an individual's career, he must then view the whole of that career as tainted with corruption.

It is possible that one should conclude from this argument that feelings of personal corruption will be strongest among those families and individuals most directly and completely involved with a regime by virtue of their special interests in the exercise of gubernaculum. Such an argument might serve to explain two facts from Calvinism's history: first, that Arminian and other more optimistic views of human nature were generally promoted not by the upper elites of Calvinist societies but by persons of somewhat lower status, and, second, that within a century after Calvin's death his darkest views on predestination most often continued as official doctrine only in those lands then ruled by a heterarchic elite (e.g., New England, the United Provinces, Basel, and Zurich). Calvinist lands then having balanced regimes were less likely to stress predestinarian beliefs in their official creeds (e.g., Transylvania, Cleves, Mark, and Bohemia).[14] The spread of Arminianism would then be explained on the ground that persons outside a society's governing elite, being less directly involved in employing the society's regime in the service of special interests, would take a more optimistic view of human nature. The association between predestination and heterarchy would be explained by the greater penetration of heterarchic than of balanced regimes by special interests.

Immanence as a Topic for Sociological Concern

If we put to one side the religious context in which the idea first arose, we find that immanence has to do with a relation between one actor, that is one individual or organization, and another: an attribute of one actor's character or "personality" coming itself also to exist in the character or personality of another. As we found, immanence is only one form in which actors influence one another.

Transcendence is not the opposite of immanence. It stands for the ability of an individual or group to influence simultaneously more than one person, group, object, or event. In traditional doctrine, God is completely transcendent. This means that he can simultaneously direct all things and events.

The data of religion illustrate the combinations possible between immanence and transcendence: there are gods who shape or create the world and thereafter ignore it. Eighteenth-century Deism is only one instance of a belief that creation was the limit of a god's direct action toward his creatures. A Deist's god could not therefore be considered either immanent or transcendent.

But if a god is presently active in sustaining or governing his creation, he may be either immanent or transcendent, neither, or both. Protestantism pictures him transcendent but not immanent. In such pantheisms as classical Buddhism or Hinduism he is immanent but not transcendent, the whole universe being a present activity of deity and coterminous with, or a part of, deity's very essence—of deity's personality or "inner" life. In these theologies there is only one time and place, and deity's existence encompasses it. The very possibility of transcendence is obliterated. Quite frequently the spirits worshipped by ancestral cults, by animists, or by polytheists are not immanent and, because they are thought limited in power to a single course of action at one place at a particular time, are not transcendent either. Catholicism pictures God as immanent and infinitely transcendent. Table II presents these combinations.

TABLE II
Combinations of Immanence and Transcendence

Active?	Immanent?	Transcendent?	Illustrations
Yes	Yes	Yes	Catholicism
	Yes	No	Buddhism Hinduism
	No	Yes	Protestantism
	No	No	Some ancestral cults and animisms
No	No	No	Deism

Although immanence is not the opposite of transcendence, it nonetheless limits the possible relations between a transcendent actor and others. If attributes of a transcendent actor's character become immanent in the character of some other actor, those attributes cannot be radically alien to the characteristics of their new owner. Protestant controversialists stressed this point. It is one of the great themes in Ernst Troeltsch's *Social Teaching of the Christian Churches* and in H. Richard Niebuhr's extension and generalization of Troeltsch's arguments.[15] As Troeltsch and Niebuhr say, when God's attributes—his purpose, will, goodness, and the like—although transcendent are also considered immanent in the Church and sacraments, God's character cannot be seen as radically at variance with the social order as it presently exists. His attributes can become immanent only if something existing in the historical world is appropriate to their nature. But anything that successfully exists in a particular time and place—the Church, for example—must, in turn, be suited to the sustenance and routines and potentialities of other things that share its time and place—for example, other groups and institutions. The divinity in the Church may seek to transform the social order but it cannot function immanently without accepting many qualities of that social order as useful and good. It cannot find them ultimately demonic. It cannot be "wholly other" than they.[16]

But there is no reason to restrict the ideas of immanence and transcendence, or of their relations, sources, and consequences, to studies of religion. All individuals and groups have a character—an organization of "personal" attributes. All actors influence the things with which they come in contact and at times that influence will be experienced as immanental. Thus Marx and Hitler were avowed atheists, but in the social order for which each fought the essential character of the society at large was to permeate every individual and institution.

Among modern sociologists, Talcott Parsons has given special stress to the pervasive importance for social science of studies of immanence and transcendence, pointing beyond religious studies to the presence of these phenomena in all social situations. For example, he introduces Weber's *The Sociology of Religion* with these words:[17]

> . . . this book is *the* most crucial contribution of our century to the comparative and evolutionary understanding of the relations between . . . society and culture generally. . . .

As Parsons there interprets Weber's work on religion, its master theme is that of the emergence in history of conceptions of God's transcendence and the decline over time of beliefs in the pervasiveness of his immanence. But Parsons generalizes the importance of Weber's analysis to include not merely the relations between social organization and religious doctrines but also all relations between "society and culture." What justifies that generalization?

I take it that Parsons' conclusion rests on a conception of culture which he shares with most sociologists. Culture, in this conception, refers to anything that serves as a criterion by means of which organizations make choices: by means of which they formulate objectives, allocate resources, select means appropriate for ends, and implement programs. As we have seen, it is only as collective actors—as social systems—that organizations undertake these activities.

An organization, Parsons and others argue, can employ some criterion in making choices only if it invests that criterion with normativity. This means that the criterion is judged relevant for the members' relations with one another and for their joint undertakings, that it is construed as proper by those who apply it and by those to whom it applies, and that it is enforced, when necessary, by agents who legitimately act on behalf of the common interest. Thus a possible criterion for choice actually becomes operative in an organization's activities when that criterion becomes a norm—a social rule. The culture of an organization is the body of norms it employs.

By this line of reasoning, norms, hence culture, are among the major attributes of an organization's character as a collective actor. They are the equivalent in a group of the attitudes, evaluations, knowledge, commitments, and acquired skills that constitute the personality of an individual. They function as "powers"—as foundations and guidelines for action—but these attributes themselves are neither the action which they shape nor the actor which bears them. On these grounds Weber's sociology of religion can be interpreted as dealing with the degree to which culture is separated from the organization which it guides and from which it grew. Transcendence represents the differentiation of culture from the organization which bears it. Immanence represents a limitation on the possible alienation between an organization and its culture and also a mode by which culture guides an organization's action and the action of that organization's members and parts.

If this idea is so important, why has it not been more fully developed since Weber wrote? One reason is that discussion of the place of immanence and transcendence in social life requires that organizations be treated as actors and, conse-

quently, that they, and not just the individuals who participate in them, be conceived as possessing purposes and as
making choices, as having commitments and as implementing decisions. It happens that exactly those approaches in
sociological theory most relevant for studies of immanence
have instead been employed on topics other than the
analysis of the total collective actor. Thus various modern
functionalisms analyze acts and their interrelations with sur-
prisingly little reference to the organizations from which
these acts presumably arise. And those analytic schemes,
strongest in characterizing properties of organizations, focus
on the detailed morphology of organizations rather than on
each organization as a whole unit and on the acts each under-
takes. My purpose is not to promote one of these several
approaches as against another, but to point to the alterna-
tives and to the relative neglect of the perspective from
which problems of immanence and transcendence arise.

The rest of this chapter is devoted to three problems il-
lustrative of those that are understood only by taking account
of an organization's wholistic character and of that character's immanence or transcendence.

1. *Collective Character and Cultus:* Let us assume that
it makes sense to speak of an organization's character as
being different from other aspects of that organization. On
that assumption it makes further sense to believe that the
collective character will be the object of efforts at understanding and conceptualization and that some authoritative
procedure will appear to declare its properties and to judge
the legitimacy of programs and proposals according to their
compatability with those properties. This is an activity we
associate in total societies with religious bodies, but not with
them alone. Institutions for higher education share in this
task, describing the essential features of a society and its culture and appraising both. Artists try to objectify and judge
these same essentials. The higher courts perform an analogous activity in relation to governmental acts. Social controversies often turn on precisely these questions. Selznick
has urged that this function of defining "character" be recognized explicitly as a major concern of the governing board

of a corporation in better articulating the corporation's structure with its purposes and character.[18] We need to understand the conditions which govern the independence, elaboration, and force of such activities and agencies. The present study suggests that the immanence of an organization's character is one such condition. The next two sections of this chapter expand this point.

2. *Institutionalization:* Groups within a society are institutionalized to the extent their functions and organization are designed and committed to serve the common interest and to the degree that the common interest is identified and authoritatively defined. It may be that the political conditions which work against immanence work also against institutionalization precisely because they make the common interest so difficult to identify in a conclusive fashion. A consequence, I propose, is that organizations under heterarchic, balanced, or limited centralist regimes must then rest their legitimation on their benefits to particular groups and interests and must make their services attractive to those special publics thus reinforcing the parochial concerns of both. I propose also that organizations (colleges or large corporations, for example) which, under these conditions, move on their own to become institutional are likely to become the objects of skepticism and even of political controversy precisely because their action implies a precise specification of the common interest that finds no counterpart in the society's constitutional structure.

3. *Secularization:* It would seem, other things equal, that an immanent order leaves open less ground for purely secular concerns. If some groups or institutions in the historical present are also divinity or the ultimately valuable itself they bear an unchallengeable authority. As agencies in history, everything they touch in the daily conduct of their affairs must shape itself to their needs. Their influence is unlike that exercised in the generalized commandments and authority of an active but purely transcendent entity. Such generalized commandments specify ends but tend to leave the means of action subject to free exploration and choice. (Moreover, when cast in the form of generalized principles

or objectives, the meaning and implications attached to commandments may appropriately be taken to vary somewhat according to the time and place of their application.)[19] When, however, divinity or something else of ultimate value is immanent in a person or organization, the current historical form of that person or organization shapes the "divine" command as communicated. Fulfillments of such commands are limited therefore to actions judged unlikely to subvert the current historical form embodying the thing of ultimate value. Thus, as in the Second Vatican Council, the divine church can legitimately change its outward form, shedding one "appearance" for another more suited to its current purpose and circumstances, but, until it has done so, the rest of the world must either adapt to its present outward form or risk finding itself cast in opposition to its god. In this manner the immanence of whatever men consider ultimately valuable limits the range of purely secular pursuits, brakes the rate of social change, and circumscribes the adaptability of a social order.

NOTES

Abbreviations used for frequently cited references.

CMeH *The Cambridge Mediaeval History,* 8 vols. Cambridge: Cambridge University Press, 1924-36.

CMH *The Cambridge Modern History,* 12 vols. New York: The Macmillan Co., 1906-25.

DHBS *Dictionnaire Historique et Biographique de la Suisse,* 7 vols. Neuchatel: Administration du Dictionnaire Historique et Biographique de la Suisse, 1921-33.

ENEC Albert Goodwin (Editor). *The European Nobility in the Eighteenth Century, Studies of the Nobilities of the Major European States in the Pre-Reform Era.* London: Adam and Charles Black, 1953.

ERE *The Encyclopaedia of Religion and Ethics,* 12 vols. New York: Charles Scribner's Sons, 1908-15.

NCMH *The New Cambridge Modern History,* series of volumes presently incomplete. Cambridge: Cambridge University Press.

Preface

1. The primary social skills are the means, necessary but never sufficient, by which every social relationship is undertaken and from which specialized varieties of social interaction may develop. A survey of relevant literature appears in Guy E. Swanson, "The Routinization of Love: Structure and Process in Primary Relations," in Samuel Z. Klausner (Editor), *The Quest for Self-Control: Classic Philosophies and Social Science,* New York: The Free Press of Glencoe, 1965, pp. 160-209.

2. The single most useful statement I have found on this topic is Paul Tillich's essay *The Courage to Be,* New Haven: Yale University Press, 1952. Important sociological statements appear in: Emile Durkheim, *Suicide, A Study in Sociology* (John A. Spaulding and George Simpson, Translators), Glencoe: The Free Press, 1951; Talcott Parsons, "The Place of Ultimate Values in Sociological Theory," *International Journal of Ethics,* 45 (April 1935), pp. 282-316;

263

Talcott Parsons, Introduction to Max Weber, *The Sociology of Religion* (Ephriam Fischoff, Translator), Boston: Beacon Press, 1963, pp xix-lxvii; Ralph Linton, *The Study of Man,* New York: D. Appleton Century Co., Inc., 1936, chapter 7. Some related works are reviewed in: Clyde Kluckhohn, "Culture and Behavior," in Gardner Lindzey (Editor), *Handbook of Social Psychology,* vol. 2, Cambridge: Addison-Wesley Publishing Co., 1954, pp. 921-76; Alex Inkeles and Daniel J. Levinson, "National Character," *Ibid.,* pp. 977-1020.

3. Ann Arbor: The University of Michigan Press, 1960.

4. Readers unfamiliar with my previous work on religion may be interested in the range of phenomena which this approach seems to explain: applied to a sample of fifty primitive and ancient societies, the present interpretation of theological doctrines led to success in predicting the presence or absence of monotheism, of pantheons of great gods, of ancestral spirits, of reincarnation, and of the soul's immanence in the body. It led also to correct forecasts of the prevalence of witchcraft, of the likelihood that a monotheistic god will be active in earthly affairs rather than removed from or indifferent to them, and of the degree to which spiritual beings are believed interested in the moral quality of human behavior.

5. Although the idea of immanence is very old, the word itself was not commonly used in theological writings until the nineteenth century. For surveys of its meaning in Christian theology, see: Arthur C. McGiffert, "The God of Spinoza as Interpreted by Herder," *Hibbert Journal,* 3 (July 1905), pp. 706-26 and his article "Immanence" in James Hastings (Editor), *The Encyclopaedia of Religion and Ethics,* vol 7, New York: Charles Scribner's Sons, 1914, pp. 167-72. See also: Borden P. Bowne, *The Immanence of God,* Boston: Houghton Mifflin, 1905; Salisbury F. Davenport, *Immanence and Incarnation,* Cambridge: Cambridge University Press, 1925; Heinrich J. D. Denzinger, *The Sources of Catholic Dogma* (Roy J. Deferrari, Translator), London: B. Herder Book Co., 1947; Jacques Maritain, *The Person and the Common Good* (John J. Fitzgerald, Translator), New York: Charles Scribner's Sons, 1947; William Temple, *Nature, Man, and God,* London: Macmillan and Co., Ltd., 1935; Paul Tillich, *The Protestant Era* (James L. Adams, Translator), Chicago: The University of Chicago Press, 1948. Statements of particular relevance for sociologists appear in Weber, *op. cit.* and in Alfred L. Kroeber and Clyde Kluckhohn, "Culture, A Critical Review of Concepts and

Definitions," *Papers of the Peabody Museum of American Archaeology and Ethnology*, Harvard University, vol. 47, no. 1, 1952, pp. viii-223. Both in nineteenth-century theology and in the theory of culture, the work of Johann G. Herder is pivotal. His basic theological statement is *God, Some Conversations* (Frederick H. Burkhardt, Translator), New York: Veritas Press, 1940. Good secondary treatments appear in Frank McEachran, *The Life and Philosophy of Johann Gottfried Herder*, Oxford: The Clarendon Press, 1939 and in G. A. Wells, *Herder and After, A Study in the Development of Sociology*. The Hague: Mouton and Co., 1959.

I. Immanence and the Reformation Controversies

1. Weber, *op. cit.* and his *The Protestant Ethic and the Spirit of Capitalism* (Talcott Parsons, Translator), New York: Charles Scribner's Sons, 1930.

2. Swanson, 1960, *op. cit.*, chapter 7.

3. Weber, 1930, *op. cit.*, pp. 104-5. My discussion of immanental doctrines in the major religions was based upon this book of Weber's and upon his trilogy: *Ancient Judaism* (Hans H. Gerth and Don Martindale, Translators), Glencoe, Ill.: The Free Press, 1952; *The Religion of India* (Hans H. Gerth and Don Martindale, Translators), Glencoe, Ill.: The Free Press, 1958; *The Religion of China* (Hans H. Gerth, Translator), Glencoe, Ill.: The Free Press, 1951. Other works of particular use for that discussion were:

Greece and Rome: Franz Altheim, *A History of Roman Religion* (Harold Mattingly, Translator), London: Methuen and Co., Ltd., 1938; Martin P. Nilsson, *A History of Greek Religion* (F. J. Fielden, Translator), Oxford: The Clarendon Press, 1949.

Judaism: Israel I. Efros, *Ancient Jewish Philosophy, A Study In Metaphysics and Ethics*, Detroit: Wayne State University Press, 1964; R. E. Clements, *God and Temple*, Philadelphia: Fortress Press, 1965. Yehezkel Kaufmann, *The Religion of Israel from Its Beginnings to the Babylonian Exile* (Moshe Greenberg, Translator), Chicago: The University of Chicago Press, 1960; Johannes Pedersen, *Israel, Its Life and Culture*, 2 vols., London: Oxford University Press, 1946.

Islam: Hamilton H. R. Gibb, *Mohammedanism, An Historical Survey*, London: Oxford University Press, 1961; Gustave E. von Grunebaum (Editor), *Unity and Variety in*

Muslim Civilization, Chicago: The University of Chicago Press, 1955.
India, China, and Japan: Robert N. Bellah, *Tokugawa Religion,* Glencoe, Ill.: The Free Press, 1957; Edwin O. Reischauer and John K. Fairbank, *East Asia, The Great Tradition,* Boston: Houghton Mifflin Co., 1960; Thomas G. P. Spear (Editor), *The Oxford History of India,* Oxford: The Clarendon Press, 1961.

4. Denzinger, *op. cit.*; Adolf Harnack, *Outlines of the History of Dogma* (Edwin K. Mitchell, Translator), Boston: The Beacon Press, 1957; Joseph Pohle, *Dogmatic Theology* (Arthur Preuss, Translator), 12 vols., St. Louis: B. Herder Book Co., 1929-34; Hastings, *op. cit.*, 12 vols., 1908-15; F. E. Mayer, *The Religious Bodies of America,* St. Louis: Concordia Publishing House, 1954.

5. Brian A. Gerrish, *Grace and Reason, A Study in the Theology of Luther,* Oxford: The Clarendon Press, 1962, pp. 9-17; John S. Whale, *The Protestant Tradition, An Essay in Interpretation,* Cambridge: Cambridge University Press, 1955.

6. Quoted in Mayer, *op. cit.*, p. 94.

7. *Ibid.*, p. 98

8. *Ibid.*, pp. 52-53.

9. Immanence-transcendence should not be confused with other abstract couples important in metaphysics: apparent-real or real-ideal or subordinate-superordinate or part-whole or specific-general. Christ is considered real and ideal whether immanent or not; he is not, as transcendent, superordinate to himself as immanent; transcendent, he is not the general class or the whole of which his immanence is a specific instance or part.

10. *Ibid.*, p. 172.

11. *Ibid.*, p. 174.

12. *Ibid.*, pp. 138-43, 158-59.

13. Gerrish, *op. cit.*, pp. 131-32.

14. Whale, *op. cit.*, pp. 14, 57-59.

15. Mayer, *op. cit.*, p. 165.

16. *Ibid.*, pp. 209-10.

17. Ronald S. Wallace, *Calvin's Doctrine of the Word and Sacrament,* Edinburgh: Oliver and Boyd, 1953, pp. 82-83.

18. *Ibid.*, pp. 20-23; H. Jackson Forstman, *Word and Spirit: Calvin's Doctrine of Biblical Authority,* Stanford: Stanford University Press, 1962.

19. Quoted in William A. Curtis, *A History of Creeds and Con-*

fessions of Faith in Christendom and Beyond, Edinburgh: T. and T. Clark, 1911, p. 175.

II. The Roots of Immanence

1. For a recent and authoritative review, see *The New Cambridge Modern History,* vol. 2, Cambridge: Cambridge University Press, 1958.

2. Michael Wilks, *The Problem of Sovereignty in the Later Middle Ages, The Papal Monarchy with Augustinus Triumphus and the Publicists,* Cambridge: Cambridge University Press, 1963, pp. 18-37, 480.

3. George C. Homans, *Sentiments and Activities: Essays in Social Science,* New York: The Free Press of Glencoe, 1962, pp. 128-30.

4. Swanson, 1960, *op. cit.,* chapters 3 and 7.

5. *Ibid.,* chapter 7.

6. There are good reviews of this problem in: Robert N. Bellah, "Religious Evolution," *American Sociological Review,* 29 (June 1964), pp. 366-70; Samuel N. Eisenstadt, "Religious Organizations and Political Process in Centralized Empires," *Journal of Asian Studies,* 21 (May 1962), pp. 271-94; Samuel N. Eisenstadt, *The Political Systems of Empires,* New York: The Free Press, 1963.

7. Guy E. Swanson, "The Effectiveness of Decision-Making Groups, A Study of the Effects of Constitutional Arrangements on Group Efficiency," *Adult Leadership,* 8 (June 1959), pp. 48-52.

8. David Easton, "An Approach to the Analysis of Political Systems," *World Politics,* 9 (April 1957), pp. 383-400.

9. My treatment of these points depends especially on: Charles H. McIlwain, *Constitutionalism, Ancient and Modern,* Ithaca: Cornell University Press, 1947; Walter Ullmann, *Principles of Government and Politics in the Middle Ages,* London: Methuen and Co., Ltd., 1961.

10. Quoted in McIlwain, *op. cit.,* p. 76.

11. Ullmann, *op. cit.,* p. 151.

III. European Regimes in the Fifteenth Century and After

1. For a more detailed discussion of this formulation, see: Swanson, 1960, *op. cit.,* chapter 1.

2. The principalities' freedom of action in foreign affairs was formally recognized in 1648.

3. I have, however, made almost no use of statements of "political theory" propounded in these several countries. Erasmus, Dante, Machiavelli, Augustinus Triumphus, Bodin, and others offer ideas important for the analysis of politics, but ideas often having little relationship to the political realities of their time.

4. In a study such as this there is no possibility of ruling out biases introduced by prior knowledge and expectations. The explanation I developed for the Reformation was grounded in some knowledge of European history. Although that knowledge was very fragmentary and quite frequently erroneous, it did exist. Similarly, although the graduate students I employed to help me cover the large literature did not know the focus of my interests or the hypotheses under study, they did bring to their work certain expectations about the character of European history, certain interpretations of its dynamics.

When one deals thus with a subject matter much of which is common knowledge, his only real safeguard against gross error will be the response of interested critics who have more thorough knowledge than he of particular societies and periods. Fortunately the data on which I have based my conclusions are available for all to examine.

How adequate are those data? As one would expect, they vary greatly in quality and completeness. Recent publications demonstrate that there is room for important reassessments and crucial new findings by historians working on even so well investigated a country and period as medieval England. Many of the basic sources for histories of Spain, Portugal, Transylvania, and even Denmark and Scotland seem not yet to be organized, let alone exploited. In several instances the countries of interest to me no longer have an important place in international affairs—and some never had such a place. The result is that one must depend too heavily on historians of a period in which these lands were of greater interest. For many, an adequate history never has been written, not to speak of a history shaped by contemporary standards of work and by present-day insights into the abstract structure of societies.

Despite these many difficulties, the required data could usually be had. Their deficiencies are important, however, because they make it more likely that future historical work will require some qualification of judgments advanced here. Indeed I have already had some experience with that possibility. The explanation for immanence and the Reformation presented here was developed in 1957-58. At that time I made an extensive reconnaisance of the better general works on European history to determine whether the theory was worth pursuing. My firm conclusion was negative. It was not until later, when, for another purpose, I read G. R. Elton's books on *England under the Tudors* and *The Tudor Revolution in Government* and F. L. Carsten's *Princes and Parliaments in Germany from the Fifteenth to the Eighteenth Century*, that I concluded my interpretation might have some merit. It seems to me in retrospect that the differences between the accounts I read first and these others consist in this: the more general accounts tend to evaluate the periods they treat against the standard of some political doctrines or against events of earlier or later periods. (Thus what by my definition is a limited centralist regime may be called absolutist in the general accounts on the grounds that it represents a constriction of the citizens' earlier rights.) By contrast, the monographic literature, while containing such evaluations, also contains detailed information concerning the actual character of political relations at a given period. It is that part of the record closer to the uninterpreted facts that I have found most valuable.

IV. Centralist Regimes

1. Marc Bloch, *Feudal Society* (L. A. Manyon, Translator), London: Routledge and Kegan Paul, Ltd., 1961; Henry St. L. B. Moss, *The Birth of the Middle Ages*, London: Oxford University Press, 1961; Joseph R. Strayer, "Feudalism in Western Europe," in Rushton Coulborn (Editor), *Feudalism in History*, Princeton: Princeton University Press, 1956, pp. 15-25; Richard W. Southern, *The Making of the Middle Ages*, New Haven, Yale University Press, 1959; John W. Hall, "Feudalism in Japan, A Reassessment," *Comparative Studies in Society and History*, 5 (October 1962), pp. 15-61. These several writers vary somewhat in their interpretations of feudalism but are in essential agreement on the facts relevant for the interpretation employed here.

2. Bloch, *op. cit.*, p. 451. The tenants of a lord's lands not subinfeudated remained under his direct control. In the case of the royal demesne of kings this led to certain privileges of both lord and tenant that were of constitutional importance. For these developments in the English setting, see: Robert S. Hoyt, *The Royal Demesne in English Constitutional History: 1006-1272*, Ithaca: Cornell University Press, 1950.

3. Arnold Luschin von Ebengreuth, *Österreichische Reichsges-*

chichte, Bamberg: C. C. Buchner, 1896, pp. 427-52; Alfred F. Pribram, "Die Niederösterreichischen Stände und die Krone in der Zeit Kaiser Leopolds I," in *Mitteilungen des Instituts für Österreichische Geschichtsforschung*, vol. 14 (1892), pp. 599-652.

4. Arnold Luschin von Ebengreuth, *Geschichte des Älteren Gerichtswesens in Österreich ob und Unter der Enns*, Wien: H. Boehlau, 1879, pp. 88-90; Henry F. Schwarz, *The Imperial Privy Council in the Seventeenth Century*, Cambridge: Harvard University Press, 1943.

5. Thomas Fellner, *Die Österreichische Zentralverwaltung*, vol. 1, Wien: Holzhausen, 1907.

6. Luschin von Ebengreuth, *op. cit.*, 1879, pp. 88-251.

7. *NCMH*, vol. 1, pp. 220-21; Schwarz, *op. cit.*, pp. 9-15, 55.

8. Gustav Seidler, *Studien zur Geschichte und Dogmatik des Österreichischen Staatsrechts*, Wien: A Hoelder, 1894, pp. 98-100.

9. Luschin von Ebengreuth, *op. cit.*, 1879, p. 286.

10. Schwarz, *op. cit.*, pp. 30-31.

11. *Ibid.*, pp. 73-74.

12. *NCMH*, vol. 7, p. 152.

13. Edith M. Link, *The Emancipation of the Austrian Peasant, 1740-1789*, New York: Columbia University Press, 1949, p. 37.

14. John B. Wolf, *The Emergence of the Great Powers, 1685-1715*. New York: Harper and Brothers, 1951, pp. 135-37.

15. Franz X. R. vM. Krones, *Grundriss der Österreichischen Geschichte mit Besonderer Rücksicht auf Quellen und Literaturkunde*, Wien: A. Hoelder, 1882, p. 509; Christian Meyer, *Reformation, Antireformation und Aufklärung in Österreich*, Muenchen: Selbstverlag, 1904, pp. 3-17; Schwarz, *op. cit.*, pp. 69-70, 80-85; Robert W. Seton-Watson, *A History of the Czechs and Slovaks*, London: Hutchinson and Co., Ltd., 1943, pp. 97-99.

16. Joseph R. Strayer and Dana C. Munro, *The Middle Ages: 395-1500*, New York: Appleton-Century-Crofts, Inc., 1959, p. 469.

17. *CMH*, vol. 1, pp. 384-85.

18. J. Russell Major, *Representative Institutions in Renaissance France, 1421-1559*, Madison: The University of Wisconsin Press, 1960, pp. 3-4.

19. *Ibid.*, pp. 24-48; *NCMH*, vol. 2, p. 455; Strayer and Munro, *op. cit.*, p. 487.

20. Major, *op. cit.*, p. 10.

21. Alexis de Tocqueville, *The Old Regime and the French Revolution* (Stuart Gilbert, Translator), Garden City, N. Y.: Doubleday and Co., Inc. 1955, p. 34; John S. C. Bridge, *A History of France from the Death of Louis XI*, vol. 5, Oxford: The Clarendon Press, 1936, chapters 29-32.

22. William F. Church, *Constitutional Thought in Sixteenth Century France, A Study in the Evolution of Ideas,* Cambridge: Harvard University Press, 1941, pp. 129-52.

23. *Ibid.*, p. 163.

24. Major, *op. cit.*, pp. 19, 24-48.

25 *Ibid.*, pp. 24-152.

26. *Ibid.*, p. 5.

27. Tocqueville, *op. cit.*, pp. 212-20.

28. Major, *op. cit.*, p. 6.

29. *Ibid.*, p. 7.

30. *Ibid.*, p. 12; Alfred Vagts, *A History of Militarism*, New York: Meridian books, 1959, p. 63. The numbers and social character of the French *noblesse* made this practice both possible and imperative to an extent unimaginable in certain other European states—England, for example. For a comparative discussion consult: Marc Bloch and Lucien Febvre, "Les Noblesses: I. Reconnaissance général du terrain," *Annales d'Histoire Économique et Sociale,* 8 (May 1936), pp. 238-42; Marc Bloch, "Sur le passé de la noblesse française: quelques jalons de recherche," *Ibid.*, 8 (July 1936), 366-78; Otto F. de Battaglia, "The Nobility in the European Middle Ages," *Comparative Studies in Society and History,* 5 (October 1962), pp. 60-75; Frederick W. Maitland, *The Constitutional History of England*, Cambridge: Cambridge University Press, 1909, p. 171. It is important, of course, to recall that many noble appointees in France came not from old noble families but from the newer "service" nobility, its role so greatly enlarged by the kings. For the development of the French nobility see Jean-Richard Bloch, *L'Anablissement en France au temps de François I*, Paris: Felix Alcan, 1934.

31. Gaston Zeller, *Les Institutions de la France au XVI⁰ Siecle,* Paris: Presses Universitaires de France, 1948, p. 27.

32. Tocqueville, *op. cit.*, pp. 27-29.

33. *Ibid.*, pp. 26-27. On the early growth of royal power over local affairs see: James W. Fesler, "French Field Administration: The Beginnings," *Comparative Studies in Society and History* 5 (October 1962), 76-111.

34. C. A. J. Armstrong, "France of the Hundred Years' War and the Renaissance," in J. M. Wallace-Hadrill and John McManners (Editors), *France: Government and Society*, London: Methuen and Co., Ltd., 1957, pp. 89-90.

35. Major, *op. cit.*, p. 6.

36. Armstrong, *op. cit.*, p. 91.

37. J. S. Bromley, "The Decline of Absolute Monarchy (1683-1774)," in Wallace-Hadrill and McManners, *op. cit.*, p. 135.

38. J. E. Neale, *The Age of Catherine de Medici*, London: Jonathan Cape, 1943, pp. 11-16.

39. Henry M. Baird, *The Huguenots and the Revocation of the Edict of Nantes*, vol. I, New York: Charles Scribner's Sons, 1895; David D. Bien, *The Calas Affair: Persecution, Toleration, and Heresy in Eighteenth-Century Toulouse*, Princeton: Princeton University Press, 1960, chapters 2, 3, and 7; Neale, *op. cit.*, pp. 24-38; Burdette C. Poland, *French Protestantism and the French Revolution*, Princeton: Princeton University Press, 1957, Chapter I and Appendices I, II, and III.

40. George C. Homans, *Sentiments and Activities, Essays in Social Science*, New York: The Free Press of Glencoe, 1962, pp. 128-30.

41. *CMH*, vol. 1, pp. 288-90. In the fifteenth century, sometimes even earlier, the internal organization and finances of several German principalities were reorganized and strengthened. These developments are reviewed in: M. M. Fryde and E. B. Fryde, "Public Credit with Special Reference to North-Western Europe," *The Cambridge Economic History of Europe* vol. 3, Cambridge: Cambridge University Press, 1963, pp. 518-26. The emphasis, in this section, on German nationalism should not obscure the pervasive, fragmenting forces at work. For a description of how even the maintenance of public order in Germany frequently depended on local alliances rather than on imperial or princely authority, see: Joachim Gernhuber, "Staat und Landfrieden in deutschen Reich des Mittelalters," *Recueils de la Société Jean Bodin*, vol. 15, 1961, pp. 27-77.

42. *Ibid.*, p. 297.

43. Geoffrey Barraclough, *The Origins of Modern Germany*, Oxford: Basil Blackwell, 1946, p. 364.

44. *Ibid.*, p. 364.

45. *CMH*, vol. 1, pp. 298-301.

46. *Ibid.*, p. 301.

47. Barraclough, *op. cit.*, p. 362.

48. *Ibid.*, pp. 365-66.

49. *Ibid.*, pp. 367-70.

50. James Bryce, *The Holy Roman Empire,* New York: The Macmillan Co., 1930, p. 457; Heinz H. F. Eulau, "Theories of Federalism under the Holy Roman Empire," *The American Political Science Review,* 35 (August 1941), pp. 643-64; Theodor Mayer, "The Historical Foundations of the German Constitution," in Geoffrey Barraclough (Editor), *Mediaeval Germany, 911-1250, Essays by German Historians,* Oxford: Basil Blackwell, 1938, pp. 1-33.

51. Barraclough, 1946, *op. cit.*, p. 411.

52. F. L. Carsten, *Princes and Parliaments in Germany from the Fifteenth to the Eighteenth Century,* Oxford: The Clarendon Press, 1959, pp. 348-422.

53. F. L. Carsten, *The Origins of Prussia,* Oxford: The Clarendon Press, 1954, pp. 229-51; Carsten, 1959, *op. cit.*, pp. 258-340.

54. Edmund Curtis, *A History of Ireland,* London: Methuen and Co., Ltd., 1950, pp. 2-3.

55. Gerard A. Hayes-McCoy, *Scots Mercenary Forces in Ireland, 1565-1603,* Dublin: Burns Oates and Washbourne, Ltd., 1937, pp. 5-8.

56. Curtis, *op. cit.*, p. 136.

57. Hugh F. Kearney, *Strafford in Ireland, 1633-1641,* Manchester: Manchester University Press, 1959, p. 2.

58. Hayes-McCoy, *op. cit.*, pp. 46-53.

59. Kearney, *op. cit.*, p. 5.

60. Cyril Falls, *Elizabeth's Irish Wars,* London: Methuen and Co., Ltd., 1950, p. 27; Eoin MacNeill, *Celtic Ireland,* Dublin: Martin Lester, Ltd., 1921, pp. 144-47.

61. William F. Skene, *Celtic Scotland: A History of Ancient Alban,* vol. 3, Edinburgh: David Douglas, 1890, pp. 137-90.

62. *Ibid.*, p. 149.

63. Penry Williams, "The Northern Borderlands under the Early Stuarts," in H. E. Bell and R. L. Ollard (Editors), *Historical Essays: 1600-1750,* London: Adam and Charles Black, 1963, pp. 1-17.

64. William C. Dickinson, *Scotland from the Earliest Times to 1603,* Edinburgh: Thomas Nelson and Sons, Ltd., 1961, pp. 8-11; Isabel F. Grant, *The Social and Economic Development of Scotland before 1603,* Edinburgh: Oliver and Boyd, 1930, chapter 9; Skene, *op. cit.*, pp. 300-366.

NOTES TO PAGES 101-109

274 NOTES TO PAGES 101-109

65. Audrey Cunningham, *The Loyal Clans,* Cambridge: Cambridge University Press, 1932, pp. 18-25; Roderick C. Macleod, *The Island Clans during Six Centuries,* Inverness: Robert Carruthers and Sons, n. d., pp. 21, 24; Duncan H. MacNeil, *The Scottish Realm, An Approach to the Political and Constitutional History of Scotland,* Glasgow: A. and J. Donaldson, Ltd., 1947, pp. 7, 63-65.

66. Charles E. Nowell, *A History of Portugal,* New York: D. Van Nostrand and Co., 1952, p. 24.

67. *CMeH,* vol. 8, pp. 525-30.

68. William C. Atkinson, *A History of Spain and Portugal,* Harmondsworth, Middlesex: Penguin Books, Ltd., 1960, p. 100; H. V. Livermore, *A History of Portugal,* Cambridge: Cambridge University Press, 1947, p. 194.

69. S. A. Dunham, *The History of Spain and Portugal,* vol. 3, London: Longman, Rees, Orme, Brown, and Green, 1832, pp. 277-78.

70. Livermore, *op. cit.,* pp. 222-37.

71. Atkinson, *op. cit.,* p. 146.

72. Livermore, *op. cit.,* p. 223.

73. *Ibid.,* pp. 340-41.

74. Max Beloff, *The Age of Absolutism, 1660-1815,* London: Hutchinson's University Library, 1954, p. 100.

75. John Lynch, *Spain under the Hapsburgs,* vol. 1, New York: Oxford University Press, 1964, p. 20; *NCMH,* vol. 1, pp. 323-24.

76. Bohdan Chudoba, *Spain and the Empire, 1519-1643,* Chicago: The University of Chicago Press, 1952, p. 86.

77. John H. Elliott, *Imperial Spain, 1469-1716,* London: Edward Arnold Ltd., 1963, p. 97.

78. *NCMH,* vol. 1, pp. 328, 332, 338.

79. Elliott, *op. cit.,* pp. 22-23, 81.

80. *NCMH,* vol. 1, p. 332.

81. Peter J. Helm, *History of Europe, 1450-1660,* London: G. Bell and Sons, Ltd., 1961, pp. 54-55.

82. Elliott, *op. cit.,* p. 22; Lynch, *op. cit.,* pp. 104-5; *NCMH,* vol. 2, pp. 323-24.

83. Lynch, *op. cit.,* pp. 12-17.

84. Elliott, *op. cit.,* pp. 84-87.

85. *NCMH,* vol. 2, pp. 320, 324, 445, 455-56.

86. Raymond Carr, "Spain," in *ENEC,* pp. 45-50.

87. Elliott, *op. cit.,* pp. 89-92.

88. Bernice Hamilton, *Political Thought in Sixteenth-Century Spain*, Oxford: The Clarendon Press, 1963, pp. 6, 11.

89. Lynch, *op. cit.*, pp. 60-61.

90. *Ibid.*, p. 61.

91. Robert E. Dickinson, *The West European City, A Geographic Interpretation*, London: Routledge and Kegan Paul, Ltd., 1951, pp. 56, 165, 187, 295, 297; Kurt Mayer, *The Population of Switzerland*, New York: Columbia University Press, 1952, pp. 19, 246-47.

92. *Ibid.*, p. 245.

93. *Ibid.*, p. 21.

94. William Martin, *A History of Switzerland, An Essay on the Formation of a Confederation of States* (Grace W. Booth, Translator), London: Grant Richards, 1931, pp. 142-51.

95. *DHBS*, vol. 4, pp. 564-73; Sebastian Grueter, *Geschichte des Kantons Luzern im 16. und 17. Jahrhundert*, Lucerne: Verlag Räber & Cie., 1945; Anton P. von Segesser, *Rechtsgeschichte der Stadt und Republik Lucern*, vols. 2-3, Lucerne: Gebrüder Räber, 1854, 1857.

96. *Ibid.*, vol. 2, pp. 172-81, 192; vol. 3, pp. 238-39, 353.

97. *DHBS*, vol. 6, pp. 232-39

98. Johann K. Bluntschli, *Geschichte Des Schweizerischen Bundesrechtes*, vol. 1, Stuttgart: Meyer und Zeller, 1875, p. 137.

99. *Ibid.*, p. 137.

100. Martin, *op. cit.* p. 152.

V. Limited Centralist Regimes

1. Vernon K. Dibble, "The Organization of Traditional Authority: English County Government, 1558-1640," in James G. March (Editor), *Handbook of Organizations*, Chicago: Rand McNally and Co., 1965, pp. 879, 881. The office of Justice of the Peace emerged under other titles in the late thirteenth century and the essentials of the system were fully established by the middle of the fourteenth century. The powers and responsibilities of the Justices were at first modest, these gradually increasing to include those described below.

2. *Ibid.*, pp. 885-86.

3. *Ibid.*, p. 887.

4. *Ibid.*, p. 889.

5. Halvdan Koht, "The Scandinavian Kingdoms during the Fourteenth and Fifteenth Centuries," *CMeH*, vol. 8, p. 555.

6. Great Britain, Naval Intelligence Division, *Denmark*, London: His Majesty's Stationary Office, 1944, p. 130.

7. Lawrence D. Steefel, *The Schleswig-Holstein Question*, Cambridge: Harvard University Press, 1932, pp. 6-7, 263.

8. *NCMH*, vol. 5, p. 525.

9. John Danstrup, *A History of Denmark* (Verner Lindberg, Translator), Copenhagen: Wivel, 1947, pp. 36, 38.

10. *Ibid.*, pp. 38, 44.

11. Auguste Geffroy, *Histoire des États Scandinaves*, Paris: Librairie de L. Hachette et Cie, 1851, p. 166.

12. F. C. Dahlmann, *Geschichte von Danmark*, vol. 3, Hamburg: F. Perthes, 1843, pp. 65-68; Danstrup, *op. cit.*, pp. 48-49.

13. *NCMH*, vol. 5, p. 524.

14. Dahlmann, *op. cit.*, pp. 44-48.

15. Danstrup, *op. cit.*, p. 49; Ernest H. Dunkley, *The Reformation in Denmark*, London: S.P.C.K., 1948, pp. 13-14.

16. Geffroy, *op. cit.*, p. 249.

17. Great Britain, *op. cit.*, p. 113.

18. Dunkley, *op. cit.*, pp. 45, 62-67.

19. *Ibid.*, pp. 67-74; *NCMH*, vol. 2, pp. 134, 141, 143.

20. Danstrup, *op. cit.*, p. 59

21. *Ibid.*, pp. 70-73; Ernst Ekman, "The Danish Royal Law of 1665," *The Journal of Modern History*, 29 (June 1957), pp. 102-7.

22. The Royal Law was not put into effect in Schleswig-Holstein. See: Great Britain, *op. cit.*, p. 130; Steefel, *op. cit.*, pp. 6-7.

23. *NCMH*, vol. 5, pp. 524-26; R. Nisbet Bain, *Scandinavia: A Political History of Denmark, Norway and Sweden from 1513 to 1900*, Cambridge: Cambridge University Press, 1905, pp. 269-76.

24. C. F. Allen, *Histoire de Danemark* (E. Beauvois, Translator), vol. 2, Copenhagen: Andr.-Fred. Hst et Eils, 1878, pp. 101, 113; John Andrews, *The History of the Revolutions of Denmark*, vol. 1, London: J. Nourse, 1774, p. 379; Geffroy, *op. cit.*, p. 269; Paul H. Mallet, *Histoire de Dannemarc*, vol. 9, Geneva: Barde, Manget, and Co., 1788, p. 156, *NCMH*, vol. 5, p. 526.

25. *CMH*, vol. 6, p. 736; Danstrup, *op. cit.*, p. 78; Great Britain, *op. cit.*, p. 121.

26. *CMH*, vol. 6, pp. 735-37; *NCMH*, vol. 7, pp. 340-43.

27. David C. Douglas, *William the Conqueror, The Norman Impact upon England*, Berkeley: University of California Press, 1964; C. Warren Hollister, *Anglo-Saxon Military Institutions on the Eve of the Norman Conquest*, Oxford: The Clarendon

Press, 1962; H. G. Richardson and G. O. Sayles, *The Governance of Mediaeval England from the Conquest to Magna Charta,* Edinburgh: Edinburgh University Press, 1963.

28. Joseph R. Strayer and Dana C. Munro, *The Middle Ages: 395-1500,* New York: Appleton-Century-Crofts, Inc., 1959, pp. 293-96.

29. David L. Keir, *The Constitutional History of Modern Britain, 1485-1951,* London: Adam and Charles Black, 1955, p. 39; Strayer and Munro, *op. cit.,* p. 481.

30. Geoffrey R. Elton, *England under the Tudors,* New York: G. P. Putnam's Sons, n. d.; Geoffrey R. Elton, *The Tudor Revolution in Government: Administrative Changes in the Reign of Henry VIII,* Cambridge: Cambridge University Press, 1953; J. E. Neale, *Elizabeth I and Her Parliaments,* 2 vols., London: Jonathan Cape, 1953 and 1957.

31. *CMeH,* vol. 7, p. 702.

32. Alexis de Tocqueville, *Journeys to England and Ireland* (George Lawrence and K. P. Mayer, Translators), New Haven: Yale University Press, 1958, p. 109.

33. Josef Redlich and Francis W. Hirst, *The History of Local Government in England,* London: Macmillan and Co., Ltd., 1958, p. 15.

34. Noël Denholm-Young, *Seignorial Administration in England,* London: Oxford University Press, 1937.

35. Frederick G. Marcham, *A Constitutional History of Modern England, 1485 to the Present,* New York: Harper and Brothers, 1960, pp. 42-44.

36. Keir, *op. cit.,* p. 36. See also: Dibble, *op. cit.,* pp. 879-909.

37. Elton, n.d., *op. cit.,* p. 60. On the growth of royal courts see: Frederick W. Maitland, *The Forms of Action at Common Law,* Cambridge: Cambridge University Press, 1936. On tenures as described below, consult Theodore F. T. Plucknett, *Concise History of the Common Law,* London: Butterworth and Co., Ltd., 1948, Book Two, Part III, esp. pp. 508-10.

38. *NCMH,* vol. 2, pp. 36-43.

39. Tocqueville, *op. cit.,* p. 19. For more extended discussions, see: chapter IV, note 30 of the present volume.

40. *NCMH,* vol. 2, pp. 226-50.

41. George C. Homans, *Sentiments and Activities, Essays in Social Science,* New York: The Free Press of Glencoe, 1962, pp. 127-44.

42. Mildred L. Campbell, *The English Yeoman under Elizabeth*

and the Early Stuarts, New Haven: Yale University Press, 1942, p. 291; Alfred L. Rowse, *The England of Elizabeth: The Structure of Society*, London: Macmillan and Co., Ltd., 1951, pp. 438-88; William R. Trimble, *The Catholic Laity in Elizabethan England, 1558-1603*, Cambridge: The Belknap Press, 1964, pp. 122-76. These same sections of the country proved loyal to the Stuart kings who sought at least to tolerate Catholicism in the seventeenth century. It was those areas of the nation first gained for Protestantism where Parliament found its strongest base of support against the Stuarts. The following summary of Christopher Hill accords with the judgment of most historians (see his *The Century of Revolution, 1603-1714*, Edinburgh: Thomas Nelson and Sons, Ltd., 1961, pp. 121-22) ". . . Support for Parliament came from the economically advanced south and east of England, the King's support from the economically backward areas of the north and west. In Yorkshire, Lancashire, and Sussex there was a clear division between the industrial areas, which were Parliamentarian, and the agricultural areas, which were Royalist. . . . often, as in London, town oligarchies were Royalist, and had to be overthrown before the Parliamentarian sentiments of the majority of the citizens could express themselves. . . . the ports were all for Parliament . . ."

43. F. L. Carsten, *Princes and Parliaments in Germany from the Fifteenth to the Eighteenth Century*, Oxford: The Clarendon Press, 1959, pp. 1-148, 191-257; Harm Wiemann, *Der Heimbürge in Thuringen und Sachsen*, Köln: Bohlau Verlag, 1962.

44. Carsten, *op. cit.*, pp. 422-44; F. L. Carsten, *The Origins of Prussia*, Oxford: The Clarendon Press, 1954; Sidney B. Fay, *The Rise of Brandenburg-Prussia to 1786*, New York: Henry Holt and Co., 1937; *NCMH*, vol. 7, pp. 292-317; Sidney B. Fay, "The Hohenzollern Household and Administration in the Sixteenth Century, *Smith College Studies in History*, 2 (October 1916), pp. 3-64.

45. Lysbeth W. Muncy, *The Junker in the Prussian Administration under William II, 1888-1914*, Providence, R.I.: Brown University, 1944, p. 7.

46. Gordon A. Craig, *The Politics of the Prussian Army, 1640-1945*, New York: Oxford University Press, 1956, pp. 1-21.

47. Muncy, *op. cit.*, pp. 18, 21.

48. Albert Goodwin, "Prussia," in *ENEC*, p. 85.

49. *Ibid.*, p. 87.

50. *Ibid.*, p. 94.

51. Hans Rosenberg, *Bureaucracy, Aristocracy and Autocracy, The Prussian Experience 1660-1815,* Cambridge: Harvard University Press, 1958, pp. 37-39.

52. Goodwin, *op. cit.,* p. 94.

53. Rosenberg, *op. cit.,* pp. 47, 53-55.

54. *Ibid.,* pp. 66, 70.

55. Goodwin, *op. cit.,* pp. 93-94.

56. Robert R. Palmer, *The Age of the Democratic Revolution, A Political History of Europe and America, 1760-1800,* Princeton: Princeton University Press, 1959, p. 33.

57. Rosenberg, *op. cit.,* pp. 117-34.

58. Goodwin, *op. cit.,* pp. 92-93.

59. Rosenberg, *op. cit.,* p. 135.

60. *Ibid.,* p. 134.

61. *Ibid.,* p. 43.

62. Carsten, 1959, *op. cit.,* pp. 149-90. Kurt Dülfer, "Fürst und Verwaltung. Grundzüge der hessischen Verwaltungsgeschichte im 16.—19. Jahrhundert," *Hessisches Jahrbuch für Landesgeschichte,* vol. 3, 1953, pp. 150-223.

63. Ingvar Andersson, *A History of Sweden* (Carolyn Hannay, Translator), London: Weidenfeld and Nicolson, 1956, pp. xx-xxi.

64. Eli F. Heckscher, *An Economic History of Sweden* (Göran Ohlin, Translator), Cambridge: Harvard University Press, 1954, pp. 37-38.

65. Michael Roberts, *Gustavus Adophus, A History of Sweden 1611-1632,* vol. 1, London: Longmans, Green and Co., 1953, pp. 14-17.

66. *Ibid.,* pp. 284-95.

67. *Ibid.,* vol. 2, 1958, pp. 1-43.

68. *Ibid.,* vol. 1, pp. 315-27.

69. *Ibid.,* vol. 1, p. 325, vol. 2, p. 48.

70. *Ibid.,* vol. 1, p. 326.

71. *Ibid.,* vol. 2, p. 10.

72. Andersson, *op. cit.,* p. 216; Roberts, *op. cit.,* vol. 2, p. 50.

73. *Ibid.,* pp. 50-52.

74. Michael Roberts, "Sweden," *ENEC,* p. 145.

75. Roberts, *op. cit.,* vol. 2, 1953, pp. 2, 54.

76. *Ibid.,* pp. 2, 35.

77. *Ibid.,* vol. 1, pp. 255-56.

78. Andersson, *op. cit.,* pp. 125, 130; *NCMH,* vol. 2, pp. 141-53.

79. Roberts, *op. cit.*, 1953, p. 19.

80. Andersson, *op. cit.*, pp. 213-54.

VI. *Balanced Regimes*

1. Robert W. Seton-Watson, *A History of the Czechs and Slovaks*, London: Hutchinson and Co., Ltd., 1943, pp. 73-75; *NCMH*, vol. 2, p. 189.

2. Seton-Watson, *op. cit.*, pp. 72, 87-88.

3. Robert J. Kerner, *Bohemia in the Eighteenth Century, A Study in Political, Economic, and Social History with Special Reference to the Reign of Leopold II, 1790-1792*, New York: The Macmillan Co., 1932, pp. 8-9.

4. *NCMH*, vol. 1, pp. 389-91.

5. Franz H. H. V. Lützow, *Bohemia, An Historical Sketch*, London: J. M. Dent and Sons, Ltd., 1939, pp. 178, 201; *NCMH*, vol. 2, pp. 468-69.

6. Kerner, *op. cit.*, p. 9; *NCMH*, vol. 2, p. 466.

7. Kerner, *op. cit.*, pp. 6-7, 9.

8. *Ibid.*, pp. 8-9.

9. Lützow, *op. cit.*, pp. 204-10; Seton-Watson, *op. cit.*, pp. 89-90.

10. Lützow, *op. cit.*, pp. 204-10.

11. Seton-Watson, *op. cit.*, pp. 90-105.

12. *ERE*, vol. 3, pp. 848, 871; Lützow, *op. cit.*, p. 214.

13. Kerner, *op. cit.*, p. 12; Lützow, *op. cit.*, p. 218.

14. *Ibid.*, p. 159; Seton-Watson, *op. cit.*, pp. 90, 99.

15. *Ibid.*, pp. 107-8.

16. *Ibid.*, pp. 107-17.

17. Lützow, *op. cit.*, p. 257.

18. *Ibid.*, pp. 292-93.

19. H. G. Wanklyn, *The Eastern Marchlands of Europe*, London: George Philip and Sons, Ltd., 1941, pp. 249-50, 259.

20. *NCMH*, vol. 1, p. 37.

21. Denis Sinor, *History of Hungary*, London: George Allen and Unwin Ltd., 1959, pp. 39-40.

22. *CMeH*, vol. 6, pp. 467, 471-72.

23. C. M. Knatchbull-Hugessen, *The Political Evolution of the Hungarian Nation*, vol. 1, London: National Review Office, 1908, pp. 70-72, 84-100; Otto F. De Battaglia, "The Nobility in the European Middle Ages," *Comparative Studies in Society and History*, 5 (October 1962), pp. 60-75.

24. Sinor, *op. cit.*, p. 104.

25. *Ibid.*, p. 128.

26. *Ibid.*, pp. 134-43.

27. Ladislas Makkai, *Histoire de Transylvanie*, Paris: Les Presses Universitaires des France, 1946, pp. 51, 88.

28. *Ibid.*, p. 94.

29. Robert W. Seton-Watson, *A History of the Roumanians from Roman Times to the Completion of Unity*, Cambridge: Cambridge University Press, 1934, p. 22.

30. Makkai, *op. cit.*, p. 87.

31. Knatchbull-Hugessen, *op. cit.*, pp. 85-86; Seton-Watson, *op. cit.*, p. 101.

32. *NCMH*, vol. 2, p. 467.

33. Makkai, *op. cit.*, p. 160; Seton Watson, *op. cit.*, pp. 105-6.

34. Sinor, *op. cit.*, p. 182.

35. Makkai, *op. cit.*, p. 89.

36. *Ibid.*, p. 155.

37. *Ibid.*, pp. 153-54.

38. C. A. Macartney, *Hungary, A Short History*, Edinburgh: Edinburgh University Press, 1962, pp. 81-82.

39. Makkai, *op. cit.*, p. 244.

40. Sinor, *op. cit.*, p. 207.

41. Makkai, *op. cit.*, pp. 165-68; Seton-Watson, *op. cit.*, pp. 122, 171-74, 180; William Toth, "Highlights of the Hungarian Reformation," *Church History*, 9 (June 1940), pp. 141-56; William Toth, "Luther's Frontier in Hungary," in Franklin H. Littel (Editor), *Reformation Studies, Essays in Honor of Roland H. Bainton*, Richmond, Va.: John Knox Press, 1962, pp. 75-91.

42. *NCMH*, vol. 2, p. 196.

43. Sinor, *op. cit.*, p. 195.

44. Seton-Watson, *op. cit.*, pp. 171-88.

45. *Ibid.*, pp. 269-80.

46. Macartney, *op. cit.*, pp. 83-88.

47. Sidney A. Burrell, "Calvinism, Capitalism and the Middle Classes: Some Afterthoughts on an Old Problem," *The Journal Of Modern History*, 32 (June 1960), pp. 129-41; Isabel F. Grant, *The Social and Economic Development of Scotland before 1603*, Edinburgh: Oliver and Boyd, 1930, p. 459; H. R. Trevor-Roper, "Scotland and the Puritan Revolution," in H. E. Bell and R. L. Ollard (Editors), *Historical*

Essays: 1700-1750, London: Adam and Charles Black, 1963, pp. 78-130.

48. *Ibid.*

49. William C. Dickinson, *Scotland from the Earliest Times to 1603*, Edinburgh: Thomas Nelson and Sons, Ltd., 1961, p. 259; James Mackinnon, *The Constitutional History of Scotland from Early Times to the Reformation*, London: Longmans, Green, and Co., 1924, pp. 188, 198; Duncan H. MacNeill, *The Scottish Realm, An Approach to the Political and Constitutional History of Scotland*, Glasgow: A. and J. Donaldson, Ltd., 1947, pp. 7, 63-65.

50. Grant, *op. cit.*, pp. 197-98, 286; Maurice Lee, Jr., *James Stewart, Earl of Moray: A Political Study of the Reformation in Scotland*, New York: Columbia University Press, 1953, pp. 12-13; David Mathew, *Scotland under Charles I*, London: Eyre and Spottiswoode, 1955, pp. 33, 95, 104, 107, 211; Robert S. Rait, *The Parliaments of Scotland*, Glasgow: Maclehose, Jackson and Co., 1924, p. 15.

51. Mathew, *op. cit.*, pp. 46-47.

52. Dickinson, *op. cit.*, p. 261; Lee, *op. cit.*, pp. 19-22; David McRoberts (Editor), *Essays on the Scottish Reformation 1513-1623*, Glasgow: Burns, 1962; Mackinnon, *op. cit.*, pp. 228-39.

53. *Ibid.*, pp. 191, 193-94, 222-24.

54. Lee, *op. cit.*, p. 8.

55. Sidney A. Burrell, "The Covenant Idea as a Revolutionary Symbol: Scotland, 1596-1637," *Church History*, 27 (December 1958), pp. 338-50; Grant, *op. cit.*, pp. 193-95, 197; Lee, *op. cit.*, pp. 8, 26, 61; McRoberts, *op. cit.*, p. 8; Trevor-Roper, *op. cit.*, p. 82.

56. Lee, *op. cit.*, p. 9.

57. Grant, *op. cit.*, p. 193; Lee, *op. cit.*, p. 8; MacNeill, *op. cit.*, p. 73.

58. Audrey Cunningham, *The Loyal Clans*, Cambridge: Cambridge University Press, 1932, p. 35; Grant, *op. cit.*, pp. 67-78, 181-83.

59. Dickinson, *op. cit.*, pp. 191-92; Grant, *op. cit.*, pp. 351, 383-93, 397, 446-47; Lee, *op. cit.*, pp. 10-11; Mackinnon, *op. cit.*, pp. 271, 289-307; Rait, *op. cit.*, pp. 5, 11-14.

60. Dickinson, *op. cit.*, p. 296; Mackinnon, *op. cit.*, p. 191; McRoberts, *op. cit.*, p. 5; Rait, *op. cit.*, pp. 47, 489; Trevor-Roper, *op. cit.*, p. 82.

61. Dickinson, *op. cit.*, p. 217; Mackinnon, *op. cit.*, pp. 275-83; Rait, *op. cit.*, p. 8.

62. *DHBS*, vol. 3, pp. 357-67; Henri Fazy, *Les Constitutions de la Republique de Genève*, Geneva: H. Georg, 1890.

63. Paul E. Martin and Others, *Histoire de Genève des Origines à 1798*, Geneva: Société d'Histoire et d'Archeologie de Genève, 1951, pp. 171-81; Georges Werner, "Les Institutions Politiques de Genève de 1519 à 1536," *Etrennes Genèvoises*, 1926, pp. 8-54.

64. Jean-Antoine Gautier, *Histoire de Genève*, vol. 2, Geneva: Roy et Malvallon Imprimeurs, 1896, p. 240.

65. Wilhelm Oechsli, *History of Switzerland, 1499-1914* (Eden and Cedar Paul, Translators), Cambridge: Cambridge University Press, pp. 130, 135.

66. Antony Babel, *Histoire Économique de Genève, Des Origines au Début du XVIe Siècle*, Geneva: Alexandre Jullien, 1963, pp. 240-71.

VII. Commensal Regimes

1. See the relevant articles in *DHBS*.

2. Wilhelm Oechsli, *History of Switzerland, 1499-1914* (Eden and Cedar Paul, Translators), Cambridge: Cambridge University Press, 1922, p. 17.

3. *DHBS*, vol. 7, pp. 471-75.

4. Jean Berchtold, *Histoire du Canton de Fribourg*, 3 vols., Fribourg en Suisse: Joseph-Louis Piller, 1841-52; Gaston Castella, *Histoire du Canton de Fribourg depuis les Origines jusqu'en 1857*, Fribourg: *Fragnière Frères, Éditeurs*, 1922; *DHBS*, vol. 3., pp. 218-34.

5. Martin, *op. cit.*, p. 152; Oechsli, *op. cit.*, pp. 275-76.

6. Martin, *op. cit.*, p. 95.

7. *DHBS*, vol. 3, pp. 440-42; *Gottfried Heer, Geschichte des Landes Glarus*, 2 vols., Glarus: Baeschlin, 1898-99; Jakob Winteler, *Geschichte des Landes Glarus*, vol. 1, Glarus: Baeschlin, 1952.

8. *Ibid.*, p. 130.

9. *DHBS*, vol. 1, pp. 356-62; Johannes Baumann, *Rechtsgeschichte der Reformierten Kirche von Appenzell A.-Rh*, Basel: R. Reich, 1897; Johann C. Zellweger, *Geschichte des Appenzellischen Volkes*, 3 vols., Trogen: Meyer und Zuberbuehller, 1830-40.

10. Irving B. Richman, *Appenzell: Pure Democracy and Pastoral Life in Inner-Rhoden*, London: Longmans, Green, and Co., 1895, p. 69.

11. Zellweger, *op. cit.*, vol. 3, pp. 181-200.

12. Richman, *op. cit.*, p. 79.

13. *Ibid.*, pp. 70-71.

14. Max Weber, *The City* (Don Martindale and Gertrud Neu-wirth, Translators), New York: Collier Books, 1962, p. 134.

15. Maude V. Clarke, *The Medieval City State, An Essay on Tyranny and Federation in the Later Middle Ages*, London: Methuen and Co., Ltd., 1926, pp. 53-67; William C. Hazlitt, *The Venetian Republic*, vol. 2, London: Adam and Charles Black, 1915, p. 454; George B. McClellan, *The Oligarchy of Venice*, Boston: Houghton, Mifflin and Co., 1904, pp. 158-68.

16. James C. Davis, *The Decline of the Venetian Nobility as a Ruling Class*, Baltimore: The Johns Hopkins Press, 1962, pp. 16-23.

17. Ferdinand Schevill, *History of Florence, From the Founding of the City through the Renaissance*, New York: Harcourt, Brace and Co., 1936, pp. 158-59.

18. Gene A. Brucker, *Florentine Politics and Society, 1343-1378*, Princeton: Princeton University Press, 1962, p. 58.

19. Schevill, *op. cit.*, pp. 152-54.

20. *Ibid.*, pp. 154-55.

21. Brucker, *op. cit.*, pp. 61-62.

22. *Ibid.*, pp. 64-66.

23. Jean C. L. de Sismondi, *A History of the Italian Republics*, New York: E. P. Dutton and Co., 1907, pp. 123-24.

24. Brucker, *op. cit.*, pp. 99-103.

25. Sismondi, *loc. cit.*

26. Brucker, *op. cit.*, pp. 66-67.

27. *Ibid.*, pp. 67-69, 89-90; Schevill, *op. cit.*, p. 223.

28. Brucker, *op. cit.*, p. 61; Schevill, *op. cit.*, pp. 210-11.

29. Brucker, *op. cit.*, pp. 97-98.

30. L. F. Marks, "The Financial Oligarchy in Florence under Lorenzo," in E. R. Jacobs (Editor), *Italian Renaissance Studies*, London: Faber and Faber, 1960, pp. 123-46.

31. *Ibid.*, pp. 123-24, 138-39; Schevill, *op. cit.*, pp. 396-97.

32. Cecil Roth, *The Last Florentine Republic*, London: Methuen and Co., Ltd., 1925.

33. W. F. Reddaway and Others (Editors), *Cambridge History of Poland from the Origins to Sobieski*, Cambridge: Cambridge University Press, 1950, p. 416.

34. H. G. Wanklyn, *The Eastern Marchlands of Europe*, London: George Philip and Sons, Ltd., 1941, pp. 137-45.

35. *Ibid.*

36. A. Bruce Boswell, "Poland," in *ENEC*, p. 155; Reddaway, *op. cit.*, pp. 150-51, 155-56, 214, 217.

37. *Ibid.*, pp. 354-62; A. E. Tennant, *Studies in Polish Life and History*, London: George Allen and Unwin, Ltd., 1924, pp. 61-62.

38. *NCMH*, vol. 1, pp. 382-85.

39. *NCMH*, vol. 2, pp. 465, 467-68, 473; *NCMH*, vol. 5, pp. 559-62; Reddaway, *op. cit.*, pp. 245ff; George Slocombe, *A History of Poland*, London: Thomas Nelson and Sons Ltd., 1939, pp. 57-58, 61-62, 70; Tennant, *op. cit.*, pp. 67-68, 92-93, 102-4, 127.

40. Paul Fox, *The Reformation in Poland: Some Social and Economic Aspects*, Baltimore: The Johns Hopkins Press, 1924; *NCMH*, vol. 2, pp. 186-87, 202-5, 208.

VIII. Heterarchic Regimes

1. Wilhelm Oechsli, *History of Switzerland, 1499-1914* (Eden and Cedar Paul, Translators), Cambridge: Cambridge University Press, 1922, p. 17; J. Planta, *The History of the Helvetic Confederacy*, 2 vols., London: Bulmer, 1900, vol. 1, chapter 8, vol. 2, pp. 284-85.

2. William Martin, *A History of Switzerland, An Essay on the Formation of a Confederation of States* (Grace W. Booth, Translator), London: Grant Richards, 1931, p. 101.

3. *Ibid.*, p. 74.

4. Norman Birnbaum, "The Zwinglian Reformation in Zurich," *Past and Present*, no. 15 (April 1959), p. 29.

5. Oechsli, *op. cit.*, p. 263.

6. Norman Birnbaum, "Social Structure and the German Reformation," Unpublished doctoral dissertation, Department of Social Relations, Harvard University, 1957, p. 270; Birnbaum, 1959, *op. cit.*, p. 31.

7. *Ibid.*, p. 40.

8. *Ibid.*, pp. 31-32.

9. *Ibid.*, p. 36.

10. Oechsli, *op. cit.*, pp. 263, 267.

11. *Ibid.*, p. 265.

12. Paul Maillefer, "Le Pays de Vaud sous le Régime Bernois," *Revue Historique Vaudoise*, 3 (January 1895), p. 15; Martin, *op. cit.*, p. 50; Planta, *op. cit.*, vol. 2, pp. 252-64.

13. Maillefer, *op. cit.*, pp. 13-23. See also the continuation of this article in the following issues of vol. 3 of the *Revue Histor-*

ique Vaudoise: (February 1895), pp. 47-57; (March 1895), pp. 74-87; (April 1895), pp. 108-18; (June 1895), pp. 161-171. *DHBS*, vol. 2, pp. 80-94, 126.

14. Oechsli, *op. cit.*, pp. 267-68.

15. *CMeH*, vol. 8, p. 332.

16. *Ibid.*, p. 348.

17. Bernard H. M. Vlekke, *Evolution of the Dutch Nation*, New York: Roy Publishers, 1945, p. 83.

18. Pieter Geyl, *The Revolt of the Netherlands, 1555-1609*, London: Williams and Norgate, 1932, p. 32.

19. Vlekke, *op. cit.*, pp. 47, 131.

20. Geyl, *op. cit.*, p. 76.

21. *CMH*, vol. 1, p. 458.

22. Geyl, *op. cit.*, pp. 23-34, 69-144.

23. Vlekke, *op. cit.*, pp. 112, 124-29.

24. *Ibid.*, pp. 133-38.

25. Geyl, *op. cit.*, p. 131.

26. Vlekke, *op. cit.*, pp. 138-42.

27. *Ibid.*, pp. 147, 169.

28. *Ibid.*, pp. 107, 112; Charles R. Boxer, *The Dutch Seaborne Empire: 1600-1800*, New York: Alfred A. Knopf, 1965, pp. 10-16, 31-53.

29. Pieter Geyl, *The Netherlands Divided, 1609-1648* (S. T. Bindoff, Translator), London: Williams and Norgate, 1936, pp. 246-47. See also Geyl's discussion in the following of his works: *The Netherlands in the Seventeenth Century 1648-1715*, London: Ernest Benn, Ltd., 1964, pp. 190-207; *Encounters in History*, New York: Meridian Books, 1961, pp. 206-25.

IX. *Religion and Regime, 1490 to 1780*

1. J. H. S. Burleigh, *A Church History of Scotland*, London: Oxford University Press, 1960, Parts III and IV; John MacInnes, *The Evangelical Movement in the Highlands of Scotland, 1688 to 1800*, Aberdeen: The University Press, 1951.

X. *A Wider View*

1. I consider the social psychology of Protestantism and Catholicism and its more general importance in a paper "To Live in Concord with a Society: Two Empirical Studies of Primary Relations. (To be published as one of the Charles Horton Cooley Centennial Lectures.)

2. References for the religious doctrines mentioned in this section were given in notes for Chapter I. I have found certain sources particularly helpful in identifying the regimes of societies associated with each doctrine:

General: S. N. Eisenstadt, *The Political Systems of Empires,* New York: The Free Press, 1963; Max Weber, *The Sociology of Religion* (Ephriam Fischoff, Translator), Boston: Beacon Press, 1963.

China, Japan, and India: Arthur L. Basham, *The Wonder That Was India,* New York: Hawthorn Books, 1963; Robert N. Bellah, *Tokugawa Religion,* Glencoe, Ill.: The Free Press, 1957; Wolfram Eberhard, *Conquerors and Rulers, Social Forces in Medieval China,* Leiden: E. J. Brill, 1952; John W. Hall, "Feudalism in Japan, A Reassessment," *Comparative Studies in Society and History,* 5 (October 1962), pp. 15-51; John W. Hall, *Government and Local Power in Japan: 500 to 1700, A Study Based on Bizen Province,* Princeton: Princeton University Press, 1966; Stanley Lane-Poole, *Mediaeval India under Mohammedan Rule,* Delhi: Universal Book and Stationery Co., 1963; Edmund R. Leach, "Hydraulic Society in Ceylon," *Past and Present,* No. 15 (April 1959), pp. 2-26; Hugh G. Rawlinson, *A Concise History of the Indian People,* London: Oxford University Press, 1950; Edwin O. Reischauer and John K. Fairbank, *East Asia, The Great Tradition,* Boston: Houghton Mifflin Co., 1960; George B. Sansom, *A History of Japan,* 2 vols., Stanford: Stanford University Press, 1958; Thomas G. P. Spear (Editor), *The Oxford History of India,* Oxford: The Clarendon Press, 1961; Max Weber, *The Religion of China* (Hans H. Gerth, Translator), Glencoe, Ill.: The Free Press, 1951; Max Weber, *The Religion of India* (Hans H. Gerth and Don Martindale, Translators), Glencoe, Ill.: The Free Press, 1958. Karl A. Wittfogel, *Oriental Despotism, A Comparative Study of Total Power,* New Haven: Yale University Press, 1957.

Byzantium and Russia: Michael T. Florinsky, *Russia, A History and Interpretation,* vol. 1, The Macmillan Co., 1953; Joan M. Hussey, *Church and Learning in the Byzantine Empire, 867-1185,* Oxford: Oxford University Press, 1937; George Ostrogorsky, *History of the Byzantine State* (Joan Hussey, Translator), Oxford: Basil Blackwell, 1956; Steven Runciman, *Byzantine Civilization,* London: Edward Arnold, Ltd., 1933; A. A. Vasiliev, *History of the Byzantine Empire,* Madison: University of Wisconsin Press, 1952.

Hebrews: Aubrey R. Johnson, *Sacral Kingship in Ancient Israel,* Cardiff: University of Wales Press, 1955; Yehezkel Kaufmann, *The Religion of Israel from Its Beginnings to the*

Babylonian Exile (Moshe Greenberg, Translator), Chicago: The University of Chicago Press, 1960; Adolphe Lods, *Israel from Its Beginnings to the Middle of the Eighth Century* (S. H. Hooke, Translator), London: Routledge and Kegan Paul, Ltd., 1932, pp. 83-142, 211-325, 424-70; W. O. E. Oesterly and Theodore H. Robinson, *A History of Israel*, vol. 1, Oxford: The Clarendon Press, 1932; Johannes Pedersen, *Israel, Its Life and Culture*, 2 vols., London: Oxford University Press, 1946; Eric Voegelin, *Israel and Revelation*, Baton Rouge: University of Louisiana Press, 1956; Max Weber, *Ancient Judaism* (Hans H. Gerth and Don Martindale, Translators), Glencoe, Ill.: The Free Press, 1952.

Greece and Rome: Arthur E. R. Boak and W. G. Sinnigen, *History of Rome to 565 B.C.*, New York: The Macmillan Co., 1965; Numa Denis Fustel de Coulanges, *The Ancient City* (Willard Small, Translator), Garden City, New York: Doubleday, 1956; Victor Ehrenberg, *The Greek State*, New York: Barnes and Noble, 1960; Kathleen Freeman, *Greek City States*, London: Macdonald, 1950; Gustave Glotz, *The Greek City and Its Institutions* (N. Mallinson, Translator), New York: Alfred A. Knopf, 1930, Part III; Alvin W. Gouldner, *Enter Plato*, New York: Basic Books, 1965; *The Greek Political Experience*, London: Oxford University Press, 1941; M. I. Rostovtzeff, *The Social and Economic History of the Roman Empire*, Oxford: The Clarendon Press, 1926; Eric Voegelin, *The World of the Polis*, Baton Rouge: University of Louisiana Press, 1957.

Islamic States: Niyazi Berkes, *The Development of Secularism in Turkey*, Montreal: McGill University Press, 1964; Clifford Geertz, *The Religion of Java*, Glencoe, Ill.: The Free Press, 1960; Hamilton H. R. Gibb, *Mohammedanism, An Historical Survey*, London: Oxford University Press, 1961; Gustave E. von Grunebaum, *Islam, Essays in the Nature and Growth of a Cultural Tradition*, London: Routledge and Kegan Paul, Ltd., 1955; Gustave E. von Grunebaum, *Medieval Islam, A Study in Cultural Orientation*, Chicago: The University of Chicago Press, 1954; Gustave E. von Grunebaum (Editor), *Unity and Variety in Muslim Civilization*, Chicago: The University of Chicago Press, 1955; Elaine G. Hagopian, "Islam and Society-Formation in Morocco Past and Present," *Journal for the Scientific Study of Religion*, 3 (Fall 1963), pp. 70-80; John S. Trimingham, *Islam in East Africa*, Oxford: The Clarendon Press, 1962; John S. Trimingham, *Islam in West Africa*, Oxford: The Clarendon Press, 1959.

3. See, for example, the previously cited works by Eberhard, Hall, Leach, and Wittfogel.

4. See also: Israel I. Efros, *Ancient Jewish Philosophy, A Study in Metaphysics and Ethics,* Detroit: Wayne State University Press, 1964; R. E. Clements, *God and Temple,* Philadelphia: Fortress Press, 1965; Pedersen *op. cit.*

5. The following are among the many important works on this topic: *Ibid.;* Martin Buber, *Two Types of Faith* (Norman P. Goldhawk, Translator), New York: Macmillan Co., 1951; Shirley J. Case, *The Evolution of Early Christianity,* Chicago: The University of Chicago Press, 1927; Franz Cumont, *The Mysteries of Mithra* (Thomas J. McCormack, Translator), Chicago: The Open Court Publishing Co., 1903; Franz Cumont, *The Oriental Religions in Roman Paganism* (Grant Showerman, Translator), Chicago: The Open Court Publishing Co., 1911; Werner W. Jaeger, *Early Christianity and Greek Paideia,* Cambridge: Harvard University Press, 1961; A. D. Nock, Conversion, *The Old and the New in Religion from Alexander the Great to Augustine of Hippo,* Oxford: The Clarendon Press, 1933; Weber, 1952, *op. cit.*

6. See, for example: Geoffrey R. Elton, *The Tudor Revolution in Government: Administrative Changes in the Reign of Henry VIII,* Cambridge: Cambridge University Press, 1953; Michael Roberts, *Gustavus Adolphus, A History of Sweden 1611-1632,* 2 vols., London: Longmans, Green and Co., 1953 and 1958; Hans Rosenberg, *Bureaucracy, Aristocracy and Autocracy, The Prussian Experience 1660-1815,* Cambridge: Harvard University Press, 1958.

7. Seymour M. Lipset, *Political Man, The Social Bases of Politics,* Garden City, N. Y.: Doubleday and Co., 1960; Robert R. Palmer, *Catholics and Unbelievers in Eighteenth Century France,* Princeton: Princeton University Press, 1939; Jacob L. Talmon, *The Origins of Totalitarian Democracy,* London: Secker and Warburg, 1952.

8. Alexis de Tocqueville, *The Old Regime and the French Revolution* (Stuart Gilbert, Translator), Garden City, N. Y.: Doubleday and Co., Inc., 1955.

9. Max Weber, *The Protestant Ethic and the Spirit of Capitalism* (Talcott Parsons, Translator), New York: Charles Scribner's Sons, 1930. For a recent survey of the complexities of economic modernization in Europe, consult: David S. Landes, "Technological Change and Development in Western Europe, 1750-1914," *The Cambridge Economic History of Europe,* vol. 6, part 1, Cambridge: Cambridge

University Press, 1965, pp. 274-601; Herbert Heaton, *Economic History of Europe*, New York: Harpers, 1948, chapters 13, 14, 15, and 16.

10. See, for example: Amintore Fanfani, *Catholicism, Protestantism and Capitalism*, New York: Sheed and Ward, Inc., 1935; Hector M. Robertson, *Aspects of the Rise of Economic Individualism, A Criticism of Max Weber and His School*, Cambridge: Cambridge University Press, 1933; Kurt Samuelsson, *Religion and Economic Action* (E. G. French, Translator), New York: Basic Books, 1961.

11. Weber, 1930, *op. cit.*, pp. 82, 102-5, 128-54, esp. pp. 132, 153.

12. David C. McClelland, *The Achieving Society*, Princeton: D. Van Nostrand, 1961. See also Robert N. Bellah, "Reflections on the Protestant Ethic Analogy in Asia," *The Journal of Social Issues*, 19 (January 1963), pp. 52-60.

13. For surveys of relevant doctrine see: John S. Whale, *The Protestant Tradition, An Essay in Interpretation*, Cambridge: Cambridge University Press, 1955, pp. 43-87; Paul Tillich, *Dynamics of Faith*, New York: Harper and Brothers, 1957; Richard Kroner, *The Primacy of Faith*, New York: The Macmillan Co., 1943; Joseph Pohle, "Justification," in Charles Herbermann and Others (Editors), *The Catholic Encyclopedia*, vol. 8, New York; The Encyclopedia Press, Inc., 1910, pp. 573-78; William Morgan, "Christian Faith," in James Hastings (Editor), *The Encyclopedia of Religion and Ethics*, vol. 5, New York: Charles Scribner's Sons, 1908-15, pp. 689-94; J. G. Simpson, "Justification," *Ibid.*, vol. 7, pp. 615-19; R. H. Coats, "Sanctification," *Ibid.*, vol. 11, pp. 181-84.

14. Relevant data are found in William A. Curtis, *A History of Creeds and Confessions of Faith in Christendom and Beyond*, Edinburgh: T. and T. Clark, 1911, chapters 10, 13, 14, 15, and 17. On the early collapse in Holland of all but "ritual" enforcement of Calvin's predestinarianism, see: Charles R. Boxer, *The Dutch Seaborne Empire: 1600-1800*, New York: Alfred A. Knopf, 1965, pp. 113-27.

15. Ernst Troeltsch, *The Social Teaching of the Christian Churches* (Olive Wyon, Translator), 2 vols., New York: The Macmillan Co., 1931; H. Richard Niebuhr, *Christ and Culture*, New York: Harper and Brothers, 1951.

16. Rudolph Otto, *The Idea of the Holy, An Inquiry into the Non-Rational Factor in the Idea of the Divine and Its Relation to the Rational* (John W. Harvey, Translator), New York: Oxford University Press, 1958.

17. Parsons in Weber 1963, *op. cit.*, p. lxvii. Emphasis in the original.

18. Philip A. Selznick, *Leadership in Administration,* Evanston: Row, Peterson and Co., 1957.

19. Georg Simmel, *The Sociology of Georg Simmel* (Kurt H. Wolff, Translator), Glencoe, Ill.: The Free Press, 1950, pp. 250-53, 256-67.

Index